Managing partnership in teacher training and development

WITHDRAWN

The trend towards partnership between higher education and other education providers is a dominant theme of 1990s teacher education. Political attention has focused on initial teacher training, but in this book the authors argue for a policy of professional development which links initial teacher education, continuing professional development, and research.

In the first part of the book, Hazel Bines and John Welton describe how the trend towards work-based training has grown out of good practice in managing professional development. They also discuss the management implications of this.

The second part, written by experienced teachers and teacher educators, explores the policy and practical management issues of partnership for education providers.

The third part sets the development of partnership in the context of broader issues of the politics of teacher education and the development of teacher professionalism.

The book ends with a section which focuses on planning and management issues which need to be considered further to establish effective practice in the management of career-long professional development in education.

Both editors teach at the School of Education at Oxford Brookes University.

Educational management series

Series editor: Cyril Poster

Managing partnership in teacher training and development

Edited by Hazel Bines and
John Welton

London and New York

First published 1995
by Routledge
11 New Fetter Lane, London EC4P 4EE

Simultaneously published in the USA and Canada
by Routledge
29 West 35th Street, New York, NY 10001

Typeset in Palatino by J&L Composition Ltd, Filey, North Yorkshire

Printed and bound in Great Britain by
Biddles Ltd, Guildford and King's Lynn

British Library Cataloguing in Publication Data
A catalogue record for this book is available from the British Library

Library of Congress Cataloging in Publication Data
A catalogue record for this book has been requested

ISBN 0–415–11399–7

Contents

Part III Partnership and professionalism

Part IV Conclusion

Figures

Contributors

Lesley Anderson is Education Services Manager and Senior Lecturer at Oxford Brookes University. Her responsibilities include the coordination of the University's licensed teachers' scheme and a contribution to the secondary PGCE course. Prior to this appointment, she worked as an educational advisor, a research and development officer and a secondary school teacher. Her present research includes a study of the first cohort of SCITT consortia.

Michael Barber is Professor of Education at Keele University. He is the author of a number of books on educational history and policy including *Education and the Teacher Unions* (Cassell, 1992) and *The Making of the 1944 Education Act* (Cassell, 1994). He is a regular contributor to the educational press.

Hazel Bines is a Deputy Head of the School of Education at Oxford Brookes University. She is responsible for academic development within the School and also teaches on both ITT and INSET courses offered by the School. Her research interests include education policy, special educational needs and teacher and professional education, on which she has written a range of publications. Previously she taught in primary, secondary and special schools in South Yorkshire.

Deanne Boydell is Principal Lecturer in Primary Education at Westminster College, Oxford. She is currently engaged in developing, managing and evaluating partnership initiatives in initial teacher education and the mentoring of newly qualified teachers in the primary phase.

George Crowther is currently headteacher of Brookside Primary School, Bicester, Oxfordshire and was previously headteacher of Cotsford Junior School, Horden, Co. Durham. He has a particular interest in the opportunities for staff development which are created when primary schools achieve a greater involvement in teacher education.

Trevor Dawn has had a long and varied career in post-compulsory education and training, in four colleges of further education, in a Local Education Authority advisory branch and in higher education. He is currently the course leader of the Certificate in Education (Post-Compulsory Education) at Oxford Brookes University.

Tony Edwards is Professor of Education, and Dean of the Education Faculty, at the University of Newcastle upon Tyne. He currently co-chairs (with Professor Jennifer Latto) the Universities Council for the Education of Teachers. He is also chair of governors at a Northumberland High School actively involved in initial teacher training. Tony Edwards' main research interests are reflected in two recently published books – *Investigating Classroom Talk* (written with David Westgate, and republished in a revised edition by Falmer Press in 1994), and *Choice and Specialization in Urban Education* (written with Geoff Whitty and Sharon Gewirtz, and published by Routledge in 1993).

Diane Gaunt is a Principal Lecturer in the School of Education at Oxford Brookes University. She coordinates award-bearing courses of continuing professional development for teachers. She has played a major role in restructuring the INSET programmes to offer greater flexibility with opportunities to accredit work done in partnership with LEAs, schools and colleges. Her research interests focus on vocational education with a special emphasis on the professions.

Georgina Glenny is a Senior Lecturer in the School of Education at Oxford Brookes University. She organises teaching studies and also coordinates the setting up of groups of partnership schools within the PGCE (Primary Education) course. She is also involved in the training of teachers working as mentors of students.

Elizabeth Hickling is currently a Senior Lecturer in the School of Education at Oxford Brookes University. She was Course Leader of the B.Ed. course for primary education and is now Course Leader of the PGCE (Primary Education). Formerly a headteacher, she is particularly interested in education for the early years.

John Howson has been a Deputy Head of the School of Education at Oxford Brookes University for the past seven years. Best known for his longitudinal study on the labour market for headteachers, he has also been closely associated with the development of the National Education Assessment Centre.

Malcolm Lee has worked in primary schools and technical colleges. Until December 1993, he was Head of School of Education and Professional Development at Doncaster College and has worked in teacher education for both school and further education teachers. He was involved in a wide range of validation work with the Council for National Academic Awards, was founding editor of the *British Journal of In-Service Education* in 1974, and is a former chair of the Association of Teachers in Colleges and Departments of Education (ATCDE) and President of National Association of Teachers in Further and Higher Education (NATFHE). He is currently chair of the Education Policy Committee of NATFHE. He now works as a part-time teacher and freelance consultant.

Bob Moon is Professor of Education at the Open University where he is Director of the Postgraduate Certificate in Education (PGCE) Programme and the Centre for Research in Teacher Education. He is a former comprehensive school headteacher and has written extensively in the area of curriculum and teacher education.

Richard Pring is Professor and Director of the Department of Educational Studies at the University of Oxford. Previously he has been Dean of Education at the University of Exeter, lecturer at the University of London, and teacher in London comprehensive schools. His main interests and publications lie in the philosophy of education.

Marian Shaw developed her interest in teacher induction as a faculty head in a comprehensive school. In her current position of Senior Lecturer in Education Management at Oxford Brookes University she has been jointly responsible for designing induction projects and leading training for mentors in primary and secondary schools for several LEAs. She has a research interest in OFSTED inspection and a training interest in management development in the UK and abroad.

Rowie Shaw, an untrained graduate, has been a headteacher for seven years, first in Tower Hamlets and currently in Bradford. Following a secondment at the University of Cambridge Department of Education in 1991, she has developed an interest in teacher education, writing and speaking regularly on the subject.

Ann Shelton Mayes is a Senior Lecturer at the Open University and Deputy Director of the PGCE Programme. She is a former comprehensive school deputy headteacher and has produced publications in the areas of mentoring and teacher assessment.

Professor **John Tomlinson CBE** has been Director of the Warwick University Institute of Education since 1985, and was Director of Education for Cheshire 1972–85. He has been Chairman of the Further Education Unit, Schools Council and Royal Society of Arts and President of the Society of Education Officers. He is currently chairing the initiative for a General Teaching Council and the Further Education Funding Council Enquiry into special education in further education.

Frank Warner is Advisory Headteacher for Oxfordshire LEA with responsibility for the induction of newly qualified teachers. For the past six years he has worked in support of newly qualified teachers through the provision of an in-service training programme and visits to the newly qualified teachers in their schools. He is also coordinator of the Oxfordshire Mentor Training Project. His past posts include headteacher of a primary school and a two-year secondment from this post to lead a language development project within a group of local primary schools and including the local secondary school.

John Welton is Professor of Education and Head of the School of Education at Oxford Brookes University. He has particular interests in the development and implementation of education policy, and in management training for senior education administrators, both in the United Kingdom and in developing countries.

Norman White spent the first part of his career teaching modern languages in secondary schools before entering teacher training. He then worked for the London Borough of Hillingdon for twenty years, first as Modern Languages Advisor and more recently as manager for Teacher Recruitment and Induction. His responsibilities in this post included licensed and articled teachers, returners to the profession and initial teacher training links with higher education institutions.

Preface and acknowledgements

Writing about teacher education during a period of rapid change raises questions about both short-term and long-term perspectives. This book, inevitably, considers aspects of policy and provision which are likely to develop and change in the next few years. At the same time, partnership will continue to be a dominant theme throughout the 1990s and will involve the issues raised in this book. We therefore hope this book will make an important contribution to debate, and to the development of policy and practice, both now and in the future.

Teacher education also involves a range of concepts and terminology. In order to ensure consistency, certain terms have therefore been used throughout the book. For example, although the editors and the contributors are committed to teacher education as well as training, the term 'initial teacher training' (ITT) has been used throughout the book, alongside in-service education for teachers (INSET) or continuing professional development. We have also referred to higher education institutions, to include both universities and colleges of higher education, and to further education colleges to represent the range of further, adult and other post-compulsory educational provision in this sector.

We would particularly like to acknowledge the work of our contributors for this book, including the commitment they have given to ensuring the quality of their chapters and their responsiveness to our editorial comments and requests. We would also very much like to thank Tricia Farrell, Daniela Lalljee, Hilary Wilson and Vince Morris for all the work they have undertaken on the manuscript and graphics. Finally, we would like to thank Cyril Poster, the series editor, and Helen Fairlie and her colleagues at Routledge, for their advice, encouragement and support.

Introduction

Hazel Bines and John Welton

During the last decade there has been considerable professional and political debate about staffing the education service. The debate has covered all aspects of staff preparation and development, from initial training to the continuing professional development of established teachers, and has been accompanied by a range of changes and reforms.

From 1984, when the Council for the Accreditation of Teacher Education (CATE) was established and strict accreditation criteria for initial teacher training were first implemented, through to 1994, when a Teacher Training Agency was introduced, a series of Conservative Government measures has continued to change the content, delivery, management and funding of teacher education. Such measures have focused on improving the perceived ineffectiveness of initial teaching training in particular and include several changes in criteria for the design and accreditation of both primary and secondary initial training courses, the development of Licensed and Articled Teacher schemes and direct funding of school-based courses. In addition, the devolution of planning and funding for INSET provision to the individual school or further education college site has had a considerable impact on induction and continuing professional development.

A variety of professionally led developments has also continued to reshape the nature and content of courses and qualifications. Teacher educators, working in conjunction with colleagues in schools and further education colleges, have introduced new courses and curricula for initial and in-service education and new teaching and assessment methods such as mentoring, profiling and resource-based learning. Attention has also been given to improving continuity between training and employment, through projects to support induction, and to extending INSET provision to include the accreditation of school-based and college-based professional development. Above all, the partnership between higher education, schools and colleges has been strengthened in a variety of ways, to ensure a wide range of practical teaching experience for those entering the teaching profession and to create stronger links between initial teacher education and all forms of continuing professional development.

Changes in teacher education have also been part of the process of substantial reform of the education system as a whole. Developments such as the National Curriculum, local management of schools (LMS) and changes in the role of LEAs have all had a major impact on the curricular, financial and organisational aspects of school education. Major structural changes have also been implemented in post-compulsory education. The binary divide between the traditional providers of teacher education, namely universities on the one hand, and polytechnics and higher education colleges on the other, has been abolished and they are all now part of a unitary system of higher education which has also expanded and changed. Further education colleges have been incorporated as institutions independent of LEA control and have initiated substantial changes in curriculum and organisation.

All these changes have had considerable impact on teacher education. The overall scenario is one of considerable instability, requiring both fast and effective responses. At the same time, few of the key issues are new. Change is interspersed with continuities of concern and intervention in relation to a number of aspects of professional formation and development, ranging from the role and amount of practical teaching experience in initial training to ensuring the right balance between individual and institutional needs in continuing professional development. Debate, research and practice have also focused on the dimensions of competence in teaching, the relative importance of specialist subject and generic teaching expertise, the development of teachers' capacity to provide for the different needs of learners and the integration of different elements of courses. In addition, some important issues continue to be neglected, such as the development of an effective system of training for teaching staff in post-compulsory education, the enhancement of management training opportunities for senior staff and the maintenance and development of a wide range of research activity.

The political and professional issues involved in teacher training and development are therefore both wide-ranging and long-standing. However, partnership is widely identified as one of the most important themes. Political attention to date has focused largely on the partnership between higher education institutions and schools in relation to initial teacher education for school education. However, political and professional changes are now extending the concept of partnership to include both initial training and qualifications for teachers in further education. Such changes have also led to the implementation of a more systematic and responsive approach to continuing professional development for teaching, management and support staff working at all levels and phases within the education system.

Such partnerships will have to be developed within the new policy and organisational structures and climate established by recent Government measures. Although many policy changes have been incremental and sometimes contradictory, there are some key directions and features that have combined to affect the ecology of teacher education. These include: the application of market principles to education; decentralisation of the strategic and operational management of the education service to individual schools and further education colleges; new forms of external accountability through formal inspection and other measures; increases in central government control, particularly in relation to the curriculum; and continuing cuts in resources available from the public purse. Such developments have also been accompanied by an emphasis on the role and rights of the consumer and a challenge to, and critique of, professional perspectives and status. The market approach to education has also altered the balance between professional and managerial conceptions of the ways in which education and other public services should be delivered and developed. Effective management, rather than traditional professional knowledge and skills, is now seen as the key to quality and productivity. At the same time, even if it is believed that professional educational expertise and collegial relationships continue to be important to the development of education, the devolution of administrative responsibilities to individual institutions, the growth of external accountability and the requirement to respond to a wide range of changes have made management a greater priority.

The development of partnership will thus require a range of political, professional and managerial responses and responsibilities, in order to continue to develop provision and practice within this new context. For example, both the structures and processes of partnership will have to accommodate the growing managerial autonomy of the range of partner providers within a market system designed to foster diversity and competition rather than equity and cooperation. Careful attention will have to be given to external requirements and definitions of quality, in ways which do not undermine other valid and effective beliefs and practices which inform the work of participant institutions. Accountability to the range of stakeholders will also need to be considered, including the interests of government, students, pupils, parents and the wider community, as well as participating institutions and their staff, in their various roles as providers, consumers, employers and colleagues. It also needs to be recognised that for many of those involved, the development of partnership may be both a perceived and an actual threat, as well as an opportunity, particularly since it is just one of a series of changes affecting roles, responsibilities, workload and resource allocation.

Partnership does provide a significant opportunity to enhance and extend professional development, and, in turn, the quality of educational provision. It has long been argued that teachers should have more responsibility for their own professional development and that there should be continuity between initial training, induction and continuing professional development, within a framework of careful planning for individual, institutional and service needs. A concept of partnership which addresses all these concerns, and which involves higher education, schools and further education colleges in all aspects of professional development, could be used to develop an enhanced model of professionalism. The policy of Conservative governments over the last decade has frequently, and often rightly, been interpreted as an attack on both teacher professionalism and the education service. However, experience has demonstrated that policy often has unintended consequences, not least because it is open to all sorts of interpretation and change during implementation. There are opportunities to shape the direction of reform and those who work in education have a responsibility to use such opportunities in the most effective ways possible.

Partnership in education is not an issue invented and owned by politicians alone. It has resulted from reflection and practice by teachers and teacher educators, working with the learners and communities they serve. The development of a professional conception of partnership is therefore one of the key themes of this book. It will, however, also be argued that such a conception must incorporate the perceptions and needs of the range of stakeholders if it is to be truly professional.

The development of partnership will also require a clear vision of the aims and desired outcomes of teacher education and a creative but realistic appraisal of structures, strategies and resources. It must also be recognised that such a vision cannot be supported within one school, further education college or higher education institution alone. Many of the changes in education over the last decade have resulted in a more competitive climate and a fragmentation of planning and services. However, most institutions still recognise the importance of a collective response and the benefit of cooperation and joint action. Partnership for teacher education offers a particular opportunity to demonstrate the value and importance of such an approach for both individual participants and the education service as a whole.

This book seeks to examine the development of partnership in teacher education in a way that focuses on the key dimensions of change, namely purpose and process. It will examine a wide range of issues in professional formation and development, together with structures, strategies and resources. It is concerned with developing and sustaining the quality of the teaching profession in schools, further education colleges and higher education. It brings together the practice and research experience of a wide range of contributors to the field of teacher education and provides an overview of the range of professional development issues and contexts involved in partnership for teacher education. It also focuses particularly on management issues, in the belief that effective management of individual institutions, partnership and professional development as a whole is a critically important dimension of teacher education.

OUTLINE OF THE BOOK

Part I of the book, Chapter 1, sets the context for following chapters, with an overview of the development of partnership over the last decade and the range of management issues involved. The chapters in Part II represent both the continuum of teacher training and development in different phases and sectors of education and a range of models and approaches in relation to provision and partnership. Each chapter also draws upon particular examples, drawn from contributors' own practice and experience in teacher education.

In Chapters 2 and 3 respectively, Rowie Shaw and Richard Pring consider teacher training and development for the secondary phase of education. Rowie Shaw outlines the approaches to professional development and partnership within a particular secondary school. Richard Pring focuses on initial training, considering the role of schools and higher education, with reference to the Internship Scheme at Oxford University and to general issues of teacher professionalism. The themes of professional development and partnership are then taken up in Chapters 4 and 5 in relation to the primary phase of education. Georgina Glenny and Elizabeth Hickling explore models of partnership between primary schools and higher education and George Crowther discusses partnership for initial training from a primary school perspective, drawing on experience of a pilot project involving a cluster of primary schools.

The next two chapters consider different models for initial teacher training. In Chapter 6, Lesley Anderson reviews the implementation of school-centred initial teacher training schemes, including the Articled and Licensed Teacher schemes and the more recent School-Centred Initial Teacher Training scheme (SCITT). Chapter 7 is concerned with open learning. Bob Moon and Ann Shelton Mayes discuss open learning approaches to teacher education, drawing in particular on their experience of developing primary and secondary PGCE courses for the Open University.

Chapters 8 and 9 focus on the induction and INSET aspects of the continuum of professional development. In Chapter 8, Marian Shaw, Deanne Boydell and Frank Warner consider the induction of newly qualified teachers, illustrating the issues involved with an account of the development of induction provision for newly qualified primary teachers in Oxfordshire. Their chapter also considers the training of mentors and the value of partnership between schools, LEAs and higher education in relation to induction. In Chapter 9, Diane Gaunt explores recent developments in approaches to INSET, as a result of changes in professional needs and patterns of funding, and considers the nature of partnership in relation to continuing professional development.

As argued earlier in this Introduction, policy for professional training and development for teachers working in post-compulsory education has been somewhat neglected. Chapters 10 and 11 focus on this sector. In Chapter 10, Trevor Dawn reviews the development of initial training and considers the implications for staff development and partnership of some of the changes taking place in further and adult education. Drawing on experience of course development at Oxford Brookes University, he argues for new approaches to initial training based on a three-way contract between the individual teacher, his or her employing institution and the higher education institution offering the training course. The impact of changes in post-compulsory education on staff development is then given further consideration in Chapter 11 by Malcolm Lee, who explores issues in continuing teacher development, drawing on experience within a college of further and higher education.

The final chapter in Part II draws together the continuum of teacher training and development with a particular focus on the role of the LEA. Drawing on experience in one London borough, Norman White considers the multifaceted contribution of the LEA to teacher education. He also considers how the new enabling, mediating and coordinating role of LEAs can be developed to support partnership in relation to teacher training and development.

Part III then develops some wider perspectives. It focuses in particular on teacher professionalism and how it should be developed given the context of partnership and the tenor of recent Government policy. In Chapter 13, Tony Edwards explores the politics of partnership, focusing on the partnership for initial teacher training between schools and higher education. He identifies the particular contribution of higher education to teacher education and the ways in which recent policy discourse and directions have distorted both issues and debate. In Chapter 14, John Tomlinson outlines the case for a General Teaching Council (GTC), focusing in particular on the issues involved in teacher professionalism. Finally, in Chapter 15, Michael Barber sets an agenda for professional reconstruction, based on suggestions ranging from the development of paraprofessional support to the need for periodic professional review, and considers how such an agenda can be developed through partnership and other means.

The fourth and concluding part of the book, Chapter 16, both draws the book together by summarising the range of partnership models and issues and also suggests ways in which the management of partnership needs to be developed in future. Focusing on key themes such as planning, funding, quality assurance and staff development, it provides some detailed basis for thinking about partnership management.

Part I

Overview

Chapter 1

Developing and managing partnership

Hazel Bines and John Welton

THE GROWTH OF PARTNERSHIP

As noted in the Introduction to this book, the development of partnership has been a dominant theme amongst the range of issues involved in teacher education. There has been a long-standing professional commitment from teachers in schools and higher education to the development of ways of working together, to provide in particular a range of practical teaching experiences for students on initial teacher training (ITT) courses for school education. More recently, the concept of partnership for ITT has widened to include further education. The shift in responsibility and funding for staff development from LEAs to individual schools and further education colleges has also focused attention on the important role of higher education in supporting the induction and continuing professional development of teachers. Partnership is thus being extended to include such staff development. Partnership should therefore be considered in relation to the range of needs and contributions of schools, further education colleges and higher education institutions.

There have been two main impetuses for such changes. The first has been largely professional and educational, resulting from a range of concerns and debate about the content of courses, including their capacity to develop and support professional competence. As Wilkin (1990) has noted, the heart of this debate is the balance and relationship between theory and practice and the way in which these have been reformulated over the last three decades.

Following the early history of an 'apprenticeship' approach, and the short, emergency teacher training programmes instituted after the Second World War, teacher education developed in two ways. First, measures were introduced to upgrade the quality and length of the academic subject components of teacher education courses, as part of the aim of achieving an all-graduate teaching profession, at least for teaching in schools. Second, the human sciences were applied to analysis of the complex processes of teaching and learning and the contexts in which they took place. Practice was seen as the application of educational theory and was rarely integrated with other learning.

However, it became increasingly clear that such a divorce between theoretical understanding and practical knowledge and competence was unhelpful to students. It also failed to reflect the ways in which professional knowledge and action actually work and develop (Schön 1983, 1987). Theory was thus reformulated as the articulation and synthesis of practice, leading to a greater emphasis on collaboration between higher education and the practice context. The apprenticeship approach, based on 'on the job' training, and the technocratic conception, based on the application of theory to practice, have been gradually replaced by a different model. This emphasises the development of understanding and expertise through systematic enquiry into, and reflection on, practice, based on experience and needs within the practice setting (Furlong 1992; Furlong et al. 1988; Whitty et al. 1992).

The development of such a model for ITT has been complemented by approaches to in-service (INSET) courses, which include action research and other forms of enquiry based on teachers' and institutions' particular professional concerns and requirements and by the growth of short courses and consultancy activities designed to meet institutional as well as individual development needs. The focus on practice has also been encouraged by the general growth of competence-based approaches to vocational and professional education, including the frameworks developed by the National Council for Vocational Education. Although notions of professional competence remain somewhat problematic, such approaches, and the accompanying requirement for a closer partnership with practitioners and employers, are beginning to inform higher education courses for a range of professions (Bines and Watson 1992). This has provided yet further encouragement for such developments in teacher education.

Thus, despite assertions to the contrary by Conservative Government Ministers and others during the 1980s and early 1990s, most ITT courses for school education developed a strong focus on practice and professional competence; involved substantial practical teaching experience; and were based on established, if varied, patterns of collaboration and partnership between the institutions involved (Furlong *et al.* 1988; Whitty *et al.* 1992). Such courses also included a number of innovatory developments, such as the use of mentors to support training (Wilkin 1992a). There was also a growing recognition of the importance of continuity between training and employment and of the induction of newly qualified teachers (Council for National Academic Awards 1992; Earley 1992a; Earley and Kinder 1994). As will be discussed in Chapter 10, training courses for further education also developed through partnership between different providers, including higher education. Finally, a range of INSET provision was developed in response to the changing pattern of individual and institutional needs and funding (Gaunt 1992).

However, the nature of teacher education, in particular the relationship between higher education and schools, continued to be subject to government policy intervention in a number of ways. The second impetus for change has therefore been political. It has taken several forms.

First, a number of specific policies have been implemented to ensure that teacher education takes place in the context of partnership. Since the introduction of the Council for the Accreditation of Teacher Education (CATE) criteria in 1984 (DES 1984), partnership in relation to ITT courses for school education, including the minimum number of weeks to be spent in school, has been made mandatory. School-based work and the partnership with schools have also become major foci of external quality assessment, as demonstrated in the Office for Standards in Education (OFSTED) working papers for the assessment of initial training for secondary school teachers (OFSTED 1993d). As discussed in Chapter 6, the development of Articled and Licensed teacher schemes, and of school-based consortia, have also reinforced the requirement of partnership and of schools taking a stronger role. Partnership with schools in relation to INSET provision has also been seen as increasingly important. For example, the quality of INSET partnerships is now examined as part of the assessment of the quality of ITT partnerships (OFSTED 1993d). As noted in Chapter

9, partnership related to INSET has also been encouraged by the devolution of INSET funding to individual schools and further education colleges.

The devolution of INSET funding is an example of the second and more indirect way in which government policy has influenced partnership in teacher education during the 1980s and early 1990s. A range of educational reforms, including local management of schools (LMS), the creation of grant-maintained schools and the incorporation of further education colleges, have all led to individual institutions taking responsibility for institutional and staff management and development, which in turn has encouraged a stronger role in partnership. Curricular reform in both school and post-compulsory education has also changed the content and delivery of courses. The increasing diversity of educational provision and services, and of institutional and individual professional development needs, has resulted in a complementary diversity of courses, qualifications and providers.

Finally, partnership has been part of the creation of a political climate of critique to legitimate reform. For example, it has been suggested that courses run by higher education are too theoretical, leaving new teachers ill-prepared for classroom teaching. The supposed left-wing bias of higher education has also been criticised (Clarke 1992; Lawlor 1990). Such attacks on teacher education have had a specific purpose, namely to legitimate reform that involves a stronger role for schools. In addition, as discussed later in this chapter, they are part of the general discourse and strategy of polarisation between different interests, and derision for professional perspectives and activities, which have characterised and accompanied recent Conservative Government policy and legislation (Ball 1990).

There are, however, some inconsistencies in such education policies and developments. First, there is no mandatory requirement to develop formal partnerships between higher education institutions and further education colleges in relation to the initial training or continuing professional development of teachers working within this particular sector. Most courses are based on such a partnership, but it has developed through professional rather than policy decisions. Second, despite long-standing concern over the transition from training to employment, the development of partnership in relation to induction has been left to local initiatives. Third, although partnership is now being recognised as an important dimension of INSET provision, recent Government policy has not encouraged responsiveness to a range of needs for continuing professional development. Nor has it facilitated development of funding, accreditation and quality assessment procedures to support the implementation of appropriate provision. Fourth, very little consideration has been given to the role of other institutions and services, such as LEAs or Training and Enterprise Councils (TECs), as discussed in several chapters in this book. Nor has much attention been given to the ways in which partnership could be extended to include the training of other professionals and paraprofessionals within the education service, as suggested in Chapter 15.

Finally, very little attention has been given to the development of partnerships in relation to research, even though research has been recognised as one of the key contributions of higher education. Research funding policy has not taken account of the close relationship between various forms of professional and institutional development and the way in which this is supported by research in higher education. Higher education research funding is focused almost entirely on supporting research by those working exclusively in higher education. Research Councils' funding strategies are based on national research priorities, and the Department for Education restricts its very limited research funding largely to the support of current policy development and evaluation. There need to be mechanisms for providing financial support to this aspect of partnership between schools, further education colleges and higher education which could help develop the research needed to improve professional practice.

Government policy on partnership, at least until 1994, has thus been both limited and partial. It could therefore be suggested that the focus on partnership does not just reflect a commitment to develop a more effective system of teacher education. Rather, as also argued in other chapters in this book, it is part of a wider agenda, including the imposition of a utilitarian view of education and professionalism and a determination to shift the responsibility and funding for teacher education away from higher education. Partnership is also closely linked to the market approach to education. One of the strongest impetuses behind recent educational reform has been the application of market principles to education, on the grounds that competition and diversity will improve standards and efficiency (Ball 1990; Flude and Hammer 1990). The existence of established centres of teacher education within higher education has thus been seen as a monopolistic restriction on the effective implementation of market approaches, which needs to be replaced by a range of diverse providers. Given that reform has also been based on the belief that teaching is a straightforward activity which can be learned largely through practice (Clarke 1992), it is not surprising that school-based and other forms of work-based training are now being put forward as the key to improving quality.

The growth of partnership has therefore been substantial. However, its development is due to a range of political, professional and educational pressures and considerations, all of which will need to be managed both now and in the future. In addition, despite the widespread view that it should be a key feature of teacher training and development, partnership remains an imprecise and problematic notion. Its application in relation to the range of professional development has not been systematic and it ranges from a rhetorical concept to a genuine focus of policy. As will be discussed later in this chapter, there may also be some contradictions in posing partnership as a major way forward within the new market approach to education. At the same time it remains a powerful metaphor for a widespread concern to improve the quality of teacher education. It is therefore likely to continue as a major issue within the management of teacher education. Some of the ways in which different aspects of partnership might be developed and managed will now be discussed in more detail.

THE FOCUS OF PARTNERSHIP

As already briefly discussed earlier in this chapter, most of the debate about partnership has centred on ITT courses for school education. Such partnership has been seen as a means of developing students' professional competences through extended practical teaching experience in schools and ensuring the integration of different elements of courses, as provided by schools and higher education. However, there are a number of other elements to partnership, including training for teachers in post-school education. In addition, both induction and continuing professional development are becoming increasingly important.

The process of inducting newly qualified teachers (NQTs) is a long-standing issue which never seems to be quite resolved.

Historically, responsibility for induction has been shared between an individual institution and the LEA. Although some institutions have incorporated the needs of NQTs into a well-planned programme of staff development for all staff, many have lacked an integrated programme. The induction of NQTs has not been a high political or educational priority.

However, partnership can play a number of roles in relation to induction. Of particular importance is the need to ensure continuity between training and employment, in order to enable students to make an effective transition from training to teaching. Experiences in this area include policies for the transfer of information, for example, a profile of competences from the higher education institution which can be taken to the first teaching post (Council for National Academic Awards 1992). As discussed in Chapters 8 and 12 in this book, there have been also significant developments in the training of teachers to act as mentors for NQTs. As also noted in those two chapters, support from higher education is becoming even more important given changes in the role of LEAs. Although students employed by schools and further education colleges in any one partnership will not necessarily have come from the partner higher education institution(s), support for induction could be seen as an increasingly crucial aspect of partnership, linking the planning and management of initial teacher education to that of continuing professional development. Involving higher education in supporting the induction of NQTs ensures that new teachers are supported by both experienced teachers and higher education staff. As well as being familiar with the local situation, the latter can also contribute a range of experience broader than that to be found in any one school or college.

Such links are particularly well illustrated by the development of mentoring in the last few years. As discussed in several of the chapters in this book, and in a range of publications on teacher education, mentoring and other professional training activities which support trainee and newly qualified teachers can have a very positive impact on the staff involved, by encouraging them to reflect on their own practice and develop a range of counselling and other skills (McIntyre et al. 1993; Wilkin 1992a). Mentoring is an important element in the professional development of experienced teachers and of the training partnership. Such mentoring also develops competence in supporting adult learning and staff development more generally within a school or further education college.

However, mentoring is but a small part of the range of professional development needs and opportunities that could be planned and supported through closer partnerships between higher education, schools and further education colleges. Such needs and opportunities have both an individual and an institutional dimension and may include:

- the needs of individual teachers for particular qualifications and programmes of professional development;
- the needs of a school or college department or team of teachers, related to a particular area of curriculum or pedagogy;
- institutional needs as identified in the school or college development plan; and
- development needs which are shared by a cluster or group of schools or colleges facing similar issues and/or wishing to develop a collaborative approach to provision.

Partnership has a role to play in all four of these aspects. For example, in relation to individual needs, a higher education institution may be able to provide a range of courses that focus on particular issues and lead to recognised qualifications. This has been the traditional form of continuing professional development. It has been led by higher education providers, albeit with some sensitivity to market and consumer needs and demands. With the decline in LEA provision, higher education has also come to have a greater role in supporting team and institutional development through the provision of INSET days and consultancy. Such partnership work has value for both partners. Higher education staff enhance their knowledge of the staff and work of partner schools or colleges, which helps in planning and managing aspects of ITT work. Schools, colleges and higher education institutions can also work together to plan activities, pool expertise and share costs. Such a partnership will, however, require a closer articulation between traditional award-bearing qualifications and short courses and development programmes in schools and colleges. As noted in Chapter 9, this is beginning to happen through the use of flexible ways of accrediting such work, including granting recognition to past learning and other credit accumulation and transfer arrangements. Nevertheless, such trends need to be encouraged through policies at both national and local level to facilitate such initiatives through appropriate funding, qualifications and programmes.

Research is a further and somewhat neglected area of partnership, despite the contribution it can make to individual and institutional professional development. Many traditional INSET courses have a research component and there is a strong tradition of full-time and part-time study by teachers for higher degrees, including research degrees. Most higher education staff also undertake various forms of research, often in partner schools and colleges. It is, however, rare for this wide range of research to be planned systematically as a resource for enquiry and development within a particular region. There is a strong argument for seeing research as an important aspect of partnership. Research has an important role in helping schools, further education colleges and higher education institutions to identify and implement the developmental agenda established in their strategic and operational plans. As noted in Chapters 3 and 13, research is one of the key contributions of higher education to both professional development and education as a whole. Effective management of partnership should include exploration of the various ways of promoting collaborative research, using the expertise, resources and networks of higher education. Following the decline in LEA resources and services, higher education has a crucial role in providing such support for schools and colleges.

Higher education also has a number of professional development needs that can be supported through partnership. Partnership can enable higher education staff to maintain their professional experience of school and further education college teaching. Schools and colleges also offer a range of resources for research activities which are important to higher education and to the development of the whole education service. Above all, partnership can strengthen knowledge, understanding and experience of professional formation and development, and the courses and learning experiences which should be developed through higher education to meet the range of needs.

Finally, it could be argued that partnership in relation to teacher education could form the basis of more paraprofessional and interprofessional training and development, bringing together the training requirements of the range of professionals who work with children and young people in services linked to education within a particular locality. These and other new foci may be more long-term, but they illustrate the potential of thinking about partnership in the broadest ways possible.

MODELS OF PARTNERSHIP

There are therefore a number of dimensions to the partnership between schools, further education colleges, higher education and others that extend far beyond a concern with the effectiveness of initial teacher training for school education. The maintenance and development of this broader partnership will, however, require a change in model, towards one based on:

• genuine reciprocity of need and expertise;
• recognition of the relationship between initial teacher education, induction and continuing professional development; and
• support for a programme of research and development activities building on the relative strengths of a range of schools, further education colleges, higher education institutions and other participants.

To date, there have been three distinct models within the more traditional approaches to teacher training and development. The first, which could be termed a *unidimensional model*, was largely dominated by higher education and comprised a 'placement' approach to school or further education college involvement in initial teacher training, supplemented by other *ad hoc* links, such as teacher attendance on courses provided by the higher education institution and the involvement of some higher education staff in research in 'placement' schools or colleges. This was replaced by a model of partnership based on some form of *equivalence* or *complementarity*, with an agreed sharing and/or distribution of roles, particularly in relation to ITT courses (Wilkin 1990). Such a partnership often included a greater involvement by higher education in providing a range of INSET courses and services for partner institutions in a more responsive way than previously. It also involved higher education staff updating their teaching and other experience, and/or developing joint research, in partnership institutions.

   This model became dominant during the 1980s, as higher education institutions, schools and further education colleges began to explore the implications of a more extended partnership over a range of professional development activities. It was encouraged by government policy in relation to initial teacher education and by changes in INSET provision, in particular the devolution of INSET funding to individual schools and further education colleges. However, it is now gradually being replaced by a more *integrated* approach comprising joint operation of a range of activities. Although the historic roots of such partnership have grown from ITT courses, they are now being complemented by a range of contributory INSET and research activities. The integrated model reflects government accreditation criteria for initial teacher training (DFE 1992, 1993b) and exemplifies government definitions of good practice in relation to partnership (OFSTED 1993d), as well as having considerable mutual value for those involved.

Most institutions are still exploring the considerable complexities of the integrated model. Nevertheless, it is important to consider a fourth *reciprocal* approach, as a further stage of partnership development. As also discussed in Chapter 4, a reciprocal approach would operate across a range of professional development and educational activities far beyond that required by recent government policy. It is a highly professional conception, based on commitment to professional mutuality and reciprocity and requires joint and systematic planning and activity across a range of areas. It also includes partnership between schools or colleges themselves as well as with higher education and other institutions and services, and may also involve collaboration between neighbouring higher education institutions. The reciprocal approach focuses on enhancing education in a locality, but also endorses the idea of education as a universal and public service requiring professional training for a career and not just teaching in one school or college or working in other aspects of the education service. It also promotes the belief that research has a wider, national import in addition to benefiting particular institutions.

Even if no model currently exists to meet all the above criteria, there are many examples of how such a model is gradually being developed. There are also a number of other initiatives, such as the courses run by school consortia discussed in Chapter 6, that have developed following the implementation of School-Centred Initial Teacher Training (SCITT) schemes (DFE 1993c). There is also the potential of extending open or distance learning to the range of teacher education, as considered in Chapter 7. Given the tenor of recent government policy, which is explicitly directed towards ensuring a diversity of courses and providers (Wilkin 1992b), the reciprocal approach is likely to be both complex and multifaceted.

There is also a danger that the combined impact of educational reforms over the last decade on schools, further education colleges, higher education and other aspects of the education service could lead towards fragmentation and competition. In particular, what Bridges (1993) has called the 'corporate' approach, that is an emphasis on individual institutional needs, may undermine provision for the full range of professional development opportunities and the assumption that such development is pertinent to a teaching career in the education service as a whole. It is therefore important to maintain a vision of partnership that transcends diversity and provides solutions to the difficulties of adapting to individual and separate policy initiatives. The desirability of the reciprocal model, based on collaboration across a range of professional requirements and activities in the interest of a united teaching profession and education service, will be a constant theme in this book. However, such a model will require creative and careful management and development.

THE MANAGEMENT OF PARTNERSHIP

Many of the detailed aspects of institutional and partnership management in relation to teacher training and development will be considered in particular chapters in this book. However, there are some important common principles and issues that can be examined now as part of this overview. They include the key dimensions of quality, control and cost (Bines 1992, 1994) together with the enabling and action aspects of partnership (Alexander 1990), which are so crucial to partnership management and development.

Whatever the model of partnership, the issues of quality, control and cost have particular relevance, at both national and local level. Those involved will have to consider both government and their own definitions of quality and how they will be achieved. In addition to the impact of professional training provision on pupils, students and teachers, the nature of the partnership itself will also be seen as a major determinant of quality.

Teacher education is subject to a large number of controls in relation to quality. These currently include:

- course validation and accreditation through higher education institutions and the Teaching Training Agency/Department for Education;
- audit of higher education quality assurance procedures by the Higher Education Quality Council (HEQC);
- inspection by OFSTED; and
- other forms of course appraisal implemented by partnership institutions, including those designed to gather evaluation from students, staff and parents.

Each party to the assessment and assurance of quality is likely to have a different expectation of how partnership should be maintained and developed and what its outcomes should be. Schools and further education colleges also have to consider professional development in the light of the quality indicators for external assessment by OFSTED and the Further Education Funding Council (FEFC) respectively.

The quality of professional development and related professional activities, and who defines the nature of that quality, are therefore central issues for teacher education and for the participants in partnership. In addition, issues of internal quality assurance and general control need to be considered. The greater involvement of schools and further education colleges in teacher education is generally regarded as having positive consequences, in that it can provide a richer experience for initial training and more systematic planning of continuing professional development needs, thus enhancing professionalism in general. However, the sharing of control between partners may create some tensions, particularly when resources are limited. It also needs to be recognised that recent reforms over the last decade have resulted in increasing central government control, through stringent accreditation criteria set by Conservative Governments and direct control of funding and other resources. In turn, although reducing costs has not been an explicit aim of such reform, proposals such as the three-year B.Ed. course and the unwillingness to consider the true costs of school-based training can be seen as reflecting a concern to reduce the costs of teacher education.

Indeed, the costs involved in professional training development are becoming increasingly important. Schools and colleges may seek to obtain the full costs of their contributions to ITT courses given the general pressure on their resources. At the same time, higher education institutions are having to manage the implications of resource transfers to schools and colleges in a context of recent rapid expansion with few additional resources and continuing expectations of efficiency gains. Similar pressures exist in relation to continuing professional development, in that schools and colleges have limited resources for such activities, while higher education institutions have to ensure INSET courses are cost-effective and that they have sufficient resources to undertake the research that is required of them. Other participants, such as LEAs, have also seen a considerable reduction of resources, including, for LEAs, as a result of financial delegation to schools and college incorporation, a major change in the resources over which the LEA has control.

There is therefore a considerable danger that without some radical reform of funding approaches in particular, issues of control and costs may dominate partnership management. As Alexander (1990) has also noted, too much attention may also be paid to what he describes as the structural, organisational and enabling aspects of partnership, to the detriment of its action and interactional dimensions. Although procedural and resource issues are important, the factors that are most likely to enhance or impede partnership centre on the attitudinal divisions arising from different roles in different institutions, the personal experiences and interactions of pupils, students and teachers and the concepts which partnership participants hold. These last may range from views about the relationship between theory and practice to definitions of what counts as good practice in both education and professional development. Once enabling structures and procedures have been set in place, the focus should be on the exchange of knowledge, the development of shared understandings and values and the enhancement of interpersonal communication and interaction within the range of professional and educational activities operated by the partnership.

If management is to be effective, there also needs to be particular clarity about the contributions that each partner makes to the partnership. For example, in relation to initial training, staff in schools and further education colleges can provide detailed knowledge and experience of a specific setting, particular learners and particular forms of professional activity. Higher education staff, on the other hand, can provide knowledge and understanding of broader aspects of school, college and teacher education and can facilitate engagement with a broad range of settings and experiences. In relation to INSET, schools and further education colleges provide the practical context for continuing professional development and can identify and provide for a range of institutional and individual needs. Higher education institutions can extend such provision through courses involving teachers from a range of institutions and can provide specialist expertise and consultancy. Higher education institutions can also provide expertise and resources to support both individual researchers and research for institutional development. Higher education can also ensure that general resources and developments in both higher education and professional education benefit teacher education. Such resources and development can range from libraries to new approaches to courses, and links with training for other professions. Other participants also have much to offer, for example the potential role of LEAs discussed in Chapter 12.

A clear understanding of such reciprocal contributions, coupled with effective structures and procedures and opportunities to share knowledge and perspectives, are therefore likely to be the hallmarks of effective partnership. Management of partnership will also need to be based on a clear understanding of those aspects that are general to all partners and those that are specific to each. Although each partner will have particular responsibilities, all partners will need to consider the need for a shared vision of professional development and the way in which each partner contributes to the whole. Each institution or service will also have its own core aims, philosophy and system of organisation, and will be subject to different forms of external control and accountability. Partnership in teacher development is only one part of the concern of each partner and other internal and external pressures may therefore work against both the spirit and letter of cooperation.

Partnership will therefore need to be worked out on a detailed basis and cannot be taken for granted. It will need to be a key component of the strategic and operational planning of each partner and will involve joint goal setting and planning, and effective resource management, communication and staff development. Its major focus, namely the curricular and other professional learning experiences of teachers at various stages of professional development, will also need to be planned and implemented in detailed ways. The interpersonal elements of partnership will also need to be fostered, particularly given that partnership remains a voluntary relationship in an overall climate of competition rather than cooperation. However, given that collaboration and partnership are seen to be valuable in relation to a number of aspects of education (Hall and Wallace 1993; Ranson and Tomlinson 1994), there is no reason why teacher education should not experience the many benefits of such an approach to provision. Moreover, such cooperation is likely to engender the professional ethos which above all is required to support partnership.

PARTNERSHIP AND PROFESSIONALISM

So far, this chapter has concentrated on models of partnership and their development by the participants involved. The wider political and educational context has also been briefly considered, particularly in terms of the ways it has set both agenda and framework for partnership at the local level. However, an important and somewhat neglected aspect of partnership concerns the need to develop an alternative discourse and policy direction at national level, focused on the needs and interests of all those involved in the education service as a whole.

The traditional concept of a national education service, locally administered, involving centralised strategic planning across a range of issues from teacher supply to continuing professional development, is at considerable odds with the determination of recent Conservative governments to develop a market approach to public welfare services (LeGrand and Bartlett 1993) and to implement an education market based on the success (or otherwise) of individual institutions and services in responding to local 'consumer' needs. However, as a number of commentators have noted, the policy of these same governments has also limited the full operation of a market approach, through imposition of a range of central controls in relation to curriculum, levels and types of national and local funding and approaches to professional training and development. These governments have also kept a tight rein on many other aspects of policy, including the ways in which quality should be assessed in school, further and teacher education. The national dimensions of partnership and provision are therefore extremely important.

However, the growing diversity of courses and providers, the ethos of competition and the increasing fragmentation of the education service have made it more difficult to identify common local, let alone national, perspectives and to reconcile the interests of the various stakeholders involved. Moreover, such interests have been deliberately polarised in order to facilitate the implementation of particular policies. Thus the supposed interests of schools, for example, have been juxtaposed against those of higher education, transforming the rhetoric of partnership into a struggle for resources and control. Similarly, the interests of parents and an undefined public have been contrasted with those of the professionals, usually to the detriment of the latter.

Some of the contradictions of, and reasons for, such political strategies have been fully rehearsed elsewhere (Ball 1990). It is also clear that their consequences have been problematic, not least for the Conservative governments that originated such strategies. The intended effectiveness of the education market has been overlaid by conflict, with little value for the children, young people and their parents whom the educational reforms were meant to benefit. The improvements in standards, which the reforms were meant to entail, have also become increasingly questionable. However, as noted in several chapters in this book, there are some indications of a truce, if not yet a negotiated peace, in relations between the Conservative government and the teaching profession, which could be used to foster a new approach to educational debate and policy. The task is to find some common ground on which to build some new partnerships at national level, in relation to the various stakeholder perspectives and interests.

There is a strong case for arguing that many of the facets of successful partnership, as identified in this chapter and discussed in the various chapters in this book, are equally appropriate in this national context. New enabling structures and frameworks need to be developed, within which a more mutual and interactive culture can be established. This will, however, require subscription to some common themes, notably quality, effectiveness and professionalism.

Inevitably, each of these terms, like partnership, is a problematic concept. As with partnership, they are also often used as metaphors of intention rather than descriptors grounded in values, practice and research. Nevertheless, as noted in Chapter 14 in relation to professionalism, they have a wide resonance. Both teachers and the public want teaching to be a profession, recognising perhaps that sterile debates about status and definition are less important than the nature of the activity involved and the guarantee of quality which true professionalism brings.

It is also now widely recognised that although professionalism implies some autonomy, it also requires both responsibility and accountability. Although the former has been emphasised in the past by some in the teaching profession, to the exclusion of the latter, most teachers recognise the importance of such a balance, particularly given the tenor of recent policies. However, continuing emphasis by recent Conservative governments on external mechanisms of accountability and control has not adjusted in turn. There is a need for a cultural change by those who exercise political control of teacher education, in order to develop the reciprocal approach that we have argued is characteristic of the best partnerships. Relationships between any government and the professions will inevitably continue to be subject to a range of pressures and constraints, and struggles over resources and control, and will be shaped by history, culture and political power (Siegrist 1994). Teacher education in Britain has been subject to particular pressures for accountability, and change has been wide-ranging and centrally instituted (Taylor 1994). Nevertheless, as in local partnerships, attention now needs to be given to how government and profession, as partners, should and can contribute to teacher training and development, and how these mutual contributions can be synthesised.

The interests of government, working on behalf of society, include the supply of trained teachers and a teaching profession committed to quality and to continuing professional development and review, in order to ensure effective educational provision in all aspects of the education service. Government also has an interest in ensuring value for the money allocated to teacher education and research. Institutions and services, as employers and providers, have similar interests, although these will be focused on their particular needs and provisions. However they also require consistent national policies and long-term planning, recognition of the value of their mutual and diverse contributions and sufficient resources to ensure their responsibilities can be carried out effectively. They also need some autonomy at the local level together with encouragement of innovation. Teachers, whether experienced or students in training, require a range of opportunities and provision relevant to their professional development needs, high-quality learning experiences and a working environment that encourages effectiveness and respects their professionalism. Finally, learners, in whatever phase or sector of education, require good quality education, which is provided by a creative but accountable professional community and which addresses both current and future needs of individuals and society as a whole.

This inter-related system of needs and requirements depends on mutual recognition of contributions and responsibilities. A professional partnership is one where the contributions and the capacities of the various partners are truly acknowledged, and above all, trusted. As many of the contributors to this book argue, such professionalism will be best encouraged in a more professional political climate.

CONCLUSION

The management of partnership thus has many dimensions. In addition, it needs to be recognised that teacher education has a complex ecology. Change in one area will inevitably have an impact on another. For example, transfers of resources for initial training from higher education to schools may limit the capacity of higher education institutions to sustain the range of expertise required for INSET courses or research. Similarly, although a diversity of courses and providers may be desirable, in terms of innovation and choice, market behaviour within such diversity may have unintended consequences, such as an unwillingness to provide for certain expensive shortage subjects or for the needs of small specialist professional groups. Strategic planning is therefore required, particularly at government level, to balance market-led diversity, and in order to ensure that the professional community, and the education service within which it works, are truly effective.

Such planning is particularly important to successful management of partnership, whether at national, local or institutional level. Too often in recent years, education management has had to focus on immediate responses to a range of initiatives and changes. Although this has resulted in a number of desirable innovations within teacher education, it has also meant the implementation of some hastily tested models and above all, some loss of vision. In particular, development of the debate about the curriculum for teacher education, and the nature of professional practice, has been constrained by constant changes in course structures to meet accreditation requirements for ITT courses and new market demands for INSET provision. Although such issues are beyond the remit of this book, they are central to partnership, and will require new paradigms to resolve the tensions involved in the rationalist, behaviourist and reflective approaches to teaching, and thus, teacher education (Elliott 1993a, 1993b). There is an equal requirement for a reflective and critical debate about the nature of teacher professionalism in the future (Avis 1994). Although there is a continuing imperative to work within the current framework in the best ways possible, there is therefore now a paramount need to reflect upon experience and consider the future in a systematic way. This book is conceived as one contribution to that debate. The chapters that follow will pursue such themes in more depth.

Part II

The range of partnership

Chapter 2

Developing teacher education in a secondary school

Rowie Shaw

This chapter describes some aspects of initial teacher training in a secondary school, indicates links with other teacher education activities and examines some management issues related to partnership. As other chapters are concentrating on the higher education perspective, here the view is wholly that of the school.

Tong School is an oversubscribed, mixed 13–19 comprehensive with over 1400 pupils. Pupils come mainly from the inner city, with over 30 per cent from the Asian communities of Bradford. Achievement is consistent with the level of disadvantage, though value-added analyses show that our pupils achieve slightly higher than predicted when compared with the rest of Bradford, and we aim to do even better.

Staff have experienced pressure from funding restraints, deteriorating working conditions, the pace of change and the extensive refurbishment works that have taken place between 1992 and 1995. Despite all this, the commitment to change, school improvement and the raising of achievement, which underpins all our teacher education activities, remains very strong.

My own interest in teacher education, together with a tradition of innovation in the LEA and the school, have enabled us to develop our particular approach. As in all staffrooms, opposing views about the value of change can be expressed with equal vigour so we do not offer for your scrutiny a perfect model. Nevertheless we have a strong philosophy based on the reflective school as a learning environment.

If pupils are to achieve more highly, teachers need to teach in a different way. Pupil and teacher achievement are therefore inextricably linked. Every individual within the school is learning, at each stage in her or his career (Barth 1991). Teacher education is a continuum stretching from one's own experience as a pupil, through initial, induction and in-service training to appraisal and further training. It is the headteacher's role to further the development of everyone in the school (Shaw 1992).

If we see the raising of achievement through improvement of teaching and learning as our central purpose, we should be able to embrace rapid and constant change more readily. We base most of our staff development on activities where we can reflect on theory, apply it to classroom practice, work collaboratively with other partners and evaluate the results before the cycle begins again. All these are important ingredients in school improvement (Fullan 1992). As Ainscow and Hopkins (1992) note, individual development cannot be divorced from institutional development and vice versa.

TEACHER EDUCATION ACTIVITIES AT THE SCHOOL

Figure 2.1 shows the intrinsic unity behind all teacher education activities at the school. In relation to ITT we work with a major local higher education provider. The induction of newly qualified teachers (NQTs) is delivered both at the school and by Bradford LEA, who now have a limited input. Both interns and NQTs have mentors. Appraisal has been running at the school for some time. This is seen as part of staff development.

School-based INSET is offered mainly, though not exclusively, through our school improvement project, Improving the Quality of Education for All (IQEA), run in partnership with an Institute of Education and a local residential training provider. I initiated this project three years ago after discussion with the LEA and it was quickly adopted by staff. It is run by a cadre of staff from main grade to Deputy Head. I selected the original three members and the cadre then increased its own membership to five persons and later to eight, of whom four are also closely involved in initial and induction training. They in turn receive high-quality training from higher education staff and cascade their expertise down into the school. The focus of IQEA, which is 'access for all to the curriculum', was identified by staff. This focus is consonant with our school mission, development plan and the recommendations in a recent LEA inspection. It is broken down into cross-curricular working groups of volunteer staff

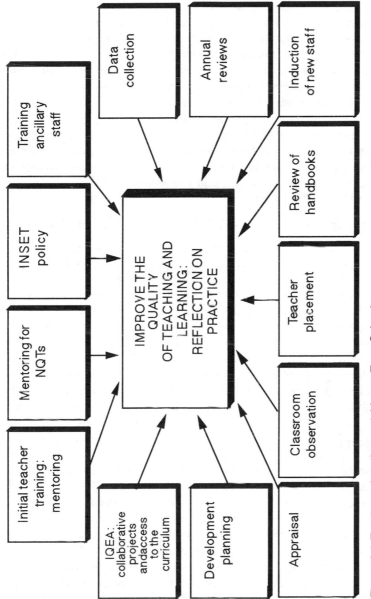

Figure 2.1 Teacher education activities at Tong School

(about 95 per cent of teachers and all support assistants) looking at issues such as differentiation, formative assessment and reading development.

These activities have the following common elements: a commitment to raise pupil and teacher achievement; a collaborative emphasis; mentoring or peer group coaching; the collection of data as part of monitoring and evaluation; the use of observation techniques; a classroom focus and the setting of personal targets to aid professional development. In all activities all participants are learning from each other. It is therefore possible to see such activities as parts of a whole rather than as a series of added extras. This is further enhanced by the fact that all staff development is coordinated by one of my two deputy heads, who is a founder member of the IQEA cadre. She is also responsible for monitoring and evaluation and the review of the school development plan. This arrangement works well and adds to the sense of unity between teacher education activities and the raising of achievement.

WORKING WITH OTHER PARTNERS

It is astonishing how the locus of decision making, control and collaboration has shifted since 1988. The development of grant-maintained schools, the delegation of budgets and government Grants for Education Support and Training (GEST) funding and the gradual weakening of the LEA have given us much more power and freedom to seek and choose other partners. This so-called 'autonomy' of schools (balanced by even greater central control) is apparent in the area of teacher education activities.

The Local Education Authority

The LEA is now almost incidental to the school's task of educating children. It is reduced to the role of contract agent and channel for some of our ever-reducing funds. At Tong School, governors stay within the LEA by choice but it has been made easy for schools to run their own affairs without reference to the LEA. Once the monolithic provider, our LEA now is a minor player in the gamut of partners with which the school works. It plays no part in ITT, a small part in providing induction for NQTs and after brokering IQEA for us, no role in that at all. We use some of our GEST money to buy consultancy from the LEA, including a link inspector, but this work is done within the framework described in this chapter and determined by the school rather than vice versa as before.

Higher education

As the influence of the LEA has decreased so has the role of higher education as a partner increased. The reduction in LEA advisory staff makes us turn to higher education and other providers for the intellectual stimulus which is essential to the reflective school. While we are engaged in theoretical activities as well as practice, it is hard to believe that the intellectual spark which will lead us to new subject knowledge or to new pedagogical theory can spontaneously ignite in the school setting. We would view with disquiet the removal of a research base from higher education Schools of Education, especially following the demise of the LEA.

Yet we note a marked disparity in the way in which our potential partners in higher education approach us and most strikingly in what they feel they can learn from us. As partnership is a two-way concept, this mutual respect must surely be a vital ingredient.

At Tong School we work with two main higher education partners, both of which we have chosen. This choice in itself is a new development. The partner for ITT is local and the other partner, for IQEA, is not. During 1992-3 we were courted by most of the four or five ITT providers we had worked with previously. There was quite a contrast in their approach to the schools in relation to funding, partnership and course structures. From our point of view, it was striking as well as understandable that all the higher education institutions seemed less ready than the schools to accept the shift in control of ITT which was apparent to us in recent reform and legislation.

We decided to sign with one provider. Funding considerations in the end weighed less heavily than the range of subjects offered, relative perceptions of quality between higher education institutions and our long-standing tradition of partnership with that institution. For the first year we decided to have only one partner for ITT in order to allow ourselves to establish procedures for the greater role we would play. In future years we may well work with more than one partner, especially in subject areas not offered by our major provider. We have not considered going it alone.

Our second higher education partner, which works with us in relation to IQEA, is explicit about its willingness to empower school staff through the partnership. The number of partner schools in IQEA is similar to the number involved in our ITT agreement but the contracting is more focused, with training being bought just like any other training package. Higher education provides the training for the cadre as well as for the whole staff, with a certain number of days being guaranteed, both in school and off-site. Planning is normally jointly undertaken and the training is felt to be of high quality and appropriate to our needs. Regular evaluation of the project is carried out by both higher education staff and the cadre and feedback is seen to be acted upon. The school is made to research and implement its own developments which are accorded value by our partners. We are also aware that we form part of a research base for the higher education institution staff and this serves as an incentive for us to try and get it right.

Other schools

Links with other schools for ITT are tenuous. This is partly due to the competitive relationships between schools fostered by educational legislation since 1988. Heads met as a group prior to ITT agreements being signed as there was some wrangling with higher education over the amount of funding to schools. However, since that time there has been little contact. Although school coordinators meet together once a term, they are not trained together as a discrete group. Mentors, on the other hand, do meet in subject groups and have felt these peer group meetings to be particularly helpful. The system of pairing schools, to enable ITT students to have teaching experience in more than one school, has in this first year been left in some schools to the student interns, which has reduced those schools' ability to cluster with other schools.

For IQEA there are regular residential sessions for the cadre with other schools on the project, some of which by chance are also involved in the local ITT partnership. Some strong links have therefore been formed, and these carry over into other activities such as joint training for mentors of NQTs.

We also considered the invitation of our local City Technology College (CTC) to join them in their initiative to train technology teachers but were deterred by the small print which would have obliged us to join the CTC Trust, as well as by the burden of other work we are undertaking.

Other partners in training

We work with an increasing number of other trainers. Some are private consultants but chief among our other partners is the Training and Enterprise Council (TEC). Most of the training and development we carry out for the pastoral curriculum, including Careers, Recording Achievement, Youth Credits and some General National Vocational Qualification (GNVQ) development, has been carried out with support from the TEC in terms of expertise, personnel, networking and funding. We see their role increasing as the role of LEA continues to dwindle.

RESOURCE ISSUES

Only a few years ago we took it for granted that all teacher education activities were free. However, we have learned very quickly in schools to put a cost on every activity and to demand accounts from our partners of what exactly we are contributing to, and possibly subsidising, in relation to the elements of ITT funding top-sliced by the higher education institution for its general expenditure. This lesson could well be learnt by the Schools of Education. Equally rapidly, we have begun to learn to cope with the bewildering array of funding sources. Schools can no longer afford to sit back passively, waiting for funding to arrive automatically from the LEA. Regrettably, we have to hustle for every penny. At Tong School we receive money for teacher education activities through higher education, Grants for Education Support and Training (GEST) through the LEA, and funding for the work-related curriculum and school-industry links through the TEC. We also had industrial sponsorship for a conference which I shall describe below.

Initial teacher training

When the offer eventually came from higher education of £900 per student, plus travelling expenses and supply cover for school staff during training, this was thought to be reasonable. Funding was adjusted for 1994-5 as teaching costs have risen by about 3 per cent. The school had started bargaining at £2000 per student, countered by an opening offer from higher education of around £300. It was helpful that the level of funding was known in time for us to build non-contact time for mentors into the timetable. It would have been impossible to provide an appropriate level of support without timetabled time with students on the specific day they are in school.

Each student costs us about £1000 per year at current costs for timetabled time with mentors and some of the additional time that other staff spend on ITT. Materials and reprographic costs run into several hundreds of pounds. This does not allow for secretarial costs. For example, each intern generates several references. Nor does it include time given by staff to contribute to the school induction programme, nor the weekly tutorials nor preparation and copying costs. Nor does it include time given by mentors, other staff or the school coordinator to prepare work with the students. Perhaps £2000 was about right!

Induction and INSET activities

These are mainly funded through GEST. Our LEA does play a significant enabling role here by delegating GEST to us and identifying how we may spend it appropriately. In addition it supports us by helping us bid for special GEST projects. Two years' extra funding for a reading development programme enabled us to finance IQEA.

Apart from these major investments, GEST for National Curriculum development is delegated by a formula to departments and a central fund of about £1000 is kept centrally for use by me and my deputy to finance management training and courses targeted in appraisal statements.

Directed time is also a resource that we use to finance IQEA meetings and some of the time spent on appraisal. We may also claim for supply cover for appraisal, although this cushioning will eventually be phased out. There has been no extra resourcing for the induction and mentoring of NQTs other than some training organised by the LEA.

THE WHOLE SCHOOL APPROACH

An important aid to articulating the links between all our training activities is the school development plan. The management team and the cadre take every opportunity to make explicit to staff and governors the links between all the projects described above. The regular evaluation and celebration of achievements through staff development activities are vital. An annual exhibition of work achieved by each IQEA project, as well as a written report, aid this process.

In November 1993, the school organised and hosted a major national conference on teacher education with speakers from schools, higher education and research organisations. This expert input was supplemented by a bookstall which did a substantial trade in texts related to staff development. The conference was attended by academics and school staff from all phases who sent in some very positive feedback. In addition, twenty Tong staff received some very high-quality input which drew together the common strands of all our training activities. The support we received from speakers and participants was only slightly tempered by the one or two highly critical letters we received before the event from senior personnel from other higher education institutions who were openly aghast at the presumption of a school which thought it could organise such an event. The conference therefore symbolised both the best and the worst aspects of the new partnerships.

THE EFFECT ON STAFF AND PUPILS

Most of the teachers who act as mentors for interns and NQTs, all of whom are also involved in IQEA, can articulate the links between these activities, which they see as collaboration, observation and focused reflection. Most of these colleagues are not heads of department. All were approached by the school coordinator following consultation with the head of department, in the first instance, and offered the role. All eventually accepted but some gave the matter a great deal of thought. All have shown enormous enthusiasm and we have been genuinely impressed with the quality of the support they have offered. Staff involved in ITT have received training at our partner higher education institution, with one introductory day to launch the partnership and the remaining days led by subject specialists from the higher education institution covering both specific curriculum topics and general studies.

Accreditation for mentors is available on this scheme. The five days' training may be used as a module on a Master's degree programme, but so far this option has not been taken up at our school. Within IQEA there is also the option of a Certificate of Professional Development, which is currently being pursued by the support assistants who work so diligently on the project.

In the main, mentors have appreciated the contact with subject and method tutors from higher education as well as with student interns and young teachers. They all feel that they have developed as teachers, acquiring new ideas, learning to reflect on their own practice and reading slightly more. Being a mentor is seen as having status and recognition and all mentors say that they would undertake the role again.

Despite fears that an influx of inexperienced teachers would have an adverse effect on pupil discipline, this has proved largely unfounded. Indeed there have been one or two cases of a group's discipline improving. There has only been one parental complaint about a student intern which led to a class change. Mentors monitor discipline closely and are made to think carefully about their own behaviour management techniques by working with trainee teachers. After the first year of IQEA we were encouraged to see a very significant improvement in achievement at GCSE. It is too early, however, to attribute this success entirely to the project.

LEARNING FROM EXPERIENCE

Some recommendations for change will now be made based on lessons learned from experience, focusing on partnership, time-tabling, resourcing and course structure.

Are we equal partners in ITT? Is higher education ready to divest itself of its lead role? In the best partnerships there does appear to be a recognition that academics can learn from practitioners. This mutual respect would seem to be the main ingredient for success.

The best partnerships will allow for course management committee members from schools and higher education to consult and inform their constituency, with a knowledge that their views are making a difference. Training programmes should use expertise to be found both in schools and higher education and documentation originating from the higher education institution should identify clearly how much teachers have contributed. Schools should have direct input into course self-assessment and OFSTED inspection and their staff should have equal access to higher education library resources. The respective roles of school coordinator and link tutor need to be more clearly defined and schools should be consulted about their link tutor, with the option to renegotiate at intervals.

There are also timetabling and scheduling issues, such as the use of time given to higher education staff for professional updating. Given that this is a resource for schools, headteachers should have a say in how this is creatively deployed as a resource for other teacher education activities.

It appears desirable to combine aspects of mentor training for ITT and NQTs with appraisal training, and indeed with general management training, as many of the skills are the same. In practice this proves difficult because of the diversity of our partners and the different time-scales required by each project. Schools need to timetable meetings for the school coordinator with all mentors, who should also meet as a peer group. It would be helpful for higher education to extend successful ITT partnerships into induction or INSET activities, especially if associated with continuous assessment or profiling of teacher performance and development.

It has proved possible to follow theoretical input from the higher education institution with practical applications in school but greater standardisation across higher education and school subject departments would help. Due regard should also be given to timetabling, including the days which students spend in school. For example, higher education staff may wish to use Fridays for their own meetings and planning. However, this may not be a useful day from the school's point of view for students to carry out teaching practice or tutorials in schools. Schools should also have systems for tracking individual pupils or teaching groups to see for how many periods in the week they are being taught by students, to ensure that some balance is kept.

When courses are planned, the teacher's pastoral role should be given more weight, playing a part in final assessments, as students do not always afford this a high priority. Some younger mentors may focus more on classroom techniques than on issues of professional expectation such as attendance and punctuality. We should afford this aspect greater emphasis in future mentor training.

Resourcing will continue to be a problematic issue as long as local bargaining persists. Will those higher education institutions which ask schools to account for the money they have delegated also give an account to their partners in schools of how exactly the sums retained by higher education are spent?

CONCLUSION

On the whole we do feel that we have moved forward as individuals and as a school and have learnt from our partnerships with higher education. How much, I wonder, have they learnt from us?

There is as yet no way of comparing views with schools in other partnerships. Will the Teacher Training Agency, OFSTED or the teachers' unions address this issue of sharing practice from the schools' perspective?

The responsibility of school managers at all levels to communicate with and develop staff within an agreed framework is an important shift in our perspective of professionalism. It has resonances in relation to Total Quality Management and other approaches to quality assurance and development, such as the Investors in People Scheme. Any innovation which improves management, increases the understanding of both theory and practice and helps staff and pupils develop, can only be welcome.

Chapter 3

School-based training for secondary initial training

Richard Pring

The University of Oxford has, over a period of ten years, developed a partnership with schools in the initial training of teachers, on the basis of which it is possible to reflect on the merits of the recent Conservative Government policy. That policy is expressed in the statement that 'the Government has decided that . . . schools should play a much larger part in initial teacher training as full partners of higher education institutions' (DES 1992: 1). Subsequently, details have been attached to that broad statement of intention. They include the requirement that at least two-thirds of the thirty-six weeks of the PGCE year should be school-based.

There have been further developments of such policy, indicating the deep suspicion of the contribution that higher education makes to initial training. Such developments include the possibility of schools or clusters of schools putting forward their own proposals for initial training. The schools, rather than higher education, would be in the driving seat.

As the director of a department that claims to have pioneered a distinctive model of initial training, I should no doubt welcome these two initiatives. Both, it would seem, suspect the 'theory into practice' model, the institutional divide and the lack of partnership which have characterised so much initial training, and it seems, share the view that initial training should be school-centred. That, however, is not how I see it. The involvement of schools and the nature of the partnership can take different forms, and characteristic of the present rush to conform to these and other recent Conservative Government requirements are schemes which are ill-thought out, and lacking in a rationale based on teacher learning or on the distinctive roles of higher education and schools.

I wish in this chapter, therefore, to argue for the distinctive roles of higher education and schools. That requires closer attention to principles of learning and to the complex nature of teaching than is generally the case as partnership agreements are hurriedly entered into. In doing this, I refer particularly to the account given by McIntyre and Hagger (1992) who have done more than most both to develop 'internship' and to draw lessons from the experience.

I shall do three things in this chapter. First, I shall argue for the principles and practices of school-focused training. Second, I shall illustrate this by reference to the Oxford Scheme. Third, I shall draw from that account certain distinctive features of teachers as professionals and the implications of this for the distinctive role of higher education.

INITIAL TRAINING

The term 'school-based' is inappropriate for the kind of partnership that I have in mind. Certainly, the majority of the time must be spent in school. Certainly, it is there, in the practical context of the school, that the most fruitful professional development will take place. But, first, there will be a substantial time spent away from that practical context – essential if the new teacher is to stand back and reflect critically on that practice. Second, and more importantly, in a genuine partnership even the school-centred part – the majority part – will have a significant higher education involvement. Higher education must not be identified with buildings. Its members can work in schools, just as teachers can work in higher education. It is more helpful to think in terms of a partnership between them and the distinctive contributions of each to the main activity, wherever that takes place.

What is that activity? It is, first and foremost, learning about the practice of teaching. The key questions are: how best do trainee teachers learn and what is it that they need to learn? Everything must relate to the quality of that learning experience – the 'how' and the 'what'.

One reason why there cannot be simple answers to those questions is that different teachers, like the children they teach, will learn in different ways. They adopt different learning styles.

Furthermore, like the children they teach, they start from different places. They come with different conceptions of the tasks, of the values to be imparted, of the nature of the subject matter to be taught, of their own talents and weaknesses, of how children learn and of what is worthwhile learning. Finally, therefore, there can be no ready-made theory upon which practice might be based or on exactly how trainee teachers should be trained.

That, therefore, leads us to the formulation of one important principle which should govern the training of teachers, namely, that it should be so organised as to enable and to encourage the learning teacher to explore, to formulate and to test out ideas of what is worth learning and how it might be learnt.

There are two dangers in the changes which recent Conservative governments have imposed. First, there is the danger that learning to teach could become nothing other than an apprenticeship to whatever practices prevail in the school to which the learner is attached. Preconceptions of teaching and of the nature of the subject to be taught go unchallenged. A set of techniques is acquired. The second danger is that learning to teach could be reduced to the finite list of competences dictated by whatever quango is given the power so to prescribe. But, as is argued by McIntyre and Hagger,

> no generalised knowledge claims about teaching can confidently be asserted as valid, and especially not prescriptions for good practice. Consequently *the central principle is that all ideas which seem valuable must be tested*. Furthermore, since teaching is a complex, value-laden, instrumental social activity, adequate testing of any ideas which are to inform practice must take account of a wide range of criteria. Some criteria . . . will generally be applied most easily in the university context. Other equally important criteria . . . can only be applied in the settings of particular school contexts.
>
> (1992: 269)

A second principle follows from this. The school must be an environment in which this exploration and testing might take place, indeed, be encouraged. It must be mature enough to allow for alternative points of view and for prevalent views to be challenged. And that may require a shift in the climate of the school, where questions are asked about the values to be promoted through the teaching of English, say, or about the most appropriate way of organising group work. Subject to the questioning of future teachers, where such questioning is encouraged, the school has to change from a merely teaching institution to a learning one.

Third, the teacher development required is too often seen to lie solely in classroom management or in the transmission of subject content. However, there is much more to it than that. The teacher is to be initiated into a form of life, a community in which there are professional responsibilities that go beyond the classroom and indeed within which classroom practices need to be understood. What happens in the classroom cannot be disconnected from a school policy on equal opportunities or from the social context of the school or from the management style of the head. Therefore, future teachers are best prepared through close attachment to a school whereby, through acceptance by the staff generally and through participation in policy discussions, they are able to acquire that wider professional perspective – and, indeed, to establish a clearer but critical picture of where they stand in relationship to these matters.

Fourth, such development and new learning, often in personally very demanding circumstances, require the mutual support of others. Such support provides not only solace when things are difficult, but also the forum through which ideas are formed and critical questions raised. The Oxford Scheme requires a minimum of eight 'interns' per school, drawn from different subject areas, a group that is large enough for the critical interchange of ideas and for the school to see itself as a centre for professional development. The school simply cannot remain indifferent to a group of at least eight, raising questions and sharing the life of the school.

Fifth, the critical questioning and the self-evaluation, as trainee teachers develop the appropriate understanding, professional skills and attitudes, require two kinds of support. There is the need, especially in the early stages, for daily supervision of the teaching, conducted by the person who, through example or critical observation or instruction, sees to the development of the craft of teaching. Such supervision, involving constant reflection and evaluation, will draw upon a wealth of experience and professional know-how, which often remains unarticulated. For this shared reflection and comment to take place, the teacher or mentor who accepts responsibility for the trainee teachers needs allocated time.

At the same time, there is a need for a broader vision, a raising of questions which go beyond the here and now of the particular classroom or school. At least, that should be the case once the initial period is over – when the trainee teacher feels sufficiently confident in classroom management to embrace a more critical stance. That wider picture and deeper questioning are supported through the links of the specific school to higher education, those links through which a school is part of a wider network of schools. And the higher education institution itself ought to be in a position to inject a more theoretical and research-based contribution to the deliberations that take place, though this might be questioned by a government committed to school-based training and by schools which have not been convinced by their experiences of higher education. This distinctive contribution will be argued in the third section of this chapter.

Reflecting on these principles, one might suggest certain practices. The first is, as I have indicated, the importance of creating schools which, in another context, might be called 'training schools', in so far as the school as a whole sees as one of its functions that of helping with the preparation of teachers and consequently adapts itself to this purpose. Such adaptation requires serious attention to teachers' learning; it requires allocated time for those teachers, the mentors, who have been assigned the task of supporting the new teachers; and it requires regular seminars which bring the various constituents together so that systematic attention might be given to the underlying principles of the practice of the school.

The second is that the development of the trainee teachers needs to be acknowledged in the phasing of the different stages of induction. Such a phasing will acknowledge the different paces at which development takes place. Initially, there is the need to gain the confidence of the classroom teacher, acquiring basic skills, knowing that one is able to work fruitfully with young people, plan lessons and organise time effectively. However, the induction needs to be gradual, carefully monitored and closely supervised. The subsequent phase is when the trainee teachers are able with confidence to explore more widely the teaching strategies appropriate to different situations, to test out ideas, and to develop their own distinctive styles. In the final phase, there should be that systematic evaluation, the acquisition of the skills and habits of reflection, which will be the basis of further and continuous professional learning in subsequent careers.

Third, assessment should be tied to these different phases, to reflect the different stages of development, including the range of skills that a competent teacher will need, the ability to think more deeply about the issues which impinge upon practice, the capacity for reflection and evaluation and the professional qualities of working within a community geared to the learning opportunities of all children irrespective of age, ability or social background.

Fourth, joint planning, implementation, teaching, assessment and monitoring are required between school and higher education – between the subject specialists and teacher mentors; between the professional tutor in the school who has overall responsibility for the school's contribution and the equivalent person in higher education relating to that school; and between the mentors and tutors from the different schools. This requires the higher education tutors to work and teach regularly in the schools, and in turn, the school mentors to be involved in higher education.

The principles and the practice that I have briefly outlined are a far cry from the practice, seen all too frequently, in which the theory is provided by higher education and the practice is an apprenticeship into the ways of teaching of a particular school. What I am arguing for is a programme of initiation in which there are different partners with their own distinctive roles, and in which the school and the mentor engage in a very different sort of activity from what they are used to. It is not something that is a mere extension of normal school activities. It is not an activity that can be simply drifted into without appropriate adjustment and preparation.

The principles and practice that I am arguing for, however, presuppose two other arguments. The first is an argument for the professional status of teaching – for otherwise why not a form of craft or technician training along lines prescribed by a very prescriptive government? The second is an argument for the distinctive role of higher education, a role that has been both attacked by recent Conservative governments and betrayed by those institutions which have scattered their students to schools with little thought given to the nature of student teacher learning, how it should be structured, how it should be contextualised and how it should be supported.

I shall then, in the final section, examine briefly the professional nature of the job for which the new teacher is being prepared, and the distinctive role of higher education, which is linked to that professional role. Before that, however, I wish to illustrate what I have said about principles and practice by reference to the arrangements, and the current thinking about these arrangements, within the Oxford University Internship Scheme.

THE OXFORD UNIVERSITY INTERNSHIP SCHEME

The shape of the year is one in which the 'interns', after an introductory period including observation in other schools, are attached to one school for the major part of the year. In that way, they become integrated into the school, and are not strangers or appendages as so often happens. The trainee teacher sees the rhythm of the school year and participates in staff meetings, parent visits and various school activities. The professional nature of the job is seen to go beyond the classroom to a community which has wider responsibilities and which embodies a set of values which need to be understood and examined critically.

The school attachment is divided into two phases. The first is partly in the school and partly in the university. In the school, there is a closely supervised introduction to classroom practice. In the second phase the intern is full-time in the school. However, throughout this phase there is a professional development programme, initially in both university and school, but subsequently in the school only, which is jointly planned and implemented by the school's professional tutor and the university's general tutor attached to that school.

There is a minimum of eight interns per school – one school has as many as sixteen. They work in subject pairs but in the larger group for their professional development. For each pair there is a mentor, and relating to each subject mentor is a university curriculum tutor. One important outcome of the Internship Scheme has been the development, based on research, of the role of the mentor (see Hagger, Burn and McIntyre 1993). Just as the professional development programme is jointly planned, so is the curriculum programme jointly planned between university tutors and school mentors. There is, in other words, a complex and beneficial network of teachers and university tutors covering the main curriculum subjects and the wider professional issues.

Jointly they plan; jointly they monitor; jointly they assess the interns at key assessment points. The emphasis, once the interns have confidence and competence in basic classroom management, is upon the exploration of learning – both the pupils' and their own – and upon development of professional understanding and self-evaluation.

Recently, this model has been subject to a thorough review, based on commissioned research. This is reported in detail in a forthcoming book (Rothwell, Nardi and McIntyre 1994). Despite the research that has already gone into the internship scheme, there is, however, still so much that is not known about how trainee teachers learn – and about how mentors, too, learn how to teach or to plan, about the support they need, and above all about what happens to pupils' learning.

TEACHING AS A PROFESSION AND THE ROLE OF HIGHER EDUCATION

The inadequacy of the traditional model of teacher training – of a theoretical introduction followed by practice and of a conception of practice in which the trainee is apprenticed to a teacher – lies in the nature of teaching as a profession. There are three aspects of this that I wish to mention very briefly, as they are developed by Tomlinson and Edwards elsewhere in this book.

First, teachers are licensed to teach because they have something special to offer and are 'an authority' in some subject matter that is important for pupils to learn. In the secondary school, that expertise or authority lies mainly in the knowledge and understanding of a particular subject, gained more often than not from having studied it at university. However, it is so often the case that knowledge of that subject gained through undergraduate studies does not involve reflection upon the nature of the subject, or indeed upon the particular value of it within the broad perspective of education. The trainee teacher, often for the first time, has to reflect upon the nature of that which is to be taught – first, because, without that reflection, it is difficult in curriculum planning to sift the essential from the contingent, the key concepts from the fringe ones and the central themes from the incidental; and second, because, if the point and value of teaching a subject do not enter into one's thinking about what to do, there can be but poor justification of what one does to the sceptical pupils, their parents and indeed to the public at large.

Second, distinctive of any profession are the values which shape the relationship between the professional and the client – in this case, the relationship between teacher and learner. In broad terms, such values must refer to the primary value of the welfare and needs of the learner, not of the economy or the parents. Just as the lawyer will serve the interests of the defendant and the doctor the interests of the patient, so too will the *professional* teacher serve the interests of the child. This could be spelt out in terms of an ethical code – concerning confidentiality, the resistance to rewards that deflect from those interests or the assertion of what is in the interests of the child, often against government or business promotions. Such values are in constant jeopardy, and yet they are reflected in countless school communities where teachers respond to pupils' needs without counting the cost or where they patiently devote time to pupils whose behaviour invites rejection by those less committed.

One should not underestimate the values that permeate teaching as a professional activity, and thus the independence of a tradition that resists the political interference of government, the blandishments of commercialism or the cultural poverty of the media. And it is that – not just classroom management skills – to which the new teacher is being introduced.

Third, distinctive of a profession is the responsibility it is entrusted with for such matters as membership, discipline, values pertaining to its activities and advice to government and others. Even without, at present, a General Teaching Council, as discussed in Chapter 14, that responsibility is exercised at many levels within the educational system, despite recent Conservative Government attempts to prescribe exactly what should be learnt and how that learning must be organised.

Initiation into the culture of professional responsibility is a lengthy process. Indeed such initiation must be part of induction and subsequent professional development, as increased responsibility is earned and given. However, the process begins with initial training, and hence the importance in that training of going beyond classroom skills to participation in a school culture where this sense of professional responsibility *vis-à-vis* government, parents and the community is clearly practised.

It has been the aim of many in recent Conservative governments to undermine the role of higher education in the training of teachers. After all, if schools are under-functioning, then who better to blame than those who trained the teachers? If standards have been compromised by pupil-centred methods, then who better to accept responsibility than those who have introduced teachers to Dewey and Froebel? Higher education institutions, however, in opposing the purely apprenticeship model that is one interpretation of 'school-based initial teacher training', must do so because of the essential role they play in the preservation of teaching as a profession.

First, given the significance of teacher expertise within an intellectual discipline, it is essential that schools are linked to those institutions whose primary job it is to maintain, through research and critical discussion, the health of those disciplines.

Second, it is inconceivable that 25,000 schools could each have the range of expertise that needs to be drawn upon for the benefit of the learner – in special needs, for example, or in equal opportunities or in a particular subject. If higher education involvement were to be abolished, then soon would develop similar centres of expertise which could be shared with hard-pressed schools, at least if the spirit of cooperation could be preserved within the context of competitive market forces. Higher education institutions at their best have aimed to become and to maintain such centres of expertise that might feed into schools, often through the contacts made through initial training.

Third, the values entailed by professionalism require an independent and critical spirit in face of pressures – whether they come from government, commerce or the public at large. Institutions of higher education remain, despite the encroachments upon their autonomy, centres of a critical tradition in a world that is increasingly over-regulated and prescriptive. It is important always to feel free to say unpopular and critical things – and to have the institutions that protect the saying of them.

Fourth, the problematic nature of education requires a tradition of systematic enquiry, a programme of research which informs the practice of teaching. Higher education should provide centres of relevant research activities in which schools, as learning communities, can participate.

These distinctive contributions of higher education (centres of intellectual enquiry, expertise, a critical tradition and relevant research), though too often lacking, provide the context in which school-focused teacher training should take place. They are the basis of the higher education curriculum tutor's relationship with the mentor, of the role of the higher education tutor in jointly planning and implementing the professional development programme, of the support for mentor and trainee teacher and of work based in higher education in which partner schools participate. In the absence of that, then we are introducing the trainee teacher to the craft, maybe, but not to the profession, of teaching. However, that partnership itself must constantly be subject to the critical scrutiny and research which is characteristic of the good higher education institution. It is a pity that this has so rarely happened.

Chapter 4

A developmental model of partnership between primary schools and higher education

Georgina Glenny and Elizabeth Hickling

The notion of partnership generated by recent educational policy indicates a determination to challenge the traditional role of higher education in the initial training of teachers. This has resulted in a rather truncated debate about partnership, focused primarily on the allocation of power and resources between schools and higher education, and has obscured the more fundamental shared core purpose of improving the quality of teaching and learning for children. Such a purpose may be implicit in policy requirements for a greater sharing of responsibility in the training process. However, the imperative to compete for limited resources and the underlying critique of present modes of training have distorted the debate. This has meant that the starting point for negotiations about partnership has been a lack of clarity about roles and responsibilities, leading to anxiety and distrust. This situation has also been exacerbated by the narrow view from recent Conservative governments, in particular, that partnership is occurring if resources are being transferred from higher education to schools.

Underlying such government thinking is a critique of higher education's contribution to the training of teachers and an endorsement of an apprenticeship model of training in schools. The wider, reflective role higher education has provided in the past is being minimised. Such an approach supports the limited public notion of the teacher's role as comprising standing and delivering the curriculum, with little sense of the much wider professional knowledge required. Both higher education and the professionalism of the teacher's role are being implicitly criticised. Partnership has been introduced in such a way that schools and higher education institutions are being encouraged to invalidate each other's roles.

In resolving on a policy in this inauspicious climate, a central premise at Oxford Brookes University has been that successful partnership should be predicated upon mutual respect and understanding. Clarity within and between roles is seen to be crucial. Successful partnership involves setting up structures and developing relationships that draw upon the different and various strengths in schools and higher education, examining their traditional roles as bases of professional training. It is clear that each has had specific roles and that partnership will only be realised and developed to the extent to which contributions can be dovetailed. However, in order for roles to be negotiated, a forum for dialogue needs to be set up.

We therefore initially held consultation meetings, which offered schools a range of options in relation to roles, relationships and levels of involvement. Our research and discussions with over one hundred primary schools have shown that they are at different stages in their commitment to training teachers and would like to be involved in a variety of ways. Although many schools have expressed a desire for a greater role in the training process, most feel that training should continue to be led by higher education. Schools have been particularly concerned that a focus on initial teacher training should not distract from their primary concern to provide the best possible learning environment for children. The schools that have welcomed a greater role in initial training see their involvement as an important pathway for staff development. Such staff development is perceived to occur in two ways. First, it is part of the necessary reflection on practice involved in supporting a student teacher. Second, better communication with higher education can facilitate access to higher education institutions and staff as a resource and as a means of meeting wider INSET needs.

From the perspective of those in higher education, good quality contact with schools is equally important. For students training to be teachers, the quality of their school placements, and in particular the model of the teaching role they experience, have an enormous impact on their professional development. The relationship between experience within school and within the higher education institution will also affect significantly the way in which students make sense of their initiation into the role of

teacher. If these two forms of experience are not properly articulated, students' professional development will be impeded. Those
involved in initial teacher training must have an overview of the
models of practice which schools can offer, to enable them to
place students where their needs will best be met.

At the same time, without good quality contact with teachers
and schools, the knowledge of staff working in higher education
may become reified. The presentation of professional experience
for study and discussion requires particular skills and expertise
developed over time, but also requires close contact with children
and schools to be maintained. The closer the links higher
education staff have with the particular concerns of particular
schools, the more likely they are to be able to support students
in the development of their professional knowledge and skills and
their capacity to reflect upon their own actions.

In the past, higher education could be criticised for not putting
sufficient emphasis on the necessary communication networks
and flexible ways of working required to facilitate closer relationships with schools. The imperative for closer partnership is a
welcome opportunity to experiment with new ways of working
together. Joint staff development can be a focus for closer
collaboration between schools and higher education. From an
enhanced relationship, the professional needs and purposes of
staff development, both in higher education and schools, can be
jointly articulated, planned, executed and evaluated in the light of
common objectives. Such principles inform the development plan
for initial teacher training for primary education, and related
INSET, at Oxford Brookes University. The core concern is seen
to be the enhancement of children's learning through the ongoing
professional development of teachers and teacher educators.
Shared staff development is therefore central to the approach.

A DEVELOPMENTAL APPROACH TO PARTNERSHIP

Our planning at Oxford Brookes is based on a developmental
approach, which aims to ensure that the relationship with
schools is reciprocal, based on shared and equivalent strengths
and expertise. It therefore contests the notion, discussed above, of
a trading relationship with schools locked into contractual obligations that are inconsistent with ever-changing school contexts.
This is not to deny the importance of an economic relationship.

However, it is anticipated that it should be subsumed within any model.

A further underlying assumption is that relationships are based on trust between individuals engaged in shared concerns, rather than on structures and systems. However, some structures and systems are more likely to develop trusting relationships than others. As relationships develop, the structural framework may also prove restrictive and therefore the possibilities for flexibility need to be considered at an early stage.

Partnerships with schools can be conceived as comprising three main stages of involvement, developing from a 'present state' through a 'transition phase' to 'active partnership'. Each stage will have characteristic qualities but may take a variety of forms. In the first two stages, the emphasis is on initial training. However, as partnership develops it should encompass ongoing professional development for all those involved in the training process. These stages and their elements are illustrated in Figure 4.1 on pages 60 and 61.

Such choices allow schools a range of levels of involvement and provide a way forward that can be based on present strengths in relationships with schools. The gradual and developmental approach avoids the problems that could result if attempts are made to involve all schools in a particular stage at the same time, especially in a climate of diminishing resources.

Drawing from the choice of stages identified in Figure 4.1, some schools may wish to continue with their present state of involvement, namely supporting students on school experience in initial training courses, with clear guidelines concerning roles and responsibilities established by higher education. At this stage, involvement is initiated by the higher education institution and communication largely comprises information about school experience. Staff development is limited and relationships between schools and higher education staff are *ad hoc*. Quality assurance remains the prime responsibility of higher education. This stage does not involve the transfer of resources. Our discussions with schools have focused on the importance of quality in teacher training and where schools have been concerned that they may not be able to fulfil additional commitments, they have resisted the temptation of additional resources.

Nevertheless, a number of schools have participated more fully in the initial training process in various ways, for example by

	PRESENT STATE	TRANSITION PHASE	ACTIVE PARTNERSHIP
UNDERSTANDING OF, AND COMMITMENT TO, PARTNERSHIP	School involvement in ITT by invitation from higher education. School experience placements by higher education on an individual school basis. Schools informed about course through information booklets. School staff teach occasional elements at the higher education institution. Involvement in selection of students for admission to ITT courses.	ITT school experience placements by higher education. Schools aware of pattern for whole course, and encouraged to work with a particular course for a period. Schools involved in ITT course design through representation on planning committees. Negotiation of ITT roles and responsibilities, including student selection, course tracking and school experience supervision.	Clustering of schools working with one ITT course. Involvement in ITT course design through a regular forum. Increased responsibility for student mentoring. Greater involvement in selection of students and in teaching higher education-based elements of ITT courses. Regular review of partnership arrangements by all involved. Partnership seen to include INSET. Development of further initiatives such as joint research.
COMMUNICATION	Initiated through school experience coordinators in higher education. Basic information about school experience. *Ad hoc* relationship between schools and higher education staff.	More comprehensive information about the course/ school experience. Designated higher education staff for particular schools. Meetings about school experience led by higher education but involving feedback from schools.	Full information about all aspects of ITT and INSET courses. Regular newsletters. ITT school experience organised with a group of schools, students and higher education staff.

STAFF DEVELOPMENT	Meetings to discuss practicalities of school experience. Some involvement of school staff in INSET provided by the higher education institution.	Partnership team developed by higher education. Some mentor training.	Joint school/higher education staff mentor training. Accredited mentor training linked to professional qualifications. Development of a resource centre for curriculum areas. Cluster-led INSET programme and conferences. Range of INSET activities planned by schools and higher education to meet individual and institutional needs.
QUALITY ASSURANCE	Triangulated assessment of school experience based on criteria generated by higher education. Assignments set and marked by higher education staff. Procedures required by higher education institution.	Triangulated assessment of school experience but with fuller involvement of school staff. Assignments set and marked by higher education staff. Feedback from schools incorporated into quality assurance procedures.	Involvement of schools in designing and implementing criteria for assessment of students. Accreditation of mentors. Range of quality assurance procedures agreed by schools and higher education institution.
RESOURCES	No transfer of resources to schools.	Priority given to partnership work within higher education staff timetable. Use of higher education staff in school to release teachers to work with students. Schools pay higher education to provide INSET. Payment to schools for particular activities such as contributions to higher education-based elements of the course.	Financial recognition of particular school roles. Monies for resource centre. Resources for mentor training.

Figure 4.1 Choices in partnership

involvement in interviews to select students for courses and by contributions to sessions with the university. Such involvement is a clear indication of the recognition that closer partnership through joint activities is a way of enhancing staff development for all staff.

Schools are therefore moving towards more active partnership through a transition phase which includes more responsibility for mentoring, contributions to course design and fuller involvement in the selection and assessment of students. This in turn requires a different response from higher education, particularly in relation to communication and staff development. For example, schools will need more comprehensive information about students' whole course experience. Staff will need to be designated to build relationships and a partnership team. To support increased responsibilities in relation to the assessment of students, mentor training will need to be developed. Appropriate resource transfer also needs to be negotiated to support additional contributions by schools. Most of our partner schools are now in this transition phase.

There has been considerable interest in moving towards the next stage, namely active partnership and in particular, the development of clusters of schools for initial training purposes. As discussed by Crowther in Chapter 5, the development of such clusters has a number of advantages. Responding to schools on an individual basis is clearly problematic and expensive in terms of time and other resources. Having groups or clusters of schools as a working unit allows important considerations to be met. It can enable a greater consistency of relationships between students, higher education staff and schools to develop over time. This in turn can facilitate agreement on ways of working as well as easing the management of school experience. The process of setting up the group and agreeing purposes helps to support and develop thinking and a common language, resulting in greater commitment to the project because of the sense of shared responsibility. In sharing ideas, schools can present a stronger and more consistent voice in dialogue with higher education and therefore be more genuinely involved in the decision making. Clusters thus provide a structure for collective responsibility. However, schools, already overloaded with their many and various concerns, will need to establish early the format and timetable for partnership involvement. If partnership is to be meaningful, it also has to be included in schools' development plans.

Active partnership should also be extended to provide a forum in schools for discussion of continuing professional development. In setting up a shared dialogue about the process of defining students' needs and developing their understandings, it is a natural step to discussion of continuing professional development for all. Such development could include joint mentor training for school and higher education staff and a range of INSET activities planned for joint and separate individual and institutional needs. We also anticipate that a further elaboration of partnership will build on the collaborative approach to enquiry about the nature of teaching and learning and develop a more explicit research focus.

Given our understanding of the range of responses by schools to present and proposed phases in the model, we needed to seek coherence and continuity in our planning by examining the following questions:

- What are our understandings of, and commitment to, levels of involvement in partnership?
- What is the nature of communication between schools and between schools and higher education?
- What forms of staff development will support the training process and the shared core project?
- How will quality assurance be achieved?
- What are the implications for resourcing?

Each of these questions will now be briefly discussed.

UNDERSTANDING OF AND COMMITMENT TO PARTNERSHIP

Partnership will fundamentally affect the power relationships between the parties involved. Traditionally higher education has firmly held overall control, particularly in relation to ITT. In a model of partnership where the various contributions of schools and higher education need to be managed, then it is important to establish the roles and responsibilities of each partner. In particular, we need to be clear which partner is taking the leading role and thus assuming responsibility for quality assurance. The leading role will also involve ensuring the design and management of a course that will fulfil the requisite demands.

Our approach assumes that higher education will continue to take this leading role in ITT and with it the responsibilities of advocacy in relation to the quality of the students' experience. It is difficult for schools to be advocates for students: although in many cases they provide excellent experiences for them, they will quite rightly prioritise the needs of the children in their care when there is a conflict of interest.

Nevertheless, collective responsibility within the partnership needs to be established. This can be achieved through changes in the management of school experience and reorganisation of course structures, enabling higher education to be more responsive to opportunities of mutual benefit often excluded at present by the rigidities of course design and timetables.

COMMUNICATION

The early stages of professional development, namely initial training, have become the focus for experiments in partnership. However, genuine involvement by schools requires a clear sense of the purposes of present course organisation. Increased involvement in the design of the training process would seem to be a prerequisite for greater collaboration.

One way of achieving this increased involvement would be to look at ways of maximising the possibilities of focusing higher education staff time in schools so that individual staff have the opportunity to develop particular relationships with teachers in schools and become more responsive to schools' agenda. Schools have indicated very strongly to us that the most effective improvement in communication would be to have the same tutor from the higher education institution liaising with particular schools, to establish and maintain ongoing relationships and the dialogue that flows from this. Schools see organisation in groups not only as an important way of aiding communication but also as a means of enabling schools to share the responsibility for supporting students.

As discussed in Chapter 5, it is clear from student feedback of a pilot project carried out this year that students also benefit from a much closer relationship with a small group of schools. The enhanced dialogue between personnel in schools and students has generated opportunities for students to take more responsibility within the training process. It has also allowed students to experience a range of different schools with clearly articulated and different perspectives and priorities.

There is a need for communication and coordination of the work of different cluster groups. It is clear that some teachers are more interested and involved than others and will increasingly become key personnel taking the joint project forward. We need to sustain such interest and commitment through the formation of an active working group. This group would not be just another committee but would identify and debate issues and monitor the process of partnership projects. An outcome of such work might be regular newsletters and the crystallisation of staff development and/or research themes. It might also be appropriate to accredit individual contributions to this group as part of a staff development qualification, thus making links between the staff development opportunities offered by involvement in ITT and traditional models of INSET. At the same time, as higher education institutions respond to the agreed needs of the partnership group, schools can have more input into the development of their own INSET programmes and can finance this more easily through joint partnership funding.

STAFF DEVELOPMENT

Current initiatives have derived from proposed changes in ITT. At the same time, as noted in Chapters 1 and 9, the pattern of contact between higher education and schools has changed in relation to INSET. Reductions in funding for courses and secondments have resulted in shorter courses, usually in specific subject areas and linked to immediate institutional needs. This has meant a decrease in opportunities for teachers to follow their own lines of enquiry and research. Alongside these changes, the role of the LEA advisory service has become truncated and increasingly inspectoral. The time is right for a new framework of partnership to support the continuum of professional development.

We have already described the ways in which interested and committed teachers in schools and higher education institutions involved in ITT can be given opportunities to debate their understanding of the nature of teaching and learning. Such debate should also provide a relevant agenda for mentor training.

Teachers have always shared their expertise with less experienced members of the profession but have rarely had the opportunity to discuss with others how they might make the most effective contribution to students' growing understanding of teaching. Working with students necessarily involves reflective activity, which supports our own professional development. The deepening of this reflective activity extends naturally into research enquiry. One way of responding to the desire of schools for INSET could be to set up networks to support individual or joint research projects, with a view to disseminating subsequent knowledge and findings through publication. These could be supported through award-bearing programmes, short courses and consultancy, drawing on the advantages of shared agenda and funding.

QUALITY ASSURANCE

We have already suggested that higher education is likely to take the lead role and be largely responsible for issues of quality assurance. However, there are many opportunities for employing schools' expertise in this area. For example, with better communication, schools can be more closely involved in course design. Given increased responsibility by teachers in schools for the mentoring role, it is also important to ensure schools' participation in the development of the criteria for assessment of students' school experience.

In order to provide a coherent framework for sharing knowledge of students' professional development, we have implemented a system for profiling students' achievement which provides a focus for discussion and shared involvement. Students' ownership of the profile provides the link between higher education and schools.

Following increased participation of school staff in course design and in aspects of the teaching in the university, such staff will be better placed to evaluate ITT courses. Increased awareness of the students' learning programme within the university should also result in a greater congruence between school and university experiences for students. Collection and evaluation of evidence on student achievement and discussion about what contributes to effective teaching will add to the quality of assessment decisions and be an important aspect of quality assurance.

Given the increased responsibility that schools will have, and the range of experience for students that schools can provide, the higher education institution should then feel confident that the criteria to ensure quality of the students' experience can be met. With closer links being made with schools, there will be more dialogue about the suitability of placements for students and a greater responsibility for negotiating placements that meet the range of students' needs.

In relation to INSET, there will be a more direct link between INSET provision and schools' needs, negotiated at the level of the partnership group. The continuing relationship with schools will allow a better view of the longer-term effectiveness of INSET provision.

RESOURCES

The particular resource implications of this developmental model include the time required for communication between and coordination of school cluster groups, the resources involved in staff development for participants and the amount and type of resources which should be transferred to schools which take on more responsibility for the training role. These resources are additional to those required to staff the course, pay for learning materials, staff and student travel, and the range of other costs involved in the delivery of any course.

The coordinating aspect will require payment to schools to support a coordinator for each partnership group. Within the university there are implications for tutor hours, including ensuring priority within the staff timetable for liaison time with each group of schools.

Joint university and teacher tutor training should be provided and ways to support this need to be explored. For those schools that take on more responsibility for the training of students, individual payments will need to be made for specified responsibilities such as teaching sessions at the university. The contribution of whole schools may be best acknowledged by offering accredited INSET opportunities.

CONCLUSION

The interactional aspects of partnership discussed in this chapter have been described elsewhere (for example, Alexander 1990).

However, our emphasis differs in some respects, in that the quality of relationships and the pathways for communication between schools and higher education are seen to be at the centre of the endeavour. Our approach is designed to ensure a genuine shift in the locus of power, proper cognisance of school and student experiences, and planning for improved quality in their interaction. It also recognises the symbiotic relationship that exists between the less and more experienced members of the profession and sets aside the demarcation between INSET and ITT. It has as a fundamental aim the support of the teacher in having both voice and influence in the development of the teaching profession.

Chapter 5

A primary school view of involvement in initial teacher training

George Crowther

All schools now find themselves in a management climate that encourages them to be more independent, more self-governing and increasingly entrepreneurial in seeking the best services and resources to enrich the education they offer their children. Local management of schools has provided a degree of financial flexibility which has been welcomed by many because governing bodies, and through them teachers, gain increased discretion to manage schools in the way they see fit.

However, alongside these freedoms lie the constraints of an increasingly prescribed curriculum, combined with greater accountability to parents and the local community for children's achievements. External assessment and monitoring of schools, including that now being carried out by OFSTED, also weigh heavily on teachers' minds.

The new climate poses difficult questions for schools concerning the selection of activities in which they should become involved. Those contemplating an increased commitment to ITT should think long and hard before being tempted by the illusory rewards which are being proffered by recent government initiatives. Before addressing some of the issues surrounding a greater involvement in ITT, and the experiences of one group of schools in particular, it is worth exploring some general principles about the activities that schools should seek to manage themselves and those that would be better left alone. Schools need to ask themselves whether they can manage and deliver a particular activity better, at similar cost, to the benefit of their children's learning.

In some cases, the answer to this question will be clear. For example, at our school, we have recently had the opportunity to manage our own grounds' maintenance. We found a local contractor who would guarantee a far higher standard of care at a cost that was only marginally more than our current contract with the LEA. We were able to negotiate a one-year renewable agreement and we know that the contractor wishes to bring the quality of our grounds to a standard that will attract other schools to seek his services in the future. The decision to become more involved in this activity was easy: we believe that an improved school environment contributes to the quality of children's learning and will prove attractive to potential pupils' parents. However, this expansion of our activities is not in an area that is central to children's learning. We shall not be involved in increased management or coordination of the activity and it will not detract from the central purpose of our school, which is to maximise the quality of our children's learning. We have little to lose and a lot to gain.

Contrast this with the notion of becoming a school that takes full responsibility for ITT. Even if we were able to select what we believe to be the cream of students, their time in the classroom may adversely affect the learning of some of our children. Schools need to count the cost of planning and coordinating the initiative, of providing sufficient and appropriate mentoring and of assessment and accreditation. Schools should also consider the time teachers will spend working with students rather than children and giving support to students at a stressful stage in their lives. We are therefore playing for far higher stakes in this endeavour.

The School-Centred Initial Teacher Training (SCITT) scheme gives consortia of schools an opportunity to design, organise and provide school-centred ITT courses for graduates which lead to Qualified Teacher Status. Funding to schools for the design and organisation of courses, payments to staff, recruitment of students and buying in expertise from higher education, including course validation where appropriate, will be up to a current maximum of £4000 per student. Schools are being offered insufficient funding to support an ambitious, and potentially problematic, initiative.

Even if funding were limitless, I feel that it is conceited for schools to believe that they have the expertise to devise and manage ITT effectively. Many teachers have the potential to become teacher educators but the further skills that they would require should not be learned 'on the job' to the detriment of students and, more importantly, children. We falsely enhance and, therefore, demean our professional abilities by assuming that we are capable of becoming independently responsible for ITT.

On the other hand, an increased involvement in a partnership with higher education institutions may be beneficial to all. However, schools must recognise their limitations as well as their strengths before making an additional commitment and they must be sure that the opportunities offered will contribute to their central aims. Such issues will now be discussed in relation to a particular initial training partnership scheme.

A PILOT PARTNERSHIP SCHEME WITH OXFORD BROOKES UNIVERSITY

Our increased involvement with Oxford Brookes University's PGCE course for primary education stemmed from an existing relationship in which we provided placements for block school experiences for students during the course. More often than not, we worked with two students on each occasion and also provided day attachments and some short-term visits for specific purposes such as curriculum consultancy training. There were a number of reasons why we sought a greater involvement.

First, we wished to provide more opportunities for teachers to broaden and strengthen their skills by working with students. We see great benefits in creating opportunities for teachers to articulate their philosophy to others and to explain the ways in which it is translated into practice. It helps them to question and clarify their thinking and to become more confident in their task. Although working closely with colleagues in school provides opportunities to exercise these skills, it can be a daunting challenge. Working alongside students allows even inexperienced teachers to be reflective in a non-threatening environment, in the same way that we often see the best in our children when they are working with their younger peers. We also wanted to increase the opportunities for colleagues to develop mentoring skills, to strengthen their ability to deliver INSET and to nurture management skills, which are important for teachers seeking senior posts in primary schools. Clearly, these aims are closely linked to our staff development policy and we believe that increasing the range of skills, which our teachers possess improves their confidence and their ability to manage the learning of children in classrooms.

Second, we anticipated opportunities for staff to pursue INSET provided by Oxford Brookes University with a degree of preferential treatment in terms both of selection and cost. We hoped to establish a reciprocal arrangement which recognised that teachers, whether during initial or in-service training, are continuing learners.

Third, we believe that students can and do enrich the learning opportunities which we offer our children. They often provide additional ideas for planning and a fresh approach to learning, and they increase contact time between teachers and children. Alongside these benefits one must balance the additional time which teachers spend supporting their partner students but we believe that there is an enhancement to the opportunities we can offer our children.

Fourth, one of the dangers for teachers of working within school, however effective and stimulating that school may be, is the loss of perspective that can result. The day-to-day challenges of teaching do not promote a broad view and tend to entrap the teacher into an excessive concentration on the immediate. One of the benefits of working with a range of students and their tutors, and indeed with a range of colleagues from other schools, is the potential to enable us to adopt a wider vision of the purpose and practice of our task. It enables us to make better decisions about how we can shape the education which we offer our children.

Finally, we also anticipated that some of the students in whom we would invest our time and encouragement might become permanent colleagues in the future, enriching our cycle of recruitment and staff development.

Although few of these arguments are quite as clear-cut as measuring the length of the grass in the school grounds, we believed that they formed a strong enough case to explore the possibility of increased involvement.

The next stage is for schools to be clear about what they have to offer to the partnership and what they want in return. We took it as self-evident that we could offer both a rich vein of classroom experiences for aspiring teachers and supportive colleagues who would be able to explore a range of issues concerning the planning of appropriate activities for children, classroom management, behaviour management, assessment and recording. We were less sure that we could offer training in subject specialisms, although we were confident that we possessed a range of expertise within the school on which students could draw.

We were also clear about some of the things that we could not and should not attempt to offer. For example, students need solid time away from the classroom to reflect on their experiences and to discuss them with others who have had similar experiences. This is rightly the role of higher education, where tutors possess the expertise to draw out the commonalities and discrepancies from varied experiences, highlighting issues and linking these to a wider debate about principles. Equally, students need to develop the ability to judge the quality of their experiences, and subsequently the quality of their own teaching, against standards to which they should aspire, may only sometimes meet and are consistently attained in only some primary classrooms. Schools should guard against a conceit that would lead them to believe that their practice, however good, is the yardstick against which aspiring teachers should gauge their performance. In addition, schools cannot offer the rich experience of eminent visiting speakers, poets and puppeteers, library resources and lectures, which are the features of the best ITT courses.

In return for our increased input, we were looking for some financial support to enable students and teachers to have the time to work together out of the classroom, facilitating our staff development aims. It is understandable that teachers have often felt guilty that they do not have sufficient time to fulfil their role as mentor to their full capability. Some funding to create this time was essential. We also wanted preferential access to INSET and the skills of the staff at Oxford Brookes University, should we need to call on them.

Armed with a clear conception of what we had to offer and what we wanted in return, we approached the staff at Oxford Brookes University with the suggestion that, as the Government's intention of requiring closer links with schools in ITT was becoming clear, we would welcome our school being part of a pilot project to investigate the possibilities of greater involvement, in partnership. Perhaps unexpectedly, our discussions were soon revolving around the logistical challenges rather than the principle since the idea of a project was welcomed by staff at the university.

Our difficulties were twofold. First, pastoral tutor groups for primary PGCE students at Oxford Brookes University are organised in sets of approximately fourteen students. It would have been very costly to manage a smaller group of students, still requiring tutor support but outside the normal pattern of organisation. Second, accreditation criteria and guidelines for ITT courses require students to have experience in at least two schools during their training. It became clear that the best way forward was to form a consortium of schools able to meet the needs of a tutor group of students.

At this point, I had misgivings about an expansion of the project to encompass a range of primary schools. A completely new level of coordination and management suddenly loomed, within which one might envisage a variety of pitfalls. Nevertheless, while discussions about the nature of the partnership were continuing, I contacted a range of schools to explain the project and to seek their involvement. This stage identified some schools who decided against involvement at this particular time. It also raised the question of the extent to which the eventual consortium would share joint aspirations for the project. Any school contemplating involvement as part of a consortium should not underestimate the cost of bringing the group together.

Over approximately three months the consortium gradually took shape, with soundings in schools being complemented by meetings between Oxford Brookes University tutors and headteachers. Eventually, it consisted of seven primary schools which were geographically proximate. They varied in size from having two to fourteen classes and ranged from rural to urban in terms of catchment area and setting. The final shape of our partnership agreement was a 'contract' between Oxford Brookes University and schools, which outlined shared commitments and the funding provided by the university. We then produced a leaflet to distribute to potential students and attracted a group of fourteen who shared our commitment to the notion of greater involvement by schools. Each school appointed a coordinator to be the first point of contact for tutors and students and we decided that any meetings would be on a need-to-meet basis, being realistic about the range of teachers' other commitments.

From September 1993, the project brought the group of students into far greater contact with our schools than students would have experienced otherwise. They visited all the schools as part of their preliminary school experience and then had an extended time in one school, before their course at the university began. Teachers visited the university to see and discuss an exhibition of work that the students produced following their first week of study, and which was based on an experiential learning project at the Pitt Rivers Museum in Oxford. The students then visited schools in preparation for their first block school experience, which took place in November and early December. In the spring term, students worked in schools to develop curriculum consultancy skills and began to prepare for their final block school experience in the summer term, which they all completed successfully. Students, tutors and teachers met throughout the year to discuss current issues and to plan for the future.

We have tried to make the partnership constant but not so time-consuming that it becomes a burden, and to ensure it is realistic in its demands on teachers, students and tutors. Equally, for those teachers who have not wished to become involved, we have expected only that they be supportive of the initiative in spirit.

We must recognise, however, that the pilot scheme was a learning experience in itself. It has not been without its teething troubles and it is to these that I now turn.

PARTICULAR ISSUES AND PROBLEMS IN PRINCIPLE AND PRACTICE

Involvement in the consortium

The nature of primary school development dictates that there will be times when a school is able to become involved in a range of initiatives and times when it must concentrate on getting its own house in order. Equally, the commitment of one group of staff to an initiative may not be there in five years' time simply because those teachers may have moved on. Any partnership arrangement needs to be flexible enough to take account of these realities. In practice, the consortium needs to be large enough for one or two of the schools to be inactive in any one year.

The quality of primary schools is another important issue, raising the question as to whether some primary schools should be excluded from student placements because they are not good enough. If our school is going to be involved in a consortium, we would wish to cluster with schools with a philosophy, practice and commitment similar to our own. While it is clear that schools and teachers can gain a great deal by working in consortia, the formation of which for ITT will be essential, bringing together a group of primary schools which are not only sharing ideas but working together to complete a shared task poses problems.

Such issues have wider implications. Given that some schools may wish to have a variable commitment, ITT could be transferred on a voluntary basis to schools that do not wish to continue their involvement later. Will school-based ITT then be made mandatory? And what will happen when OFSTED inspectors produce a critical report on the quality of teaching and learning at a school which currently has a group of students halfway through their training? If, according to some politicians, standards of teaching and learning in schools have reached an all-time low, is the solution to entrust those schools with the initial training of the next generation of teachers?

Funding

We sold the initiative to our governing bodies on the basis that it would take place at no cost to our budget. We expected necessary funding to come from Oxford Brookes University, particularly in the area of providing supply cover costs to enable our teachers to work with students. Our funding is increasingly tight and Oxford Brookes University has similar problems. This year the project has thrived on the enthusiasm, commitment and goodwill of many teachers, tutors and students. However, this is not a basis for future years when the project must be seen to be properly funded. At present, it appears that there is no mechanism which enables partnerships of schools and higher education to be jointly funded. Unless we can find a way of funding such partnerships properly, they will wither on the vine.

Management and planning

Working within a consortium of schools creates considerable management tasks for someone. Ideally, the project needs an overall coordinator for the consortium, a tutor coordinator at the higher education institution and a coordinating teacher in each school. If the people concerned are accepting additional responsibilities, they should be paid for them.

There are a number of potential planning problems in relation to matching students' needs to schools' capacities. Within our group of students we had those with a clear interest in teaching a specific age group in primary schools as well as those who were undecided at the start of the course. Within seven primary schools we had a range of offers of placements for the first school experience, including larger schools willing to take three or more students and our smallest schools able to take only one. Obtaining the best fit between students' wants (and needs) and schools' offers is not easy.

We had made a bad mistake early in the year when, having allowed the students to make their choice for the preliminary school experience, one school found itself without a student. Understandably, that school felt that its commitment to the consortium was not valued or needed.

Our solution for first block school experience placements was to ask schools to provide some flexibility by stating the range of their expectations. For instance, one school's parameters were:

At least one student but not more than four. Age groups offered in order of preference: Key Stage 2 rather than Key Stage 1 and a nursery place if you really need one.

All the offers from schools were funnelled to the university tutor, who then decided on placements in consultation with students and schools. This system encouraged both schools and students to be flexible but recognised that some choice for students, and the fulfilment of expectations in schools, are both desirable.

The problems of placement became more difficult as the course progressed because, for the final block school experience, the students needed to select a different school from that of their first block school experience. They also needed to have a change from other schools in which they had spent a good deal of time already. This narrows the possibilities while not narrowing schools' expectations or students' preferences! It also needs to be recognised that students may drop out of their training, which will then affect the planned pattern of school involvement.

There are therefore all sorts of logistical problems in relation to the optimum size for a consortium of schools and a group of students. These problems need to be considered carefully during planning.

Maintaining momentum

When schools and teachers become involved in a new initiative they are enthusiastic, a quality for which teachers are seldom given sufficient credit. Having become involved, teachers are easily disappointed when an initiative wanes and, in my experience, this is more problematic than making too many demands on staff. During the first term of our project, the rhythm of activities and contacts between students and teachers was consistent but during the second term, which was more university-based and with no block school experience, the contacts were too few to sustain momentum. It seemed that schools' involvement was either famine or feast. The pattern of the course has therefore been redesigned to overcome this weakness.

Partnerships must make sure that there is regular contact offered between students and schools. Such contact would normally focus on professional activities but could also include informal visits to keep relationships fresh.

Momentum can also be sustained by making the benefits for all participants clear. The interested but busy teacher may ask, 'What's in it for me?'. Benefits need to be made clear from the outset to teachers, and indeed, students. A leaflet to all involved, outlining the additional opportunities that are created for both students and teachers, may help to sustain commitment.

Although accreditation requirements leave little room for manoeuvre, the pattern of an ITT course needs to fit the increased expectations in schools which develop following their growing involvement.

CONCLUSION

The notion of schools playing an increasingly active part in ITT is still in its infancy. Our experience suggests that there are potential benefits for primary schools but that they are better exploited in partnership with a supportive higher education institution.

Our students have also recognised benefits. They have commented on the increased security conferred by working with a consistent group of schools and teachers with whom they are able to build relationships. They have also appreciated our commitment to their development and have reciprocated by their enthusiasm for the project.

Teachers would do well to remember that recent government pressure to establish initial training in schools is set against a background of certain politicians feeling that 'good mums' can teach Key Stage 1 classes effectively, a squeeze on funding for higher education institutions and constant sniping about weaknesses found in schools. In these circumstances, it is prudent to question the motivation of those who encourage schools to go it alone in training teachers. The SCITT initiative sets out neither a rationale for ITT in schools nor a developmental plan. It is assumed that schools will be able to deliver ITT effectively and that financial incentives will persuade them to become involved. As with grant-maintained status, additional funding is tempting but schools must count the cost of accepting additional responsibilities which may detract from their central purposes and they should question the permanency of funding.

Our experience suggests that a pattern of closer collaboration with higher education promises to be the best way forward but that the basis for this new partnership needs to be established carefully and methodically. If the process is rushed or goes badly wrong, it will be students, teachers and ultimately children who will suffer. Schools should therefore not just 'take the money' that may be available for developing ITT courses in schools, but should rather 'open the box' and carefully consider the benefits, issues and problems inside.

Chapter 6

Conceptions of partnership in school-centred initial teacher training

Lesley Anderson

Since 1989, various schemes for initial teacher education have been introduced that stress the importance of 'partnership' involving two or more of trainee teachers, schools, LEAs and higher education institutions and emphasising varying degrees and types of workplace development.

One such scheme is the Articled Teacher initiative. This scheme, first introduced in 1990 and now no longer available, was founded upon a partnership between LEAs, schools and institutions of higher education. It was set up as an alternative approach to the traditional Postgraduate Certificate in Education (PGCE) and comprised a two-year programme. Although articled teachers spent considerably more time in schools than students on conventional courses, the involvement of higher education was required. The award of a standard teaching qualification was ensured, as well as some form of quality assurance and academic integrity.

In contrast, the Licensed Teacher scheme, also introduced in 1990, was founded upon a contractual partnership involving unqualified teachers. It is left to the discretion of the LEA or school as to whether an institution of higher education plays a role in the training process. This route into teaching was designed with two purposes in mind, namely to regulate the acquisition of qualified teacher status by overseas-trained teachers and to encourage career-changing new entrants into teaching. It differs markedly from the Articled Teachers initiative and other routes into the teaching profession in that it does not lead to a teaching qualification awarded by higher education. Licensed teachers receive a licence to teach in schools. After a specific period of time teaching 'under licence', which is usually two years, they are assessed for Qualified Teacher Status. Since there is no absolute requirement for higher education institutions to be involved in the training of licensed teachers, the introduction of the scheme meant there were no longer standard requirements for entry into teaching in the maintained sector of education. The scheme is primarily school-centred. Licensed teachers are recruited by the school or the LEA and are based in one school for the whole period of their training. Importantly, licensed teachers are not supernumerary, but are appointed to fill specific vacancies; they train literally 'on the job'.

In a more recent initiative, the School Centred Initial Teacher Training (SCITT) scheme, consortia of schools are in the lead. They take prime responsibility for course development and delivery, and for student assessment, and are funded directly by government. Higher education institutions play a role only if invited.

This chapter explores these developments. It reflects upon three aspects of school-centred ITT, each of which has significance for understanding the likely medium- and long-term implications of moves to increase the involvement of schools in initial teacher education and the possible associated downgrading of the significance of higher education in the training and accreditation of the next generation of entrants to the teaching profession.

First, consideration will be given to extant evaluations of the Articled and Licensed Teacher training schemes, which point up some difficulties in making such partnerships effective. Second, school-centred courses will be discussed in the light of the implications of a recently conducted survey of schools involved in the first round of SCITT, carried out by the author in January 1994. The results of this survey indicate that the success of this initiative will depend on the extent to which it can be easily accommodated by schools already busy implementing other reforms. The survey also highlights the need for these schools to provide a form of training that commands universal respect in terms of practical and academic credibility. Finally, the chapter will analyse some of the opportunities and problems of mentoring, a central feature of school-centred approaches to initial teacher education.

THE ARTICLED AND LICENSED TEACHER SCHEMES

As noted earlier, the Articled Teacher scheme was set up as an alternative approach to the traditional PGCE and required explicit partnership arrangements between schools, higher education institutions and LEAs. Courses were set up by sixteen consortia comprising LEAs and higher education institutions and the trainees received a bursary rather than a means-tested grant. Throughout their training period, the trainees remained super-numerary to the staffing of the schools in which they were placed. The scheme was used to prepare teachers for both primary and secondary phases, with training for the latter confined mostly to shortage subjects, including mathematics, science and modern languages.

The first cohort of articled teachers began their training in September 1990. Recruitment to the scheme amounted to less than 4 per cent of the total number starting conventional PGCE courses that year. The fourth and final cohort, which comprised only primary articled teachers, began in September 1993. In each year the intake included a higher proportion of mature and, in some consortia, of ethnic minority, entrants than conventional PGCE courses.

The HMI report on the scheme (OFSTED 1993a) highlighted a number of key findings which, it suggested, should inform the planning and implementation of such approaches to initial teacher education. In particular, the report emphasised the importance of partnership between higher education institutions and schools in effective school-based training and the time that this takes to develop. Additionally, the report discussed the need for clearly defined roles and systems and for courses to be organised around a well-structured hierarchy of skills. It also recommended that all staff should be prepared for their particular contribution to the training process and that trainees need to see good practice and have teaching experience in more than one school.

Data collected by the author about an Articled Teacher programme offered in one secondary school between 1991 and 1993 reinforce these findings. Early discussions took place between the participating LEA and higher education institution, the school only becoming involved because of a desire to address specific recruitment needs. Consequently, there was little room for any choice about the subject specialisms of the articled teachers based at the school. The intention was that articled teachers would be both full members of the particular higher education institution's PGCE course and valued members of the LEA's teaching force. As it was, the major part of the support for the articled teachers came directly from the school staff. The LEA's contribution was limited and the practical problems of the partnership between the school and the higher education institution, including the hour-long journey between them, undermined the intention that the articled teachers should be fully integrated with students on the standard PGCE course. The scheme lasted less than three years and was closed down in 1993.

An evaluation of the Licensed Teacher scheme by HMI (OFSTED 1993b) highlighted that most licensed teachers were appointed to LEAs and schools with recruitment difficulties. The report also pointed out that, of those licensed teachers performing poorly, many were in schools that were considered unsatisfactory for the training of teachers. Moreover, few schools provided well-structured training for the licensed teachers. Where training was provided out of school, it did not always match the training needs of the different categories of licensed teachers. LEA support for these teachers was basically limited to training courses and finance.

The experience of a group of licensed teachers studied by the author again reinforces these findings. All of the teachers were recruited to vacant posts which the schools concerned were experiencing difficulties in filling. Similarly, the training of the licensed teachers, beyond day-to-day classroom support, was sketchy. Although the LEA did make a commitment to offer training opportunities for its licensed teachers, chiefly by making it a requirement that they were attached to an institution of higher education during the period of their licence, in practice this meant that the licensed teachers were integrated into existing courses. This was less than satisfactory as the background, experience and needs of the licensed teachers were so varied that each required individual provision for such support to be effective.

A key similarity between the schemes for licensed and articled teachers is that such teachers are not required to spend time in other schools. They have therefore tended to lack experience of a wider range of institutions. This restricted school experience raises issues about the accountability of such training, particularly when special arrangements may also be made to accommodate individual needs and difficulties, reducing aspects of the content or length of training.

SCHOOL-CENTRED INITIAL TEACHER TRAINING

The recently introduced School-Centred Initial Teacher Training (SCITT) scheme places total control of ITT in the hands of schools. As mentioned earlier, this scheme differs from traditional courses in that consortia of schools are the key players in the training and are funded direct from central government for this purpose. There is, currently, no requirement for the consortia to involve higher education, although they are encouraged to do so. The schools can be of any type – primary or secondary, maintained or independent.

The principles underlying this scheme extend those put forward in other recent reforms of ITT, including the requirement that schools should play a much larger role. Six consortia of schools were approved by the Department for Education to begin the training of teachers in September 1993. A further three consortia commenced SCITT programmes in January 1994 and additional schemes are now being implemented. Each consortium within the scheme is required to identify a 'lead' school to receive and manage government funding.

The following findings are based upon telephone interviews conducted with the lead school coordinators from five of the consortia which commenced in September 1993. The interviews took place in January 1994 and involved the collection of factual data about each consortium, the student cohort, the course, mentoring, evaluation procedures and resources. Additionally, the coordinators were asked to give their perceptions of the advantages and disadvantages of the scheme for both the student teachers and the schools as well as an overall view on progress to date.

The consortia, all of which were secondary, varied in size from four to eight schools. They comprised LEA and grant-maintained schools, city technology colleges (CTCs) and one sixth-form college. Two consortia comprise CTCs as lead schools together with TSI (Technology Schools Initiative) schools affiliated to the City Technology College Trust, the latter being a mixture of grant-maintained and LEA-controlled schools. They had no previous experience of working together. The CTC consortia only offered initial teacher training in technology, receiving additional funding through the Smallpeice Trust for this purpose. The schools in the remaining consortia did have experience of working together and in some cases, such relationships were well developed. These consortia accepted students training in a range of National Curriculum subjects, although the greatest emphasis was placed upon mathematics, science and technology. The range of subjects on offer appeared to depend on the experience, enthusiasm and standard of achievement of the departments involved.

The number of student teachers in each consortium varied from eighteen to twenty-eight. There were forty-nine women and sixty-four men involved, the majority of the men being based in the CTC consortia or the one consortium that offered training for the physical education of boys. In the main, the student teachers were in their twenties or thirties and ethnic minorities were well represented within each group.

The courses led by CTCs were forty-four weeks long, although in one consortium it was suggested that this would be reduced to forty for the next round beginning in September 1994. The other three courses were thirty-six weeks long. All provided experience across the 11–18 age range though for some of the students in one consortium, training for parts of Key Stage 4 in the National Curriculum was omitted because the CTC did not yet have its full complement of pupils of this age.

Five out of the six September 1993 starters were working with at least one higher education institution which validated the course. These consortia offered a PGCE qualification in addition to Qualified Teacher Status for those student teachers who reached the required standard. In addition, students following the Smallpeice Technology Teacher Training programme may also be awarded the Smallpeice Technology Teacher Training Certificate. The remaining consortium did not work formally with any higher education institution, although it bought in higher education lecturers from a range of institutions to deliver part of the training. On satisfactory completion of the course, student teachers on this programme were awarded Qualified Teacher Status and the consortium's own postgraduate teacher certificate.

The consortia led by CTCs offered the same course, devised by the CTC Trust's Director of the Smallpeice Programme, together with the partner higher education institution. Additionally, recruitment, selection, financial and other aspects of management of this course were handled by the CTC Trust. Courses offered by the other consortia in each case were designed by the schools, usually in association with higher education, and recruitment and selection were mostly managed by the consortia. Generally, the number of quality applications in 1993 was high and consortia were able to select well-qualified graduates and reach their target numbers. However, a few students withdrew at the last moment, leaving these consortia unable to fill places.

There was evidence from the telephone interviews that involvement in the scheme, particularly in the consortia which were not led by CTCs, was dependent upon one or two enthusiastic individuals, usually at deputy head level. In most cases, these people had previously coordinated other initial teacher training based within their schools, notably in relation to licensed teachers. They were also responsible for getting the scheme under way within the very tight time-scale involved. Indeed, most of the comments and concerns expressed by the consortia coordinators were connected with what they considered to be a lack of preparation time and, therefore, the need to iron out problems as they came up. For example, it had been necessary for one consortium to suspend a student teacher without knowing in advance what procedures to follow.

For similar reasons, the marketing of the courses was fairly low key as there was little time to do more. The courses tended to be advertised through the local press, the *Times Educational Supplement* and the General Teacher Training Register (GTTR). Most of the consortia were still in the process of putting together course and publicity material. The CTC Trust, however, produced separate course information on the Smallpeice Technology Teacher Training programme.

Discussion about resources inevitably centred on the need for more. In each consortium, all permanent staff facilities and resources were available to the students. In addition, most consortia were in the process of creating a resource base and some were attempting to obtain sponsorship from industry further to develop this. Students working within the consortia with explicit higher education involvement all had access to the higher education institution's library. The consortium 'going it alone' purchased student access to a library in a higher education institution even though it did not have a specialist education section.

When asked about their perceptions of the course to date, most of the consortia coordinators indicated they were aware that the students were 'guinea pigs' and that there could be no certainty about the credibility of the training beyond the consortium. One consortium coordinator suggested that there was some concern amongst the student teachers as to whether they would achieve employment in schools beyond those that were part of the scheme. Another coordinator indicated that involvement at this early stage was both an advantage as well as a disadvantage for the students. Additionally, the coordinators felt students missed the opportunity to mix with other students in a higher education environment. The other problems mentioned were more practical. For example, in some consortia, travel between schools was difficult for the students. Even so, they were required to meet regularly together in one place. It was also felt that the sheer number of extra bodies within particular schools had created a feeling of overcrowding.

However, a number of benefits were perceived. All the coordinators stressed the extent to which student teachers were able to get 'hands-on' experience from the very beginning of their course. They also stressed the way in which the scheme enabled student teachers to learn about how schools operate and about the working life of a teacher. They considered these opportunities to be superior in kind to those offered by conventional PGCE courses. One coordinator commented on the students' awareness of what goes on in school and another emphasised the fact that, during their time in school, students had access to people 'trained to develop them over a long period of time, who could provide good role models and act as mentors as well as tutors'. He suggested that the students appreciated the greater integration of all parts of the consortium programme compared with courses led by higher education. Another coordinator highlighted the aim of his consortium – to create 'thinking, reflective people', rather than 'teacher-technicians'.

There was also much enthusiasm about the wide range of benefits gained by the schools through involvement. One co-ordinator described such benefits as 'immense'. He suggested that the professional satisfaction and morale of permanent staff had increased significantly and that colleagues were reading much more about both their subject and education in general. Other coordinators also agreed that the student teachers' presence in school had engendered a positive effect on permanent staff, one commenting that 'new blood had brought the school alive'. It was also suggested that those adopting a mentoring role had become more reflective individuals.

All the consortia had provided some training for mentors and other staff directly involved. Due to the lack of start-up time, this training had been limited to date and had largely comprised one or two occasions led by the consortium coordinator or by higher education tutors. Payments to staff were being made either in money, time or both, but tended to be relatively small. Some consortia coordinators hoped to improve incentives in future years, particularly through more specific timetabling for student teacher support and mentoring.

MENTORING

The schemes outlined above all highlight specifically the role of the mentor in the trainee's support. However, as noted in Chapter 8, there is a lack of consistency about the precise meaning of mentoring as well as the characteristics, responsibilities and training required of an individual fulfilling the role of a mentor. This is true for individual schemes and also from scheme to scheme and extends beyond mentoring for initial teacher training. Indeed, any quick review of the literature on mentoring reveals considerable ambiguity about its meaning and implications. Its use in school-centred initial training therefore needs careful consideration.

In the Licensed Teacher scheme, it is unlikely for training to be given to teachers prior to, or while they fulfil, a mentoring role. This is mainly because licensed teachers are usually appointed to a post that has proved difficult to fill and the head of department becomes the mentor by virtue of his or her managerial role rather than for any other reason. The responsibilities given to mentors in this scheme reflect the inconsistencies already suggested, and may not recognise the different, potentially conflicting, aspects of the role. For example, although there was at least one example among the schools studied by the author of an institution distinguishing between the mentoring and the assessment aspects of the scheme, in many instances these processes were carried out by the same person.

Mentors working as part of the Articled Teacher scheme studied by the author were provided with guidance from the higher education institution in the form of a handbook. This was introduced to them at a meeting. However, as one co-ordinator pointed out, 'you could not call it training'. Attempts were made by the schools to avoid appointing heads of department to the role although this was not always possible. No specific criteria were used for the identification of likely mentors.

The organisation of mentors within the SCITT programme may vary from school to school within one consortium. The research indicates that some schools held interviews for the posts while others used senior staff recommendation to identify the people to take on the role. Yet another group invited staff to put themselves forward. All the consortia studied mentioned some mentor training and all but one had commissioned such training from an institution of higher education. In the one consortium that did not, the deputy head had considerable experience of mentoring for initial training. Mentor training was therefore provided 'in-house'. A number of coordinators mentioned that the training is ongoing.

There were differences amongst the consortia with regard to the precise activities undertaken by mentors. One coordinator stated that the mentors were involved in the assessment of students' competences, while another emphasised that mentors are never in an assessment role and are regarded as 'critical friends'. Only one consortium has a job description for its mentors. The consortium led by the deputy head with mentoring experience made much of its 'structured mentoring' approach which was 'devoted to developing classroom skills'. An in-house handbook led the mentors through the process which was well defined and used for providing feedback as well as 'signing-off' competences. At the time the research discussed in this chapter was undertaken, the Smallpeice prospectus did not mention mentors or mentoring as a feature of their scheme.

With regard to incentives for SCITT mentors, again there was no consistency. Some were receiving a small time allowance (the equivalent of one period per week), others a financial payment, while another group had nothing in addition to their usual salary. The coordinator explained that as most mentors were senior members of staff, they were already receiving an allowance.

The research highlights the range of interpretations of the role of a mentor within the schemes as well as the emphasis placed on it. It also puts into sharp focus the issues of accountability and quality of these different approaches to ITT.

CONCLUSION

Alternative routes into teaching such as Articled and Licensed Teachers and SCITT schemes are clearly attractive to some potential trainee teachers, especially mature entrants, and to those schools with recruitment difficulties. It is apparent, too, that some schools enjoy their new 'training' status and derive considerable benefit from it as a result. Significantly, these benefits have been achieved in partnerships with higher education.

These initiatives, however, draw attention to some of the challenges that need to be met in the course of designing and implementing programmes of teacher education that are primarily school-centred. These challenges include:

- the need to define and agree a lead player in the partnership;
- the need to establish credible and recognisable criteria of teacher competence and professional development standards;
- the need to clarify the role of the mentor; and
- the need to cost accurately the time and resource implications, bearing in mind that school-centred schemes for teacher education tend to be very labour-intensive and hitherto have depended significantly on goodwill offerings.

The challenges highlight the practical constraints entailed in making partnerships effective between schools, LEAs and higher education institutions. They also articulate with that aspect of school-centred programmes of teacher education which stresses the mentoring of trainee teachers rather than their supervision.

It is clear that the major challenge facing all those involved in ITT is that of resources linked to quality. Put sharply, government, in collaboration with schools and higher education, needs to calculate accurately and meet the real costs involved. It must also establish national criteria for accrediting trainers and measuring teacher competence. Only in this way will all concerned be able to help ensure a high level of teacher professionalism for future generations of children.

Chapter 7

Frameworks, competences and quality: open learning dimensions to initial teacher education and training

Bob Moon and Ann Shelton Mayes

Britain's Open University was founded in 1969, one of the symbols of the 1960s' technological revolution. It has since prospered. With nearly one hundred thousand undergraduate students, and the same again on a range of postgraduate courses, 'the OU' is far and away the largest institution of higher education in the country.

Teacher education was, from the first, one of the major activities of the University. In the 1970s, tens of thousands of teachers raised their qualifications to graduate status through OU study. In the 1980s, thousands more went on to qualify professionally at Master's level through a range of education courses. In the 1990s, the programme is extending to doctoral level and, in a move that has attracted widespread interest, to initial teacher education and training, the focus for this chapter.

The OU's move into ITT preceded the highly political debates about teacher education of the early 1990s. Pressures from the student body were at the heart of the initiative. They argued strongly that the same needs that brought them to OU study in the first place (geographical distance from conventional institutions, personal circumstances, career and financial interests) were every bit as relevant to studying and preparing for a vocational and professional qualification. If the OU could prepare undergraduates and provide Master's degrees in education, then why not extend the provision to initial training? In the mid-1980s, the University took a first step by providing a professional studies course that other institutions could incorporate within a conventional part-time course. The take-up, however, went little way towards meeting the demand, and institutions were slow or reluctant to adopt existing models into a more open and flexible framework.

A deepening crisis in both the overall numbers and qualities of recruits into teaching at the beginning of the 1990s presented a further opportunity for the OU to review its policies towards ITT. Two market research exercises showed the extent of the possible takes-up. Fifty per cent of OU undergraduates were interested in becoming teachers and 30 per cent were seriously interested. The interest split evenly between primary and secondary teaching, with mathematics and science teaching attracting the most interest amongst the latter. Aspiring primary teachers had a much higher level of mathematics and science in their qualifications than the usual B.Ed. or PGCE primary entrant and they lived, in substantial numbers, where the turnover of primary staff represented a major problem (particularly, for example, in the south-east of England). There was also evidence that an OU route to Qualified Teacher Status would be attractive to applicants from ethnic groups currently under-represented in the teaching force nationally. The market research showed that the cohort of people interested in becoming teachers in their early thirties had different characteristics from their contemporaries who had made the decision a decade earlier. The multiple aims, therefore, of widening access, opening up opportunity and contributing to the quality and supply of teachers, represented an attractive option and gained financial backing in terms of a start-up grant totalling £2.5 million from the Department for Education, with support from the Welsh Office and the Department for Education in Northern Ireland. The course planning and the production of materials took place between April 1992 and March 1994 and the first cohort of over a thousand students was admitted in February 1994. The admission numbers were heavily oversubscribed and the characteristics of those admitted were in line with all the market research predictions indicated above.

The launch of an OU Postgraduate Certificate in Education (PGCE) involved the development of new forms and styles of education and training. While the national criteria set out in Circulars 9/92 and 14/93 (DFE 1992, 1993b) had to be met, the means of doing so would inevitably depart from conventional provision. Here you meet one of the central dilemmas for an institution like the OU.

It was impossible, and undesirable, to try to replicate all aspects of the criteria and practice of conventional providers. Yet, inevitably, initial evaluations and judgements of a programme are heavily influenced by established conventions. The task was to define planning criteria congruent with the philosophical and logistical rationale of the programme. We needed to differentiate between regulated input factors (the minimum number of weeks to be spent in schools, for example) and discretionary input factors (how the school experience was sequenced). We had also, however, to look at this in the same way with regulated outcomes (competences, for example) and discretionary outcomes (the form of any achievement profile developed through the course). In doing this we were aware that initial teacher training currently represents an uneasy compromise between a traditional wish to control and uphold certain styles of input while at the same time attempting to place the emphasis of evaluation on outcomes. Course design is therefore circumscribed and not always in ways that appear to have a substantial foundation in empirical evidence.

A number of key decisions provided a foundation for the planning framework. First we established a common framework for the course, allowing for phase and subject variations, but ensuring a logic and coherence to the development of partnerships with schools and the design and production of the course resources. In planning the frameworks we also established the principle that all activities associated with the course had to link directly in some way to the practical experience in schools. All the readings, assignments, observations and so forth were selected and designed with that in mind. If a link could not be made, they were excluded.

The second area of decision making was in relation to entry characteristics of students, assessment and profiling. We were comfortable with the idea of a broadly defined competence model, but we wanted to ensure that the advantages were fully exploited in a formative way by students as the course developed. Entry to the course was set out on the basis of a threshold level of qualifications and personal qualities. Students were accepted in the order they applied provided this threshold was met, a process that reflected the spirit of a move towards recognising 'outcome characteristics' rather than trying to second guess the 'input characteristics' most likely to lead to success. We acknowledged, however, that the assessment model should go beyond competences in recognising the development of professional 'qualities' and in reflecting the need for conceptualising competence and qualities within an ongoing process leading to induction and further professional development.

The third set of decisions related to students and quality assurance. A programme taught across the country (and extending to Cyprus, Germany and a number of other European countries) and involving thousands of schools had to evolve robust measures to secure quality. The programme framework and the assessment model were important features of this but additional processes of moderation and monitoring would be essential. In many respects this would be a new departure for teacher education generally, and could provide some pointers to the new types of quality control arrangements required in the move to more school-based programmes of training.

THE COMMON COURSE FRAMEWORK

This framework is at the heart of the OU's PGCE. Figures 7.1 and 7.2 on pages 95 and 96 outline the form this takes for the secondary and primary courses. Each stage and each block of the course has been developed against a further and more detailed specification. Although the different course lines (primary/secondary) and subjects (English, mathematics, science, technology, history and French) have distinctive activities and materials, the order and sequence in which they are addressed is common. The framework specifications extend to the student's school experience at each stage of the course. A series of observations, activities and teaching sequences is prescribed and cross-referenced to the study programme as a whole. A feature of the course is the emphasis placed on understanding pupil learning. Students are therefore introduced to the main theories of learning and progressively, as the course develops, they observe and practise how these ideas can be integrated into different teaching strategies.

A wide range of open learning resources has been developed. Central to the course is a study guide which sets out the routeway through the materials and crucially links this to the experience prescribed for the periods of time in schools (the course provides for experience in two schools). Additionally, students are provided with two resource boxes in the style of an attaché case, each containing a wide range of documents, facsimile materials and other texts that are used at different stages of the

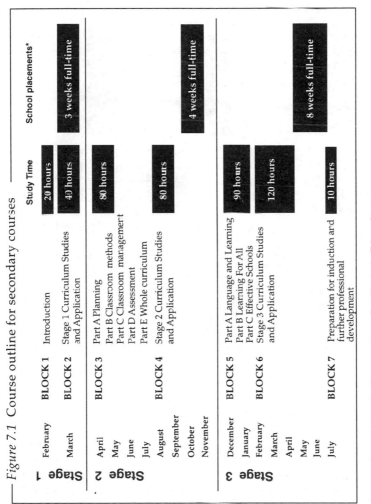

Figure 7.1 Course outline for secondary courses

Source: Open University/Postgraduate Certificate in Education
Note: *Involvement in school-based activities across the ~ 8 months (e.g. parent evenings, drama, music and sport) – 3 weeks.

Figure 7.2 Course outline for primary courses

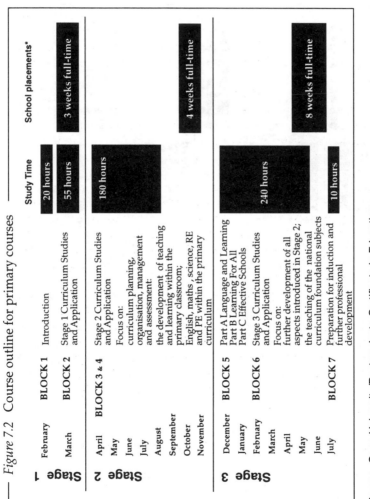

			Study Time	School placements*
Stage 1	February	**BLOCK 1**	Introduction	20 hours	3 weeks full-time
	March	**BLOCK 2**	Stage 1 Curriculum Studies and Application	55 hours	
Stage 2	April	**BLOCK 3 & 4**	Stage 2 Curriculum Studies and Application	180 hours	
	May		Focus on:		
	June		curriculum planning, organisation, management and assessment;		
	July				
	August		the development of teaching and learning within the primary classroom;		
	September				
	October		English, maths, science, RE and PE within the primary curriculum		4 weeks full-time
	November				
Stage 3	December	**BLOCK 5**	Part A Language and Learning Part B Learning For All Part C Effective Schools	240 hours	
	January				
	February	**BLOCK 6**	Stage 3 Curriculum Studies and Application		
	March				
	April		Focus on:		8 weeks full-time
	May		further development of all aspects introduced in Stage 2;		
	June		the teaching of the national curriculum foundation subjects		
	July	**BLOCK 7**	Preparation for induction and further professional development	10 hours	

Source: Open University/Postgraduate Certificate in Education
Note: *Involvement in school-based activities across the 18 months (e.g. parent evenings, drama, music and sport) and teaching in another school = total 18 weeks' school experience.

course. Each primary student receives two such resource packs, one focusing on primary school organisation and curriculum and the second on the teaching of reading. Secondary students have a pack focusing on their specific subject as well as the general issues of secondary education. Videos, filmed in over thirty schools across the country, and audio-cassettes are also linked into the course framework as are readers and set books appropriate to the course as a whole and subjects within it. Finally all students are provided with a home computer (that is subsequently, in part recognition of the support given, passed on to the major placement school). This allows the development of IT capability, both personally and in terms of classroom applications, facilitates inter-student and student–tutor support and communication locally, permits local and national noticeboards/conferencing and gives students access to a wealth of resource data held centrally on the OU system.

The common framework, and the student activities associated with this, provide a template against which mentors and others in school can provide teaching and advice. The terms of the partnership are therefore explicit within the framework and the advice and training given to mentors can be planned across the course to parallel the sequence of the student's activities. Mentor support is given face-to-face, in terms of day or half-day sessions around the beginning of each stage of the course and through a professional development pack with text, video and audio resources. This is set out in two parts, which explore the generic issues of mentoring in ITT and then apply them to the specific requirements of the OU's PGCE.

The designing of the framework, and of the resources and students' school-based activities, was all carried out with teachers experienced in the mentoring and student support role. Such teacher involvement is now in operation, formalised through a series of regional and national advisory groups that look at all aspects of programme development, initiating suggestions for change and responding to feedback from all aspects of the quality assurance process.

ASSESSING COMPETENCE AND PROFESSIONAL QUALITIES

Assessment in ITT, in part because of government regulations, has provoked fierce controversy (Kerry and Shelton Mayes 1994). Our

OU perspective was that competences can be broadly defined to take account of the complexity of teaching: we recognised that the merit of such a model lies in providing an explicit shared framework about learner outcomes that students, mentors and tutors can use for formative and diagnostic as well as summative assessment purposes. A major concern in developing a model of broad statements of competence was how to include a professional values dimension. In making values an explicit part of the assessment model we hoped to ensure that mentors, tutors and students address issues of 'professionalism' firmly within the context of assessing teaching competences. In deciding to explicate the professional values dimension as part of a competency model we built on other assessment models – in particular the ASSET model for social workers developed by Anglia Polytechnic University and Essex County Council (Winter 1991) and the Northern Ireland Working Party on Competence (DENI 1993).

The assessment model was developed with primary and secondary teachers working within the framework of national regulations (DFE 1992, 1993b). From the outset we created a number of guiding principles:

- that explicit learner outcomes must provide a structure for formative, diagnostic as well as summative assessment purposes;
- that outcomes presented in broadly defined competences terms must incorporate an explicit values dimension; and
- that students had to be responsible for presenting evidence of achievement.

The model of assessment is conceptualised in terms of two dimensions of assessment. Five broad areas of teaching competence were identified and these were disaggregated into no more than four or five sub-categories. Students are required to provide evidence that they have demonstrated competence at the level of these sub-categories and, at the final stage, of having fulfilled the requirements of each of the major categories. This ensures that evidence is presented and judgements made at a level commensurate with the complex nature of teaching. In parallel, however, students are required to demonstrate professional qualities in the way that teaching competence is displayed. The assessment model comprises five areas of teaching competence:

- curriculum/subject planning and evaluation;
- classroom/subject methods;
- classroom management;
- assessment, recording and reporting; and
- the wider role of the teacher.

Evidence is submitted by the student to illustrate competence in the elements of each area.

There are some important points to be made. First, the defined professional qualities are not assessed separately from the normal day-to-day tasks of teaching. Professional qualities do not exist in a vacuum but they must have some context for their realisation. Evidence presented to demonstrate competence must, therefore, simultaneously demonstrate professional qualities (see Figure 7.3 below). Second, the competency model is used by mentors and tutors at each stage of the course to provide informal and formal feedback (for example, via school reports) on current progress within competency areas and by students for self-assessment

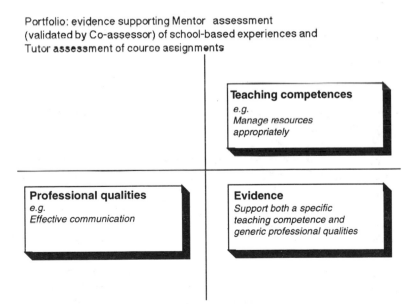

Portfolio: evidence supporting Mentor assessment (validated by Co-assessor) of school-based experiences and Tutor assessment of course assignments

Teaching competences
e.g.
Manage resources
appropriately

Professional qualities
e.g.
Effective communication

Evidence
Support both a specific
teaching competence and
generic professional qualities

Figure 7.3 Competency-based assessment
Source: Open University/Postgraduate Certificate in Education

Submitted to Examination and Assessment

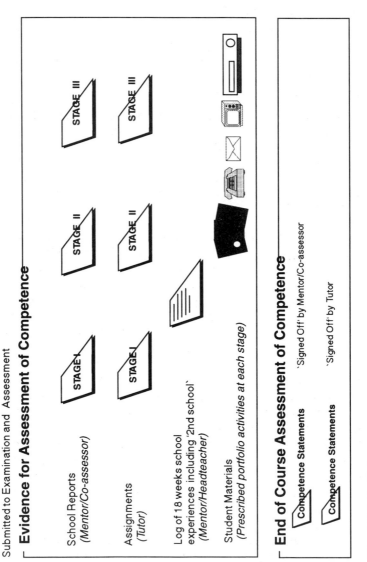

Evidence for Assessment of Competence

School Reports
(Mentor/Co-assessor)

Assignments
(Tutor)

Log of 18 weeks school
experiences including '2nd school'
(Mentor/Headteacher)

Student Materials
(Prescribed portfolio activities at each stage)

STAGE I   STAGE II   STAGE III

STAGE I   STAGE II   STAGE III

End of Course Assessment of Competence

Competence Statements   'Signed Off' by Mentor/Co-assessor

Competence Statements   'Signed Off' by Tutor

Figure 7.4 Portfolio
Source: Open University/Postgraduate Certificate in Education

opportunities. The model is therefore seen primarily as formative and diagnostic during the student's progression through the course. Finally, summative judgements are made at the point when all necessary evidence is accumulated. This stresses the importance of the interrelation of the teaching competences and professional qualities and disavows an attempt by assessors to 'tick off' competences in a discrete and isolated way.

Within the competency framework we then looked at the nature of evidence required to support judgements. The responsibility here in presenting evidence was, properly, seen to lie with the student. A professional development portfolio was designed to serve two purposes, by providing:

- evidence for summative assessment for the award of the PGCE; and
- a profile of professional learning to take forward into induction.

Figure 7.4 on page 100 shows how this develops at each stage of the course. A number of issues arise from this. First, we felt it was important to provide a structure to support the student in identifying and presenting appropriate evidence. Second, we needed a mechanism that would allow moderation between a range of school contexts as part of the quality assurance procedures. It was therefore important to prescribe the overall structure of the portfolio and, in particular, require the student critically to analyse a number of portfolio activities arising from his or her work in schools. Third, mentors are expected to base their judgements on all the work carried out in schools. As well as materials generated by students within their school experience file and professional development portfolio, this includes observations on student teaching and discussions with students – an important point in allowing for context-dependent issues to be considered. Mentor judgements are validated internally by another senior teacher in the school and externally by monitoring arrangements. Finally, the tutor applies the same competency model when marking assignments. All assignments arise out of school experience and thereby reinforce the interconnected nature of the assessment system.

Initial reaction by mentors and students on the course suggests that they find this explicit competency model supportive in structuring individual training activities during school placements; in providing a shared language for analysing class-rooms; and in formal reporting on progress at each stage. We believe it offers a rigorous assessment of teaching competences and professional qualities while providing straightforward procedures for all those involved in the assessment process.

STANDARDS AND QUALITY ASSURANCE

Standards in teacher education and quality assurance (although the term came relatively late to this sector of higher education) have been traditionally based on two measures. Externally HMI have played, and continue to play, an important role in monitoring and reporting on individual institutions and issues in general. The former polytechnic and college sector had direct experience of this over a longer time-scale than the 'older' universities, but across the higher education sector the involvement of HMI in some form, and subject to certain protocols, appears generally accepted. The Council for the Accreditation of Teacher Education (CATE) developed a range of criteria, including latterly a competence assessment framework, against which external inspections by HMI or peer appraisal could be used in forming judgements.

Internal quality assurance was, and to some extent still is, based heavily on three or four measures, namely: course assessments (in a PGCE perhaps four, five or six pieces of marked work); teaching assessments (most commonly assessed on a pass/fail basis); choice of schools (and choice of departments with some secondary courses); training of key staff in schools (although the higher education institution rarely has the choice of such staff); and the moderation of an external assessor or examiner (usually, but not always, covering school experience). Some institutions, though our experience suggests not many, make explicit links between the different components and set out a quality assurance framework. Some, but again only a minority, include a moderating element within the framework to ensure some comparability of standards. This was an area ripe for rethinking. The selection of schools, for example, while widely recognised as important at a rhetorical level in practice, has often been carried out against minimal criteria. In some areas the urgency to provide placements has overridden any question of selection and in other areas the need, at secondary level, to 'cluster' students has often meant the relinquishing of long-established subject ties in certain schools and taking on much less experienced departments within the cluster school. It appeared highly unlikely that an 'ideal type' situation of good school, strong department (or in primary schools, year team) and experienced mentor, all sustained over time, was going to exist in many courses. The quality assurance model had to be cognisant of this. Equally it was clear that the two or three (sometimes fewer) unmoderated lesson observations that commonly supported most teaching 'practices' offered an inadequate base for making comparative judgements of quality.

The stronger frameworks built into programmes and practice through the evolving influence of CATE, the increasingly explicit inspection criteria of OFSTED, and the move to a more widely dispersed range of school and other institutional bases for training, have now given greater prominence to issues of standards and comparability.

Quality assurance, therefore, in the OU model, is reflected in a range of interconnected measures. Examples include:

- the working of a common course framework;
- the prescribed format of school activities linked to the progressive course assessment requirements;
- the stage by stage reporting by schools against the assessment model, monitored on the ground by a national programme of visits and checks and the scrutiny centrally of all school report forms;
- intensive observation and visiting of students identified as within the borderline or fail categories;
- sample visiting and cohort-wide written surveys to evaluate the experience of students, mentors, school coordinators and tutors;
- tutorials and scrutiny of marked assignments in line with normal OU procedures;
- training and support programmes, centrally and regionally, focusing specifically on tutors and mentors; and
- external examining of all aspects of the programme including the assessment of the quality of resources prior to their adoption in the course.

Alongside this internal quality assurance comes the external scrutiny of an HMI specialist inspection team versed in the principles and procedures of open and distance learning and evaluation, and therefore, the same range of indicators. The cross-referencing between internal quality assurance and external inspection provides a further measure of the quality of the programme. This is an area for further exploration. To what extent can, or should, institutional procedures in this area attempt to mirror these other much more explicit approaches adopted by HMI? The relationship between internal and external systems urgently needs to be examined. This point illustrates, as does the preceding discussion, the convergence between quality assurance in open and distance course programmes and more conventionally taught models, both within higher education and schools. Much of the monitoring and survey work that has existed within institutions such as the OU since its inception is now increasingly relevant to the rapidly changing world of higher education and teacher education generally. The moment is propitious for developing a dialogue around this theme.

OPEN LEARNING AND TEACHER EDUCATION: CONVERGING WORLDS?

The increasing convergence of open and distance learning and quality procedures extends to other aspects of teacher education. The need to provide flexible and part-time in-service and higher degree programmes is pushing more and more institutions into developing self-study materials. Distance learning, formerly almost wholly the preserve of the OU, has been developed in a number of higher education institutions in a variety of ways. And so just as the OU is entering worlds such as ITT and doctoral programmes, so other institutions are developing more accessible and open teaching strategies. This we see as a healthy basis on which to build cooperation, although it will mean some rethinking of course planning and presentation and the thinking through of new evaluation criteria for higher education in general and for open and distance learning institutions such as the OU.

Looking forward a few years, therefore, we could see the sorts of strategies and resources developed, by necessity, for an OU part-time ITT course as equally relevant to a full-time conventionally structured programme. The whole constructivist agenda around learning cries out for the sort of multi-media text, video and audio resources developed within an open learning context. The move to a greater emphasis on school-based experience within ITT (a shift in direction that preceded the political controversies over ITT in the early 1990s) indicates the importance of coherent course frameworks. Systems need to be in place, for example, that avoid some of the idiosyncratic quality differences between subject method courses that exist in secondary ITT, or the divergence that can exist between B.Ed. and PGCE courses for the primary phase. For the OU, the advent of new forms of technology and communication poses a challenge to the sorts of methodologies developed so successfully in the last twenty-five years. Facing that challenge in the next twenty-five, in much closer relation to the teacher education community generally, opens up some exciting possibilities.

Chapter 8

Developing induction in schools: managing the transition from training to employment

Marian Shaw, Deanne Boydell and Frank Warner

This chapter examines how the newly qualified teacher (NQT) is inducted, focusing on the progress from studentship to competent professional. It is widely recognised that induction concerns more than just the first year of teaching; thus, although this chapter focuses predominantly on the skills and practices needed to make this link as seamless as possible, it does so within the context of the teacher as lifelong learner in institutions that take the development of all their staff seriously. At a time when LEA funding and influence are waning, it is important for the profession that schools, as they become increasingly self-managing, identify and accept fully their responsibilities towards their new teachers. An induction project for newly qualified teachers in primary schools in Oxfordshire will be described, to illustrate how a productive partnership between LEA, schools and higher education can develop the processes needed to establish sound school-based induction. The project was evaluated carefully, which has enabled us to conclude the chapter with transferable lessons and to identify good practice. Before moving on to the project, we will first review briefly some of the principles of induction in the context of the changes that are currently taking place in education.

THE CONTEXT OF TEACHER INDUCTION

In any profession, transition from training into the workplace generates certain tensions, both for employee and employer. After appointment, new employees need to know at an early stage that the contributions they make are both valued and appropriate. Employers are equally keen to ensure the acquisition of practical knowledge and skills needed to achieve this, and to get the new member on task. On a longer-term basis, however, employees need to be supported in sufficient depth to continue their professional development, establishing a sound framework for future challenges in their career. The challenge for the employer is to find the right balance of emphasis and activity between these long-term and short-term needs and to reconcile any conflict of interest between the two.

In many professions, these issues are addressed by new appointees having a clearly identified period for induction into both the organisation and the profession. During this time, they are not expected to contribute significantly but rather to tune in and learn. The teaching profession is, in this respect, different from most other jobs. Far from having such a transition period, teachers are largely on their own with the responsibility of teaching full classes of pupils from the first day of employment. Induction has therefore to take place while the teacher is fully engaged in work. This creates the need for structured support, not just for the NQT, but also for the teacher in the key supportive role, namely the mentor.

Teaching is an increasingly challenging career, and induction, optional at one time, is now seen as vital if teachers are to fulfil their roles professionally. Induction is often managed in a variety of ways, such as LEA advisory support in schools, courses for NQTs run or commissioned by the LEA, and school-based mentoring. When LEAs employed the teachers directly, induction was largely assumed to be their responsibility. Now that schools are taking more of the responsibility for the appointment and professional development of their new teachers, mentoring in the school is taking on more significance.

The use of the word mentoring needs defining in the specific context of NQT induction. We understand it to be the comprehensive support given by more experienced teachers to enable new teachers to function at a higher professional level than they would otherwise do. It includes induction into a particular school and into the teaching profession in general. In order to be fully effective, mentoring has certain requirements. Both mentor and NQT need to understand their relationship, the school needs to allocate resources, mentors need to have the appropriate knowledge and skills to initiate and develop the relationship, and other staff in the school need to understand the role that they can play. While the need for mentoring is widely accepted, whether or not it happens in practice has often been left to chance.

Since the James Report (DES 1972), recommendations for effective induction have been implemented in a fragmented way. In part this may be due to lack of understanding of what the process entails. Experienced teachers, for example, do not always recognise the need for induction. Even if they do, educating children is different in significant ways from mentoring colleagues, which may involve the acquisition of new skills or the transfer of existing skills to a new context. It also involves the acquisition of new knowledge, such as a theoretical understanding of how beginning teachers develop professionally.

Time is another issue. Some aspects of mentoring have to take place during the school day. This raises questions of organisation and priorities among competing resources. Attitudes are also significant. Much induction takes place informally, on a trouble-shooting basis, and needing support has often been seen as an indication of failure. Even LEA training courses for NQTs, though highly valued in some areas, were found by HMI to be inconsistent across the UK (HMI 1988).

In order to identify the elements of sound induction, it is helpful to analyse the new context. Changes in ITT, the reduction of LEA support and the increasing prevalence of short, fixed-term contracts for NQTs in the aftermath of local management of schools, are all having an effect on the management of induction.

The development of school-based ITT is presenting schools with new challenges. Whereas this should enable more continuity between training and employment, it can only be achieved if sufficient attention is paid to both the similarities and the differences between initial training and induction. Although the mentoring of students and NQTs has certain similarities, such as the skills of listening, questioning and giving feedback, there are also substantial differences, particularly in accountability. These differences have implications for the management of induction and the training of mentors for this purpose.

New teachers, with a range of school responsibilities in addition to teaching a class of their own, are mentored as colleagues. Students, on the other hand, practise in someone else's class. They need to develop and demonstrate competence across a broad spectrum of skills and knowledge and they undergo formal assessment, and receive constructive feedback about their performance, from both class teachers and higher education tutors. Under the new criteria for primary teacher training (DFE 1993b), primary school teachers will be required to have greater formal responsibility. A greater variety of models of training may evolve. In effect, this means that there will need to be a broader spectrum of training for mentors in schools where there are both students and NQTs.

Teacher induction also needs to be considered in the context of the declining influence of LEAs. The number of advisory staff has been cut, and many of those remaining are turning to OFSTED inspection as part of their job, leaving less time for those aspects of their work that are neither statutory nor profitable, such as induction support. They also have no influence over schools that have opted for grant-maintained status. This means that LEAs no longer have responsibility for induction; whether or not individual schools accept this responsibility is another matter.

The induction scene of the future is also characterised by disturbing changes in the pattern of NQT employment. For example, local surveys have shown that NQTs are being given far more temporary contracts than used to be the case before local management of schools, a trend that is being repeated nationally (Earley and Kinder 1994). Since the 1988 Education Reform Act, headteachers and governors have realised the importance of the investment they (rather than the LEA) are making in selecting a member of staff. An untried NQT, particularly with the abolition of the probationary year, can represent a real risk. This, together with the uncertainty surrounding staffing requirements as a result of pupil-driven budgets, has led to employers engaging NQTs on what is, in effect, a trial basis. Although an understandable practice in the current financial context, there are severe consequences for the NQT's performance and development. The mental energies of temporary teachers are likely to be diverted outside the school for much of their contract, searching for, and then focusing on, the next job, just at the time when they should ideally be working single-mindedly for the school and the profession, consolidating their own professional learning. The mentor of a temporarily employed NQT therefore needs to be prepared to offer a different kind of support.

In identifying some of the key issues in the changing context of NQT induction, the need to look afresh at the whole process has been established. Projects that amalgamate the two dimensions of the LEA and the individual school, and also draw on higher education, appear to offer ideal practice at the current time. We next describe such a project.

THE OXFORDSHIRE PRIMARY GEST INDUCTION PROJECT

The project was supported by government funding, from the Grant for Educational Support and Training (GEST) scheme. It built on the sound practices that Oxfordshire had already established for the induction of NQTs. It was designed and implemented for the first time in 1992-3, and refined for 1993–4. The stages of the primary phase of the project are summarised here, outlining its development from concept to practice.

Working within the agreed framework of a steering committee established by one of the LEA's senior advisers, a Primary Mentoring Working Group was formed, composed of four experienced headteachers, a primary LEA adviser, an experienced mentor, two teachers who had been NQTs the previous year and two key personnel from each of the two higher education institutions involved in the primary project. The project was designed by this working group and publicised to schools by the primary adviser, building on his historical LEA role of support for NQTs and their schools. Training courses were led by higher education and LEA personnel. In 1992-3, one full day of training was provided for each mentor at the end of September, focusing on the principles and basic skills of mentoring, examining some challenging NQT situations and anticipating possible difficulties and problems. Mentors were involved in the development of a personal development profile for the NQT. A folder of support materials was designed, written so that such materials could be converted into a distance learning pack for the future once the GEST funding had ceased.

Three skills-focused twilight sessions for mentors were held in each county division, and a further twilight session for mentors, headteachers and NQTs was organised at the end of the summer term, to consider the next stages of the induction process and to help inform the process for the following year.

The progress of the project was monitored informally by the working group throughout the year and more formally at two stages during the year, namely halfway through and again at the end. As part of the formal evaluation process, the views of mentors and NQTs were sought by questionnaire (Boydell and Bines 1994). After evaluation, certain issues became clearer. Mentors requested a training event earlier in the term. They also wanted quality time with their NQTs, picking up on the issues explored on the mentor training day. Adjustments were made by the working group and the 1993-4 programme evolved. The mentor training day was in the first week of term, and a full day for mentors and NQTs together in the second week replaced the twilight mentor training sessions, giving structured time for mentors and NQTs to establish their relationships and key needs. Twilight support sessions were operated by the LEA adviser, complementing the training programme and providing continuity throughout the year.

The training for mentors in the Oxfordshire project was based on two fundamental principles which underpinned the whole process. First, there was a heavy focus on building the NQT's confidence. This was seen to necessitate confidentiality within the relationship, ruling out the accountability and reporting back model implemented by some LEAs. Second, training was geared specifically to the emerging needs of the NQT and the identification of an agenda of developmental issues jointly negotiated by the NQT and the mentor. The mentor was not expected to interfere or to be prescriptive.

Mentor training was designed to help establish a trusting relationship based on a clear understanding of these principles. It recognised the experience that mentors brought with them, and built on this, highlighting a large range of skills, such as listening, sensitive questioning, analysing and handing back responsibility to the NQT to make up her or his own mind about what action to take. Mentors needed to choose the appropriate response at the right time. Too much direction and support would make the NQT dependent on the mentor, but too little would leave the NQT floundering. Mentors were encouraged to help their NQTs analyse the underlying issues, discuss various possible ways forward and challenge them to decide for themselves. The joint use by mentor and NQT of the personal development profile lent rigour to this process. Throughout the training, it was emphasised that there was no single Oxfordshire model of mentoring or induction, but that each school should develop its own system within the framework of the LEA policy.

Given the principles described, it was clear that good mentors wore many hats, and the training therefore addressed the various roles needed to provide NQTs with all-round support. These included vocational roles, such as informing, consulting, coaching, giving feedback when asked, helping the NQT to network with other helpful people and protecting them when necessary from taking on too much. Interpersonal roles included encouraging, praising, reassuring, sharing one's own dilemmas, using counselling skills, and, as the year wore on, helping the NQT to become more independent.

The formal project evaluation investigated how these different roles were perceived by the participants and in which order they were needed. The findings throw more light on the process of mentoring for effective NQT development. At the start of the year, NQTs felt their main need was plenty of reassurance from their mentors, for which they tapped their mentors' interpersonal roles. To a slightly lesser extent, but still importantly, they also needed help from mentors in a vocational role, particularly in relation to provision of information and support with curriculum planning, organisation and classroom management.

As the year progressed, the NQTs gained in personal confidence and became more familiar with curriculum planning. By the end of the year, not only were NQTs seeking less support from their mentors but the emphasis had changed. The help they predominantly needed was firmly based on the vocational side, this time rooted in assessment and record-keeping issues which they had seemingly pushed aside when coming to terms with the enormity of teaching at the start of the year (Boydell and Bines 1994).

There have been a number of benefits from the project. Not only did NQTs gain in confidence, skills and professionalism, but mentors also benefited from enhanced professional development. For schools, the project helped to reinforce the expectation of continuing staff development. For the LEA, less remedial action for failing NQTs meant that more effort was able to be deployed on proactive support. It seems that with an integrated induction project of this type, the profession as a whole might benefit, with more teachers performing to a higher level and fewer teachers leaving the profession disillusioned.

ISSUES ARISING FROM THE PROJECT

The project highlights important issues relevant to successful induction.

Partnership

A joint initiative, such as the one described, has many merits. At a time when resources are scarce, it offers coordinated support, with a clear structure, designed by professionals 'on the ground'. Each member of the partnership plays a specific part, for which clear expectations need to be made at the start. Higher education staff, for example, can take the lead in developing appropriate materials and delivering and accrediting training. LEA staff can use knowledge of existing networks and of schools to coordinate all activities, and are particularly well placed to identify where supplementary support is needed. Schools advise on the needs of both mentor and NQT, making an input to the content, approach and timing of the various elements of the induction process. In this way, everyone gains.

Successful partnership facilitates the transfer of accountability for NQT induction from the LEA to the schools. Nevertheless, such a partnership does not have a mandate: schools may still choose not to take their new responsibilities seriously. OFSTED inspection, which collects evidence from NQTs rather than mentors, may provide some incentive, although indications so far suggest that there is perhaps less monitoring going on here than expected (Ormston and Shaw 1994). Partnership can also ease another tension. There is evidence that where schools are faced with a LEA adviser who doubles as inspector, they may be less likely to acknowledge the source of induction difficulties in case more fundamental weaknesses are exposed. Productive partnerships can help defuse these situations where the personnel involved in induction are not exclusively LEA employees.

Selection and training of mentors

Given that it is usually not feasible for NQTs to select their own mentor, schools need to consider carefully who is the most appropriate teacher for this important job. It needs, among many attributes, someone who can listen, help NQTs articulate their concerns, accept other people's ways of doing things, and, of course, practise what is preached. The mentor will also need to be someone who fully supports the ethos of the school, and is able to influence decision making. Consideration also needs to be given to whether more senior teachers and direct line managers should become mentors, given trends to separate professional evaluation from the more supportive aspects of mentoring in order to avoid conflicts in role (Earley and Kinder 1994: 62).

Although training is dependent on the school's decision, NQTs usually have an entitlement to professional staff development. Mentors should also have such an entitlement. Experienced staff, who have inducted probationary teachers for years, still recognise that good training greatly enhances the value of their job as mentor. Joint training of mentors and NQTs, placed at the start of the NQT's employment, is also useful in establishing the relationship on a sound basis. The recognition by mentors that they too benefit from both the relationship and the training is encouraging, and is becoming a motivating factor for accepting the role of mentor.

Training that is run in mixed school groups ensures that there is a broad basis of experience on which to build, and that NQTs, isolated in their own schools, can draw support from others, an aspect of training that NQTs find particularly helpful. This is largely, at present, a LEA function, but it may founder unless someone takes it on. In areas where the impact of the LEA is declining fast, there is already a growth in training led by higher education institutions to fill the gap. This is important, as school clusters often have neither the time nor resources to organise such training themselves.

The induction process

It is helpful if mentoring has a formal structure, where there is agreement about respective roles, confidentiality, function and frequency of meetings, observations and reviews. Without this structure, mentoring becomes solely 'advice on the hoof', as there is no time to have a professional discussion, tease out the issues and make real progress. Although the many spontaneous interactions are invaluable, the space to reflect and to plan needs formal recognition. The role of the headteacher in supporting the mentoring relationship is crucial.

A good scheme also plans for continuity, ensuring that the support offered during the first year takes into account the student experience, preparing both NQT and mentor, where possible, in the period between the NQT's appointment and the start of his or her post. Although formal mentoring may have ceased at the end of the year, awareness of the need for some support into the second year ensures that teachers do not feel suddenly isolated. It also provides the expectation of lifelong learning.

All parties need to be aware of NQTs' changing needs as the year progresses, and structure the year accordingly. Once a productive relationship is set up, the needs of the NQT have to be met in a way that is suitable and sustainable throughout the year.

Developing whole school understanding and management

Only one-third of the schools in the survey carried out by the National Foundation for Education Research (NFER) had policies for induction of NQTs (Earley and Kinder 1994). Yet having a NQT on the staff is very much a whole school issue. Mentors cannot supply all the support needed single-handedly, and, indeed, part of their function should be to help the NQT network with other staff as appropriate. For this, staff have to be aware of the needs of NQTs and of the principles of mentoring, even if they are not acting currently as mentor. The school that takes professional development seriously for all its staff is better placed to support NQTs and may even learn from them! Many schools are in the process of creating a policy on induction and most still have a LEA framework to guide them.

Good induction has to be resourced, and governors, as well as staff, need to understand that this implies certain budget commitments, such as time needed for observation by and of a NQT. In Oxfordshire, the issue of induction has now been placed on the governor training agenda. It is interesting that although few of the NFER sample schools saw a NQT appointment as a cheap option, money for induction tends to be buried in the school budget and rarely earmarked. This may imply the need for a political battle to prioritise such funding for induction purposes (Earley and Kinder 1994).

CONCLUSION

This chapter has described a project reinforcing the partnership between a LEA, schools and higher education, while placing ownership firmly with the participants. Projects such as these enable schools to take an increasingly leading role in induction as LEA influence wanes.

Some of the complex forces at work in the changing pattern of NQT induction have been identified. The basic need, however, is constant, namely to offer new teachers sufficient support to bridge the gap between initial training and confident performance and growth as a professional. With staffing absorbing an average of 70 per cent of school budgets (Audit Commission 1993), it makes economic as well as professional sense to ensure that new entrants into the profession are fully equipped to develop into the sort of teachers our society needs.

Chapter 9

Supporting continuing professional development

Diane Gaunt

Partnership in the continuing professional development of teachers began to develop on a substantial scale in 1987, when changes in funding altered the balance of power controlling in-service education and training (INSET). At first these partnerships were forged between higher education institutions and LEAs but following the implementation of local management of schools, the growth of grant-maintained schools, the development of school-based initial training and the incorporation of further education colleges, partnerships are developing directly between higher education institutions and individual, or consortia of, schools and colleges.

The growth of such partnerships, together with changes in INSET funding and in higher education in general, have had a considerable effect on the pattern of INSET provision. This in turn has generated a range of management issues. This chapter will first outline the systems and approaches that have emerged in this new context and then identify some of the management implications. Reference will be made to the development of INSET provision by the School of Education at Oxford Brookes University, to illustrate the issues involved. Finally, the chapter will consider future needs and developments and the way in which these may be met within the context of partnership.

NEW SYSTEMS AND APPROACHES FOR CONTINUING PROFESSIONAL DEVELOPMENT

Until 1987, continuing professional development largely meant courses leading to qualifications together with some provision for shorter specific training. Financial resources were available to

LEAs through a national pool system to support a relatively small number of teachers seconded to take long award-bearing courses run by higher education institutions. The demise of this system was heralded in the White Paper *Better Schools* (DES 1985) which asserted that INSET resources were not being used to best advantage and shorter, less traditional activities would be more effective for many purposes. Funds were to be used to benefit more teachers by targeting priorities identified by central government and LEAs in order to match training both to the career needs of teachers and to curricular changes in schools and colleges.

Under the subsequent Local Education Authorities Training Grants Scheme (LEATGS), grants were made to LEAs either to provide training using their own staff or to buy in expertise from higher education or the growing number of private trainers. A report by HM Inspectors (HMI 1989) on the first year of the scheme observed that planning, organisation and delivery of INSET had been approached more systematically and that generally INSET was in better health than ever before.

The Education Support Grant (ESG), which came into operation in 1984, was the second new source of funding for INSET, providing the means for purchasing materials and equipment, the employment of advisory teachers and the training of non-teaching staff and governors. Following a scrutiny of the two schemes, they were merged in 1992 to form Grants for Education Support and Training (GEST).

The effects of the new funding arrangements on higher education were profound. Staff found themselves trading in an INSET market and were faced with new concepts such as business plans, product design, income generation and customer care. Survival depended increasingly on the development of short courses to be delivered in a range of venues: schools, colleges, teachers' centres and hotels. Some staff were also employed as consultants, giving advice to teachers, schools, colleges and LEAs in relation to the range of changes being brought to bear on education.

Many higher education providers worked hard to redesign their award-bearing courses to offer greater flexibility and accessibility in order to appeal to teachers studying in their own time and often at their own expense. This challenging process involved changing course structures, content, modes of delivery and assessment while maintaining academic rigour. The majority of institutions have changed from linear to modular courses which are seen to offer greater scope for individualised programmes of study, flexibility in pace and mode of attendance, a variety of entry and exit points, recognition of prior and parallel learning and credit accumulation and transfer schemes (CATS). Such courses may also facilitate the opportunities for shared learning created by the new partnerships between schools, colleges and higher education.

The first part of many courses now involves programme planning during which teachers reflect on their professional development, identify their prior learning and make a statement explaining the coherence, balance and progression of their proposed programme. A module on research methods is included early on in most programmes in order to equip teachers with the techniques to conduct investigations in their own professional settings (Williamson 1989). There is a strong trend towards ensuring that teachers have the opportunity to produce coursework that is of direct use to them. Many elements of courses are therefore assessed through assignments which encourage teachers to research and evaluate their own practice. In addition, the majority of modular schemes include independent study modules and the final element for most awards is a dissertation or project, often involving practice-based enquiry.

The professional demands made on teachers have altered. In particular, affective skills such as teamwork and managing change have become more important. These changes have been reflected in new assessment strategies. Whereas traditional assignments focus on individual written work, such approaches to assessment may now be supplemented by group projects and seminar presentations which are often assessed by fellow students as well as tutors.

The central tenet of a credit accumulation and transfer scheme is that credit points may be assigned to learning wherever it takes place provided that such learning is demonstrable and thus assessable. The most widely used scheme has evolved from that developed by the Council for National Academic Awards (1986). This scheme has now been adopted by many higher education institutions, including the old universities, the new universities (former polytechnics), the Open University and the remaining colleges of higher education. The UK credit system articulates with those used in Europe and other parts of the world.

The scope for credit accumulation and transfer within modular INSET schemes is enormous since accreditation can be given for courses run by higher education, courses run by employers and work-based learning in the form of school or college development activities and projects. There is a growing demand from teachers and their employers that this work should count towards certificates, diplomas and degrees as part of INSET partnerships with higher education.

The accreditation of structured INSET provided by higher education or the partner organisation is straightforward inasmuch as the creditworthiness can be determined using clear criteria. Professional development that occurs in a teacher's day-to-day work can also be recognised through the accreditation of prior experiential learning (APEL). Assessment of such learning must be as valid and reliable as the procedures used to assess coursework. The most common instrument is the portfolio, normally comprising a narrative which demonstrates reflection on experience in order to identify the learning outcomes together with supporting documentation. Guidance on the identification of prior learning and the preparation of a portfolio may be provided by a formal class, tutorials or a manual. However, warnings have been given on the danger of making the whole procedure so mechanistic and time-consuming that it becomes a barrier rather than a means of broadening access (Usher 1989).

There are a number of mechanisms used by higher education institutions to accredit or validate short courses of professional development run by their own staff or other providers. A crucial factor is speed of response. The traditional course approval procedures used in many higher education institutions, which involve a number of committee stages, external assessors and elaborate documentation, have had to be streamlined without sacrificing quality assurance. Such accreditation has many advantages. For example, Triggs and Francis (1990) found that accreditation gave recognition to teachers whose work had previously been unrecognised, promoted the recognition of INSET as a valuable activity, attracted teachers to award-bearing courses and enhanced teachers' confidence. The inclusion of an assessed component generally enhances the effectiveness of an INSET activity in that it requires teachers to read around the subject and undertake research in the workplace.

A number of approaches and procedures have therefore been developed to facilitate partnership in relation to continuing professional development. By offering choice, flexibility, links to the teachers' own professional responsibilities and accreditation for a range of INSET activity, higher education providers can support partnership in relation to continuing professional development in a number of ways. Nevertheless, the implementation of such models raises a number of management issues that need to be resolved. Some of these will now be discussed.

MANAGING PARTNERSHIP

Management issues include resources, information systems and staff development. The sharing of financial and human resources is inevitably one of the most contentious aspects. The majority of INSET partnerships with individual schools and colleges or consortia have grown from partnerships in initial teacher training. Even before the shift to school-based training, some schools began to look at their devolved budgets and ask whether providing school experience placements was cost-effective and often came to the conclusion that it was not. Some higher education institutions have thus repaid schools with INSET vouchers to entitle teachers to attend modules from the award-bearing INSET programme offered by the institution while others have provided training to meet particular school needs. Although such approaches reinforce the importance of partnership across the continuum of professional training and development, and recognise the contribution made by schools to initial training, they can be both difficult to administer and costly to provide.

As noted in Chapter 1, the resources available for initial and in-service training are closely linked. The transfer of resources to schools for initial training may have a considerable impact on the range of expertise available within the higher education institution for INSET work. At the same time, the range of demands on higher education providers to offer not only award-bearing courses but high-quality training and consultancy means that such expertise must be both protected and developed. Further pressures arise from the need for INSET provision to be both cost-effective and yet cheap enough to be attractive in the INSET marketplace.

The need for effective information systems has a number of dimensions. Managing a complex modular scheme requires substantial administrative backup. Ideally a computerised student management system should be used for record-keeping, with transcripts produced at the end of each term or semester. Records also need to be kept of accreditation arrangements and decisions in relation to school-based or college-based INSET and the procedures and outcomes associated with APL for individual teachers. The information systems developed by higher education for such purposes may also need to articulate with staff development systems within individual schools and colleges and partnerships as a whole. For example, each teacher may be issued with a professional development portfolio, designed to enable the teacher to record and give an account of the reflective practice and enhanced professionalism derived from various situations (Graham 1989). Since profiling has become an integral part of initial teacher training it is likely that profiles will become increasingly significant in continuing professional development (Bolam 1993). The National Commission on Education recommended that 'all teachers should have a personal development plan (PDP) in the formulation of which they should have an active role and which should be linked to their profiles. . . . The plan will continuously evolve as INSET courses and other experiences are credited' (National Commission on Education 1993: 219–20). The development and maintenance of such profiles will require collaborative approaches within the INSET partnership with regard to documentation and other forms of recording.

Staff development is another important aspect of partnership. As noted in several chapters in this book, an important development has been the enlarged and more defined role of the school mentor under the new arrangements for initial teacher training and for the induction of newly qualified teachers. Similar arrangements are made in colleges of further education for the mentoring of their staff who are attending part-time courses of initial teacher training. Mentors are experienced teachers who have generally welcomed their new role and have seen their responsibilities as a new professional opportunity. Nevertheless there is a need for training that can also be accredited by the higher education partner, to enable such training to lead to a further qualification if wished. Although mentorship is another illustration of the links between initial and continuing professional development, and brings the concept of the master teacher advocated by Warnock (1979) closer to reality, the costs of training and accreditation need to be met. The development of mentor training through INSET funding, as well as through funding for initial training and induction, could be a particularly fruitful approach.

Staff development is similarly required for the higher education members of the partnership. Higher education staff now have to undertake more guidance and negotiation with teachers and are required to provide a greater diversity of teaching modes and settings than ever before. They also need to develop their skills in training and consultancy (Gaunt 1992). However, there are few sources of funding or expertise for such staff development, other than those that can be provided by higher education institutions themselves.

The management of INSET partnerships also needs to be articulated with the management of partnership in relation to initial training. However, staffing and management structures may be distinct for these different aspects of the work of higher education institutions. Policy development and coordination are thus extremely important if the higher education institution is to work effectively with its partner schools and colleges across the professional development continuum.

THE DEVELOPMENT OF INSET PROVISION AT OXFORD BROOKES UNIVERSITY

The development of INSET provision by the School of Education at Oxford Brookes University reflects many of the issues discussed above. For example, the award-bearing courses offered by the School have been redesigned to offer greater scope for flexible and part-time study and for the recognition of other professional development activity. The modular INSET scheme now includes MA, Postgraduate Diploma, BA and Certificate awards based on specialist and open programmes (Gaunt 1992). Procedures for credit accumulation and transfer, and for accreditation of prior experiential learning (APEL), are well established and are requested by an increasing number of teachers wishing to enrol on the INSET programme. The School also undertakes a range of short course and consultancy work for LEAs and for individual schools and colleges and consortia. Teachers who have taken GEST courses run by the School for various LEAs are awarded a Certificate and also have the opportunity to have the work credited towards a degree or diploma. In relation to the accreditation of INSET activities other than award-bearing courses offered by the School or other providers, a fast and responsive system has been developed based on a simple pro forma which is considered by a committee within the School and the Faculty quality assurance committee before being passed to the University's CATS Committee for final approval. An established system is therefore in place to extend partnership in accreditation in future.

The management of INSET has also received considerable attention. For example, in relation to information systems, Oxford Brookes University is well known for its pioneering modular undergraduate course with its sophisticated system of information management (Watson 1989). It is now committed to modularising most of its post-experience and postgraduate courses, and to this end it is developing a new computerised management information system which will extend the facilities previously restricted largely to the undergraduate programme to all courses. The School of Education's INSET scheme has acted as a useful model and example of information needs in such developments.

Within the context of resource transfer to schools for initial training purposes, the School has protected its range of expertise by expanding short course and consultancy provision, building in particular on strengths in areas such as education management and special educational needs. However, the management of such work remains complex, given the unpredictability of demand over the academic year. It is therefore difficult to balance with any certainty the range of demands on staffing and other resources across all programmes and to ensure that each member of staff is engaged in a secure, and yet flexible, timetable of work. Currently, most members of staff are involved in both ITT and INSET courses and it is intended that all staff should take on more short course and consultancy work. As a result, most members of staff are aware of, and involved in, the continuum of professional development. Management structures are based in part on a distinction between ITT and INSET courses. However, the committees and personnel involved are also aware of the importance of seeing partnership with schools and colleges as an entity, despite the difficulties of coordination and unified policy development.

As noted in a recent publication on developments in professional education within the University (Bines and Watson

1992), the successful implementation of a flexible and responsive approach within higher education to continuing professional development is dependent in large part on the work of individual staff and departments. However, such developments can also be facilitated by effective management within the institution as a whole. Such management recognises the potential of modular schemes; encourages new approaches to teaching, learning and assessment; responds positively to the accreditation of individual prior learning and of courses offered by other providers; and gives credence to the importance of partnership with employers and the local community. Institutional encouragement, and the expectation that new approaches within higher education will be applied to teacher education, can thus be seen as an important part of developing INSET partnerships. At the same time, the quality of INSET provision, and of relationships with schools and colleges, will remain the most important factor in successful partnership.

CONCLUSION

The teaching force in this country is currently beset by a crisis of confidence. Radical curricular and administrative changes have placed new burdens on the classroom teacher. The long-term professional development of the individual teacher has been subordinated to short-term imperatives of central government. Gilroy and Day (1993) have pointed to an increasing tendency to regard 'development' as 'training', which may be achieved in short sharp bursts and which must be directly related to policy implementation. Partnership between schools or colleges and higher education is designed to meet institutional needs in response to changes in policy. The continuing development of individual teachers may be a secondary consideration but in a well-managed scheme, institutional needs and individual needs should be viewed as complementary rather than conflicting.

Chapter 10

Partnership in initial training for further and adult education

Trevor Dawn

The further and adult education system is expected to meet a multiplicity of demands: from individual students with aspirations for qualifications or the desire for personal fulfilment; from government, which requires both high-quality vocational training and a safety net for social pressures; and from employers and other groups in the community for whom such education meets a variety of needs. The pressures generated by these different demands and expectations have created a parallel need for staff development and formal teacher training.

However, it is often the case that a substantial course of staff development is undertaken by a lecturer before formal initial teacher training, with the possible exception of a short introductory course. This chapter will examine the related nature of staff development and initial teacher training and the partnership implications for both.

THE TRADITIONAL SYSTEM OF INITIAL TEACHER TRAINING FOR FURTHER AND ADULT EDUCATION

The majority of teachers in further and adult education enter the profession without a recognised initial teacher training qualification. It is perfectly possible for them to remain as untrained teachers for as long as they are employed. There is no statutory obligation to train. Since the early 1970s, however, most teachers have gained recognised qualifications through courses of part-time study concurrent with employment as a teacher. A minority have entered the profession after undertaking a year's full-time initial training similar to the PGCE for graduates intending to teach in primary and secondary schools.

Provision for part-time courses has varied according to the way in which individual regions in England and Wales responded to the recommendations of the Haycocks Committee which reported three times to the Secretary of State for Education and Science between 1975 and 1978 (DES 1975, 1977, 1978). For full-time teachers, or those with a substantial part-time contract, initial training courses have normally comprised a two-year part-time programme, with a pattern of weekly day release and a four-week block release in each year, leading to the Certificate in Education in Further Education (Cert.Ed.FE), provided by higher education. Since their inception, such courses have qualified for mandatory award status.

For other part-time teachers, regional schemes have developed, often based on the City and Guilds of London Institute (CGLI) 730 series of training courses, in line with the three-stage process recommended by the Haycocks Committee. Stage One normally comprises a short induction course of about thirty hours of attendance to enable teachers to survive in the teaching environment. Stage Two is a more substantial course with successful completion of Stage One as a prerequisite for entry. It involves 180 hours of attendance and a programme consisting of a balance of underpinning knowledge and practical teaching skills. Such teachers can then progress if they wish to Stage Three, namely the Cert.Ed.FE.

Recently, a number of providers have adopted a model whereby Stages One and Two can be accredited to a Cert.Ed.FE programme, thereby shortening the final period of study for this qualification. Such an option is normally made available to both full-time and part-time teachers in further and adult education. This development has been based on the growing partnership between higher education and its partner colleges and other organisations within the further and adult education service.

The traditional ethos of the various patterns of teacher training has been one of cooperation, often through *ad hoc* committees of staff development officers and senior management staff from colleges together with higher education providers. The models put forward by the Haycocks Committee involved a partnership approach which was designed to be different from full-time, pre-service models of attendance. First, it was an entry requirement in all cases that the trainee teacher should be employed in a teaching capacity so that he or she could be observed teaching a regular class. In practice this meant that employing institutions had to be consulted about the training needs of the trainee for whom remission of class contact time was allowed. Second, all Stage One and Stage Two courses were subject to validation by a panel of the Regional Advisory Councils (RACs). This applied whether the course was submitted by an individual institution or, as was more common, by a local authority consortium. This insistence on regional approval raised the status of the courses for part-time teachers. The CGLI provided nationally managed validation and moderation. Finally, at Stage Three, the Council for National Academic Awards (CNAA), the then validating body for higher education providers, required evidence of local consultation and local participation in the planning of Cert.Ed.FE courses. Practising further and adult education teachers formed the backbone of the teaching teams and many centres ran both Cert.Ed.FE. and CGLI 730 courses, thereby benefiting from an interchange of ideas and staffing.

STAFF DEVELOPMENT IN FURTHER AND ADULT EDUCATION

Since the late 1970s, the further and adult education system has had to enhance substantially its staff development provision to cope with fundamental changes in the economic and social fabric of society. For example, the international shift towards information technology, which has now permeated all facets of economic life in most Western countries, has involved a total reappraisal of the nature of the skills which young people now need for work. As Lee notes in Chapter 11, the decline of certain industries has also changed the nature of vocational training. In addition, further and adult education were required to respond to a national crisis of mass unemployment and the accompanying focus on youth training schemes, retraining and other forms of vocational education.

The subsequent changes in curricula were substantial and involved a number of organisations, generating a range of staff development opportunities. Courses, publications and a range of open learning materials and other resources were developed at local, regional and national levels, spearheaded by the Further Education Unit, which favoured regional networks, and the Manpower Services Commission (later the Training, Employment and

Education Directorate), which preferred to subcontract the delivery of training to a variety of agencies. The Further Education Unit in particular pioneered the concept of curriculum-led staff development, which for many lecturers was vital as they struggled to meet the new challenges. The Department of Education and Science also recognised the urgency of staff development by prioritising a number of items in its Grants for Education Support and Training (GEST) programmes and by encouraging the examining boards to develop new qualifications. The Further Education Staff College also contributed significantly to staff development opportunities in terms of courses and publications. Finally, in 1988 it became obligatory for LEAs to institute staff development schemes in the colleges under their control, which in many cases led to the appointment of staff development officers and accommodation for staff development activities. As will shortly be discussed, changes in courses, qualifications and approaches to teaching, learning and assessment have continued into the 1990s, requiring yet further staff development. In addition, staff development is now linked with formal appraisal requirements and with recruitment and promotion issues.

The responsibility for training staff has therefore been thrust upon colleges and centres and they have responded very professionally. A culture of entitlement and expectation in relation to staff development has permeated the perspectives of teaching as well as management staff. Such changes have also altered the nature of initial teacher training, from an approach based mainly on initiating lecturers into the ways of teaching and behaving in further and adult education, which is at the heart of the pre-service model, to a model which gives coherence to the experience and commitment of the existing practitioner.

THE FUTURE OF INITIAL TEACHER TRAINING AND STAFF DEVELOPMENT IN FURTHER AND ADULT EDUCATION

Lecturers have thus become used to rapid change. However, they now face a revolution on two fronts: the curriculum front, with the drive towards competence-based qualifications through National Vocational Qualifications (NVQs) and General National Vocational Qualifications (GNVQs); and the institutional front, as a result of the incorporation of further education colleges and the demise of the LEA role.

The Further Education Funding Council (FEFC) has added performance criteria and strict outcome-focused conditions to the successful 'throughput' of NVQ and GNVQ passes. This has had an impact not only on the resource allocation per student but also on the professional skills of some lecturers. It is quite common to hear lecturers of vocational subjects talk of being deskilled as their role is concentrated into the managing of prepackaged learning materials followed by the assessing of evidence of competence.

This development is affecting the rationale and design of initial teacher training and ultimately its financing, with some strategists seeking to bring teacher training qualifications more into line with competence models which satisfy the criteria specified by the Training and Development Lead Body (TDLB). Not all teachers, or indeed, providers of teacher training, feel this trend is in the best interests of the teachers or their students and they await the emergence of an Education Lead Body. Meanwhile, there is a real danger that the inherent tensions of the 'training' and 'education' dimensions of post-compulsory provision will lead to a polarity of training expectation and need, whereby the vocational teachers are in one teaching and learning culture and the academic and non-vocational teachers are in another.

Finally, the Further and Higher Education Act of 1992, which led to college incorporation, was based in part on the assumption that the efficacy of the market and the benefits of deregulation will have a positive bearing on quality and cost-effectiveness. Concepts of competence and fitness for purpose may therefore undermine the belief currently underpinning many initial training courses that a broad range of knowledge and the skills of reflective practice are fundamental to the notion of the trained teacher. Curriculum-led staff development has demonstrated the capacity of those working in further and adult education to respond to change, albeit at the level of coping mechanisms. Furthermore, there are fewer checks and balances in a system based on greater freedom to determine local priorities and local solutions. Should the mandatory award for the Stage Three or Cert.Ed.FE level of training cease to be available, the consequences are likely to be a deterioration in the resources given to teacher training, particularly once it becomes evident that the costs of training will have to be borne entirely out of college or adult centre budgets. Deterioration in resources does not necessarily mean a deterioration in quality but the danger is that the accepted level of competence will turn out to be lower than the Cert.Ed.FE threshhold to which we have become accustomed. The overall effect of these trends is that a radical reappraisal of the nature of partnerships between colleges or other post-16 providers, and higher education institutions providing training for the sector, needs to be undertaken to ensure a well-trained teaching force.

THE FUTURE PATTERN OF TRAINING

It is evident that a professionally recognised qualification is required to develop and accredit the immediate competences needed so that lecturers can cope with the demands of their existing workload. This qualification should also provide a structured exposure to ideas and information that go beyond current staff development issues and enhance the teacher's ability to be flexible and to adapt to changing circumstances. This may well be best served by a type of three-part contract (English 1975) between the teacher, his or her employing institution and the higher education institution, in order to meet the range of needs, expectations and requirements involved. As identified in Figure 10.1, each partner has a relationship with, and an obligation to, the other two partners. The contract can only work when it has been designed in a holistic manner so that the obligations and the expectations of all the parties are recognised and formalised.

On the A–B axis in Figure 10.1, the partnership will involve mentorship, management, access to wider opportunities and regular liaison with staff development systems. On the A–C axis, the college, or other form of post-compulsory provision employing the teacher, should ensure that the actual teacher training programme meets the needs both of the individual teacher and of the institution, within the latter's overall human resource policy. On the B–C axis, the higher education institution should ensure that there is a core to the professional development which is consistent with national requirements while allowing scope for the desires of individual teachers and their institutions. The core should centre on key principles and approaches and the knowledge which underpins them, and how they

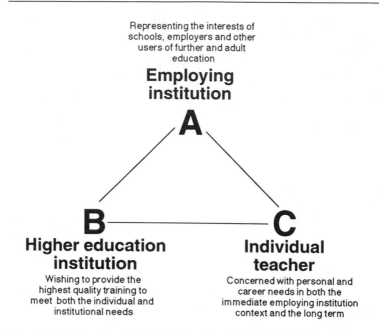

Representing the interests of
schools, employers and other
users of further and adult
education

**Employing
institution**

A

B ———————————— **C**

**Higher education   Individual
institution   teacher**

Wishing to provide the   Concerned with personal and
highest quality training to   career needs in both the
meet both the individual and   immediate employing institution
institutional needs   context and the long term

Figure 10.1 A contract for initial teacher training for further and adult
education

impinge upon the practical nature of the teacher's role. It should
also conform to the structure of competence-based schemes while
allowing for the possibility that the really well-trained teacher
goes beyond the confines of competence. The non-core elements
of the training should cater for the needs and interests of both
individual teachers and their employing institutions.

Such an approach can be illustrated by developments at Oxford
Brookes University. The Cert.Ed.FE course offered by the School
of Education, now renamed as the Certificate in Education (Post-
Compulsory Education), has been redesigned to put the principles of the three-part contract into action. Course participants
will be expected to complete a core of professionally agreed learning outcomes in the form of a competence profile. However, they
will have a wide degree of choice as to how the evidence is
assembled, that is, whether by conventional course assignments
or by other means including the accreditation of prior learning
(APL). This core will form two-thirds of the course requirements.

In addition, course participants will have the opportunity to
negotiate the non-core parts of the programme. These may be

undertaken through units of study designed by the course team, through work-based tasks which are then rated for credit or through direct access to other programmes, notably the BA (Professional Studies in Education) programme offered by the School. The exact nature of a participant's programme will be finalised in a learning contract, which will reflect a balance between the duty of teacher training institutions to ensure standards, the wishes of employing institutions to provide a focus with a direct bearing on the role of the teacher, and the needs of the participant in terms of career development, coherence and progression. The partnership links with each employing institution will be maintained in three ways: by informal liaison committees; by membership on the course committee which manages the course; and through the development of a mentorship scheme to help each participant make the most of the opportunities for integration of learning afforded by this approach to partnership.

IMPLICATIONS FOR PARTNERSHIP

This form of contracting and course design will change the relationship between each of the partners. Each higher education institution will need to ensure adequate arrangements for the accreditation of prior and parallel learning and offer tutorials and guidance so that individuals can manage substantial elements of their own programme. It will also need to liaise with each employing institution to secure coherence of training with other aspects of staff development. Finally it will have to provide high-quality teaching and learning opportunities to challenge and stimulate the teachers on the programme being offered.

The employing institution will need to ensure that the teacher in training has the necessary support to derive maximum benefit. There may well be resource implications such as remission from class contact time for the teacher, payment of mentors to support the teacher and allowing the teacher access to materials in order for the teacher to demonstrate competence and/or complete required work. However, the benefits for the institution will include a greater involvement in the management and organisation of the training and a greater guarantee that both process and outcomes reflect the institution's needs.

The major impact, however, will be on the individual teachers, who will be the axis on which the training is focused. With guidance and support, they will manage their learning in ways which will ensure that they not only complete the core requirements, thereby achieving the highest level of teaching skill and knowledge, but also enhance their immediate staff development for the benefit of their institution and its students or trainees.

CONCLUSION

The pressure for change is already being felt and acted upon, as the potential partners cope with new demands. Such a flexible and user-friendly concept of contracting and partnership will do much to convince all interested parties of the possibility of a holistic approach which can preserve the best traditions of the past while catering for the rapid and immediate changes that face post-compulsory education and training.

It is in such an environment that we should resist attempts to be minimalist in outlook. Although direct skills for direct ends is currently a dominant policy imperative, it is important to ensure a commitment to a model of reflective practice which exemplifies a more extended view of staff development. The institutions best equipped to thrive in the new market context will be those whose staff are the most flexible and the most fully trained. The best way to ensure these criteria are met is through the approaches and partnership described above.

Chapter 11

Opportunities for continuing teacher development in a college of further and higher education

Malcolm Lee

THE CONTEXT OF CONTINUING PROFESSIONAL DEVELOPMENT IN FURTHER EDUCATION

A characteristic feature of the further and higher education service in the last decade has been the concern for the provision of quality education and training. A range of literature has been generated in relation to the definition, enhancement and measurement of quality. Because the qualifications awarded in further education relate to the needs of business, industry and the professions, some of the quality measures applied in those fields have an attraction for use in this area of education. Concerns about Total Quality Management (TQM) and quality assurance have concentrated the minds of many committees within the further education service, leading to weighty documentation. However, as Müller and Funnell (1991) have pointed out, there is a danger that quality documentation may become more significant than commitment to quality management, including staff development.

Further education provision can be constructed using a three-dimensional model as in Figure 11.1, with one dimension representing governance, funding and control, another the curriculum and a third the different providers, which are spread more widely than the traditional further education college. Any discussion of continuing teacher development in post-school education needs to refer to such dimensions.

The dimension of governance, funding and control has changed radically since the 1988 Education Reform Act was passed. Like a number of large further education colleges, the institution which will be discussed later in this chapter receives its

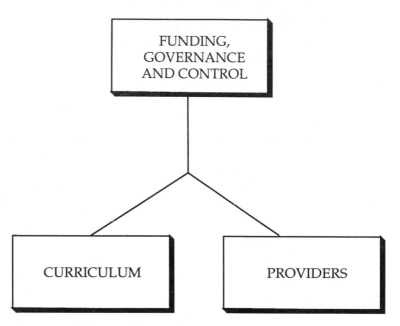

Figure 11.1 A model of further education provision

funding from a number of sources, including the Higher Education Funding Council, the Further Education Funding Council, the regional Training and Enterprise Council (TEC), the Home Office (for the provision of prison education), full-cost course income from industry and student fee income. In terms of governance and control, Section 152 of the 1988 Act stated that not less than 50 per cent of governors should represent employment interests and not more than 20 per cent be selected and appointed by the LEA. The 1992 Further and Higher Education Act created independent further education corporations which were established in April 1993, completing the reforms of governance begun in 1988. The independent status of colleges will have far-reaching effects on educational provision as such colleges prepare to compete in the marketplace. Theodossin (1992), in considering further education in the market place, identified little reliable data about how the general public perceive the further education college but noted that such data as existed were not very positive. This must give some cause for concern. The guidance given to the embryo further education corporations focused almost exclusively on the detail of plant, financial, personnel and general aspects of management. Very little attention was given to educational provision or curriculum or staff development.

The 1980s saw the gradual development of a new ideology about education and training and the emergence of a new vocationalism. This was influenced by high levels of unemployment, especially among young people, loss of confidence in the educational system and government intervention to change policy direction. In the 1960s and 1970s, higher education had been expanded significantly but almost nothing had been done to develop the system of post-school education for the majority of school-leavers or the adult work-force in general. Thus only a low percentage of the work-force was formally trained, even though many of them clearly had skills and competences to perform the required tasks at work.

The development of the curricular dimension of further education is now undergoing radical change in response to such issues. However, such curriculum reform is largely taking place under the aegis of the National Council for Vocational Qualifications (NCVQ) which is seeking to develop a curriculum based on what a student can do in terms of performance. As detailed in a range of publications from this body, the emphasis now is on systematically setting out 'performance criteria' and 'range statements' as a basis for the development of programmes of education and training. Such an approach has departed from the established curricular practice of stating what was to be learned, known and understood. It appears to be accepted that if students can show what they are capable of doing, knowledge and understanding must have been acquired, although some recognition has more recently been given to the need for competence to be underpinned with knowledge and understanding. In a critical examination of this radical curriculum change, Smithers has suggested that the three main awarding bodies in the field of vocational education, namely the Business and Technology Education Council (BTEC), the City and Guilds of London Institute (CGLI) and the Royal Society of Arts (RSA) 'feel constrained in expressing public criticism because they believe their commercial survival depends upon marketing the new qualifications to as many students as possible' (Smithers 1993: 10). The problems associated with this approach to curriculum therefore have a number of implications for student learning and staff development.

In relation to providers, the use of a National Vocational Qualification (NVQ) for the accreditation of vocational education and training through the assessment of competence has widened the range of education providers. In addition to the further education corporations there are a large number of private providers marketing programmes leading to the awards of different levels of NVQs. Those who teach and assess students on courses where the award is specified in terms of a NVQ level require a Training and Development Lead Body (TDLB) Assessor Award. This involves the teacher in providing evidence of competent performance in the assessment process. The full implication of this type of activity for continuing professional development has still to be thought through.

Another aspect of the NVQ system of awards is the use of prior learning and achievement in giving credit to the student. This means that a student may have been deemed to have achieved part of the course requirements by virtue of demonstration of successful learning in some activity prior to the course. The use of such schemes of accreditation of prior learning offers both an opportunity and a challenge to those who plan for the continuing development of further education teachers. It is an opportunity because recognition can be given to the reading, curriculum development, production of learning materials and problem-solving in which many teachers engage as part of their work. The challenge to the awarding bodies is to provide an award system which will enable such developments to take place while ensuring the maintenance of the standard of awards.

This brief account of changes and developments provides a framework for the consideration of continuing teacher development of those who work in the system. There are, however, a number of other factors which need to be noted. These include the diversity of courses provided across a wide range of fields of study in the institutions offering vocational education and training and the ways in which such diversity impacts on both staff and institutions as a whole. In addition, the teaching force itself is very diverse in terms of background. Staff have a wide range of academic, vocational and professional qualifications together with varying amounts of industrial and professional experience and many have not been formally trained as teachers. Moreover, the range of teaching qualifications extends from the basic subject-specific RSA teaching certificates and the more general CGLI 730 series of teaching certificates to the Cert.Ed.FE and PGCE awarded by higher education institutions. The programmes leading to these various qualifications are very different and hence prepare teachers in ways which provide a range of levels of skill and competence in relation to their professional responsibilities and future development.

Organisation of the employment-specific areas of the curriculum into fairly closed units can create the potential for internal divisiveness and the development of micro-political systems which may create tensions between different subject areas and undermine performance. This can be illustrated by an example taken from a further education college. The college in question located its information technology section in the electrical engineering department on the grounds that the technological hardware was electronically operated. This department purchased software on business accounting and although the business studies department had the necessary hardware and the expertise, the electrical engineering department ran the business accounting course. Because keyboard skills are essential for the operation of computers, the same department proposed to teach typing, even though the business studies department had skilled teachers in this field. It requires little imagination to realise the tensions created by such decisions and the ways in which they may seriously impede planned programmes of both curriculum development and teacher development. However, more cooperative working does occur and, where it happens, is testimony to the value of integrated development.

Developments in the post-school system, driven by the changing framework of provision, highlight the need for education and training of the staff working within the system. This training is necessary to help them respond to the changing clientele created by the widening of opportunities for students with many different needs, as a result of the new vocationalism and other reforms in British education. As Lauglo and Lillis (1988) have argued, the complex requirements which have to be met in providing a new practical and vocational curriculum cannot be easily handled if attempts to introduce such a scheme on a wide basis are undertaken too quickly. The trail of vocational education initiatives which are a part of recent educational history provides some support for this position. The implications for continuing teacher development are significant.

In addition, the vocational skills which were developed in the further education system of earlier decades are fast becoming redundant as certain industries decline. The classic example is the decline of the coal industry and the consequent demise of courses to train the work-force for that industry. The Responsive College Programme was launched in the 1980s to help respond to the changing demand for skills and the college discussed in this chapter was part of that project. The development of open-learning centres and resource-based learning are other initiatives aimed at widening access and opportunity. Valuable as some of these initiatives may have been, there has been no clear vocational curriculum developed that carries conviction; rather the approach has been to devise a national assessment scheme through National Vocational Qualifications. This is a poor substitute for a meaningful vocational curriculum and presents certain problems for staff development.

Finally, approaches to the organisation of staff development within colleges need to be considered. One of the responses of the early 1980s to the need to promote curriculum development was the addition of staff development provision to each curriculum proposal. As a consequence, certain individuals were identified as staff development tutors. However, the role of such tutors has been highly problematic. For example, when the role was investigated in the Yorkshire and Humberside region by Marsden and Tuck (1988), they identified sixty-eight distinctive functions of such tutors in the region, including the facilitation of courses and curriculum development. The varying and complex nature of the role has led to differences in provision between colleges, with a range of implications for continuing professional development. In particular, more attention needs to be given to planning and facilitating continuing professional development related directly to the curriculum, particularly in the light of the range of current curricular change.

There are therefore a number of issues concerning continuing professional development in further education, including the overall context for the provision of further education, the nature of the teaching force and the importance of planning. The rest of this chapter will explore a particular college's approach to continuing professional development.

APPROACHES TO CONTINUING PROFESSIONAL DEVELOPMENT AT DONCASTER COLLEGE

Lee (1990) has conceptualised professional development in further education as the interaction of individual, institutional and managerial factors. This is illustrated in part by the college's 1983 policy statement that

> the established policy . . . affirms that teaching at all levels should derive from up-to-date scholarship and familiarity with current professional and commercial practice. This requires that staff should be conversant with the development of their disciplines, current research findings and the methodologies of research and current commercial, industrial and professional practice.

Although this policy was pursued, it was limited by the availability of resources.

The introduction in 1986 of the Government's training grant scheme, set out in Circulars 1/86 and 6/86, formed the basis for policies of staff development in further and higher education. A central feature of such policies was that they must be managed within a framework of institutional goals. The objectives of the college plan for in-service training were to:

- undertake INSET activities to develop and improve pre-vocational work for the 16 to 19 age group;
- support curriculum development for maintaining and developing courses for local industry, commerce and the professions;
- foster activities leading to updating of knowledge and expertise;
- encourage work placement as part of the updating experience;
- develop skills and knowledge in the area of micro-technology and computing;
- develop skills relating to course provision for students with special educational needs;
- support management development at different levels;
- improve the quality of the teaching of courses through initial training and the utilisation of some of the above experiences;

- support study for diplomas, degrees, higher degrees and other forms of research; and
- improve the marketing of the institution's services.

To a large extent these matched the individual needs identified by staff as the result of the analysis of individually completed questionnaires. They still remain the focus for managerial, institutional and individual aspirations.

Future plans were built on this first plan as submitted to the Department of Education and Science in 1986. Priorities were determined by a twofold process. Senior management and heads of department identified college needs while individual staff, through discussion with line managers and the staff development tutor, tried to match institutional needs with personal aspirations and professional interests. Evaluation of the programme was also required to support bids for future funding, ascertain the future development needs of the staff and understand better the process of teacher development.

The number of training events provided in any one year was considerable, for a full-time staff of over 300 and a part-time staff approaching twice that figure. In 1988–89, for example, data collected showed that 86 per cent of the staff undertook some form of training, which was an increase of 3 per cent on the previous year. These staff participated in 790 training events representing 3659 training days. One individual participated in fifteen events and fifty-six staff participated in five or more training events.

Evaluation was based on qualitative analysis using a small number of performance indicators assessed largely by the individual members of staff undertaking the training activity. The five performance indicators selected were participant satisfaction, the degree to which training objectives were achieved, the applicability of the training to the current work of the participant, the ways in which the training was used to develop teaching and courses and finally, how much further training was required and whether the participant was willing to undertake it. These were built into a simple questionnaire so that individuals were able to consider how the training might be used and identify for themselves their future training needs.

Analysis of the 1988–89 programme showed that 88 per cent had used, or would be able to use, their training in their work.

The applications of the training to their work could be grouped into seven categories, as follows:

• enrichment of teaching and the promotion of greater student awareness;
• provision of new course material and the improvement of the content of courses;
• provision of ideas to inform curriculum development and course planning;
• development of insights into new technologies and raising awareness of the potential for the future;
• facilitation of new courses to be offered to industry and commerce as the result of the acquisition of new knowledge;
• support for the validation of courses and the writing of new course proposals; and
• help with the development of better information systems to promote new courses.

Such data provide very important guidelines on continuing professional development needs.

College policy has always stressed the importance of further study and research. This may in part reflect the considerable amount of higher education provided in the college. Since 1979, a substantial number of staff have taken the Cert.Ed.FE, or the in-service B.Ed. or B.Phil. degree programmes, all of which are available in the college. This has provided an internal partnership between the section of the college which provides in-service education for a wider market and those who work in other departments delivering the post-school curriculum offered in the college. The Cert.Ed.FE is an initial training qualification, as discussed in Chapter 10. The B.Ed. is a first degree and as well as enabling non-graduates to obtain a degree has provided a basis for curriculum development, since projects for this degree have enabled work to be done which relates to the developing educational programme within the college. The B.Phil. is a two-year research degree designed by the education section to develop the teacher as a researcher. The first year of the course develops research skills and the second year is devoted to a piece of research related to the teacher's work. One example of such research, undertaken by a member of the construction department, was concerned with a system for the development of integrated assignments for BTEC courses.

One of the problems of further education is the potential

isolation of an individual college from the other educational provision within an area. The participation of college staff in award-bearing courses involving teachers from local schools or other post-school providers of education is one of the ways of enhancing personal learning. The approach within the college has encouraged the value of working with others to be recognised, as also noted by Hargreaves:

> Teachers do not develop entirely by themselves, however. They also learn a great deal from contact with other people who are knowledgeable about and have experience of teaching and learning.

> (1992: 216)

The opportunities for the professional development of the teacher in a mixed further and higher education college are considerable if the award-bearing system is part of a credit accumulation and transfer scheme (CATS) and in-service training courses are so structured that they are compatible with such a scheme. This makes possible the development of an INSET programme from which staff can gain credit for their work towards awards which will enhance their professional profiles and which can be transferred, if required, to programmes and awards offered by another institution.

CONCLUSION

In this chapter the context in which teacher development takes place in further education has been identified as having a number of factors which shape the nature of staff development programmes. At this stage it is not possible to predict how the newly incorporated colleges will manage their staff development. The momentum of the past may continue for a time. The flexibility that managers of the colleges are seeking in the process of redefining the working conditions of the teachers in the service could significantly enhance opportunities for continuing professional development, as long as such flexibility is constructively applied to curriculum and staff development.

The National Council for Vocational Qualifications will also have a range of effects, which can only be speculated on at present, on both the traditional further education curriculum and the training and continuing professional development of those who teach such courses. For example, a number of teacher training courses have been redesigned in terms of competency outcomes. Another related question is how far the TDLB type of award will alter the nature and style of continuing professional development and the nature of award-bearing courses offered by higher education. The National Association of Teachers in Further and Higher Education has argued for the establishment of a Lead Body for education, comprising a majority of serving teachers (NATFHE 1994) but although discussions have taken place, no firm proposals to establish such a body have been made. Certainly it could make a significant contribution to continuing professional development in the post-school provision of education and training.

Chapter 12

The role of LEAs in initial training, induction and continuing professional development

Norman White

Ever since the 1944 Education Act, LEAs have played a key role at local level to ensure that schools and colleges are properly equipped and resourced to provide an appropriate education for local children and young people. During the ensuing fifty years, they have been subject to considerable pressures from central government, whatever the party in power, to ensure that statutory duties were fulfilled. Such responsibilities were largely concerned with administrative matters, such as educational provision for the area, admissions procedures, upkeep of buildings, staffing appointments, contracts and conditions of service and other legal obligations.

Perhaps inevitably over this period, the 'provider and decider' LEA incurred the wrath of many who found its *modus operandi* frustrating. The face of compassion was hidden behind a mask of bureaucracy in relation to the schools which needed more efficient central heating, well-drained playing fields or replacements for the eyesore huts, or the parents who took issue over the admissions policy or the departments which continually missed out on equipment and resources. This resentment has spilled out in the 1990s, encouraged by a Conservative Government which, motivated by its own centralist brand of right-wing dogma, has been clearly determined not only to curtail the powers of LEAs but also to threaten their very *raison d'être*.

However, those who decry the LEA for its failings ignore the extraordinary new curricular and staff development movement which began during the 1960s and 1970s, when significant new developments in the role and influence of the LEA took place. There arose a growing LEA involvement in the professional ethos of schools and colleges, in the content of the curriculum and in the nature and quality of teaching and learning in the classroom, as distinct from previous LEA concern for what were largely administrative issues. Subject and phase advisers were appointed to support the work of teachers in the classroom. In addition to their vital brief to monitor levels and standards across the LEA, such advisers were expected to bring teachers, schools and colleges together in order to share ideas and experiences, to create, in best 1944 Education Act fashion, a 'community' where good practice could be appreciated and disseminated. As a consequence the role of advisers, advisory teachers, professional development officers and teachers' centre wardens was crucial in the introduction of new approaches, courses and examinations, fostering a new era of professional work and development in a very special partnership between the LEA, schools and colleges which began to flower from the mid-1960s onwards.

This is a long way from a power-conscious, power-seeking LEA. The key words then and now are 'share', 'enable', 'encourage', 'coordinate' and 'give'. All those engaged in the challenge were partners seeking to enhance the quality of teaching in the classroom and to facilitate the learning process for children and young people. This philosophy must cause us to reflect upon the terminology of the current so-called trading market in which we work. The heart of the LEA role has always been to work with the customer (teachers, schools and colleges) for the sake of the client (child or young person). The LEA trilogy has always been that of provider, enabler and advocate. To believe otherwise is to misunderstand totally the role the LEA has had the privilege of playing over the past three decades.

As Taylor so rightly states, 'the education service can only flourish when there is a genuine partnership of the authority, governors, heads and teachers, clients and communities; this should be based on openness, trust and a clear understanding of responsibilities and entitlements' (1993: 348). Waterman and de Lyon confirm and extend that view by suggesting that 'the strength of the LEA will derive from its *unique* (my italics) ability to provide an efficient and effective network for governors, head-teachers and teachers, and to involve them in developing policies for education' (1993: 213).

Network is a key word. The LEA has always been at the heart of a network of customers, clients, ideas, initiatives, programmes, shared policies and beliefs. This is more true than ever now that local management of schools (LMS) has given schools the freedom to care for their own individual learning environments according to their own beliefs and priorities, relieving LEAs of the need for distant and bureaucratic decision making which tended only to alienate those it sought to serve. As Bines and Thomas note, 'although a number of LEA responsibilities have now been delegated to schools, this may allow the LEA to find its true role, focusing on the quality rather than the administration of education' (1994: 64).

It is also quite clear that over the past three decades, these new approaches and partnerships have been developed across the country. Ranson's research into the changing role of local government in education reveals a widespread understanding by LEAs that their role must change from a dominating and controlling model to one of collaborative practice. The beliefs of a chief education officer quoted by Professor Ranson summarise most appropriately the new overall LEA philosophy in arguing that 'the partnership scheme is intended to bring schools together in an organised co-operative system which enables the schools to support each other and the LEA to support the schools' (Ranson 1992: 35).

It is a strange paradox that during the 1980s, when LEAs were striving to maintain the goodwill of schools and colleges while struggling to manage reduced budgets, vital network links were nevertheless being forged. The LEA saw that it was now required to enable rather than control, to encourage institutions to work together and to provide them with advice and support. Ironically, this new enabling vision was fostered further through government intervention in the form of various government grants and initiatives in relation to curriculum and staff development, such as Grants for Education Support and Training (GEST). As the government identified priority areas for LEA activity, the partners in the education service were brought closer together to respond to fresh challenges.

This was certainly the case with regard to teacher recruitment. The government's decision to utilise GEST funding to help alleviate the acute recruitment problems encountered by schools contributed significantly to the partnership ethos between LEAs and schools. Working parties of headteachers, teachers and LEA officers once again came together to address the need to attract and retain newly qualified teachers. The effect of improved LEA recruitment policies on subsequent induction programmes will be considered later in this chapter but the implications of a shared approach to recruitment and induction for relationships across the local community cannot be underestimated.

THE LEA AND INITIAL TEACHER TRAINING

It was at this moment of growing partnership and rapprochement that the government chose to unveil a most significant initiative in ITT, namely the Articled Teacher scheme. With only a few exceptions, LEAs had hitherto played little part in teacher training programmes. However, the DES letter of 27 June 1989 changed all that. The Secretary of State announced that he welcomed recent moves to extend the amount of time student teachers spent in school during their ITT courses. He wished to see this trend continued and invited LEAs and schools to join higher education institutions in a scheme which would pioneer a more school-based approach to teacher training. LEAs were thus given a key coordinating role within the new scheme. The concept of partnership, long nurtured by LEAs with regard to their local schools, now took on a tripartite interpretation, as this revised teacher training structure brought the LEA into this new school-based development.

In Hillingdon, the LEA and schools saw this as a welcome opportunity to work together in the training of future teachers, recognising it as an enriching experience for schools and a challenging responsibility for all. Most importantly, and this is true not only of Hillingdon but of all the other LEAs which grouped in consortia across the country, the challenge was successfully taken up for the very reasons highlighted by Tomlinson:

> By supporting innovation, encouraging good practice, giving freedom of action to imaginative professionals, the LEAs have been the seed-bed for significant educational advances, including many now generalised by central government policy. . . . Consider any catalogue of significant education developments in this country this century and I suspect you will find LEA involvement.
>
> (1986: 220)

This extract sums up all I have been trying to convey so far about the providing, but also the enabling, coordinating LEA.

It is now the moment to consider the respective roles of the different partners as we examine the nature of the initial teacher training partnership. What particular strengths does each bring to the process and what role must each play in its management? Perhaps we should first eliminate any possible misunderstandings. Hillingdon LEA and its schools did not respond to the Articled Teacher initiative, and would not respond to comparable future school-based initiatives, in order to 'take over' from higher education. The LEA views with the greatest concern any move to deprive teacher training of the accumulated experience, knowledge and commitment of higher education colleagues. Indeed, our schools seem to recruit from year to year an ever-improving quality of newly qualified teacher while we have come to know, over the past few years, a group of colleagues with whom it has been a professional pleasure to work. We would therefore endorse the views of HMI in their report on school-based initial teacher training (HMI 1991b) which noted the importance of higher education expertise and, given the scale of initial training, the difficulties of devolution to a large number of schools. We would also agree with Tomlinson, who has argued that

> the extreme forms of the ideology which advocates total school-based, apprenticeship-style training or excessive proportions of it in training-courses . . . betoken an impoverished or dismissive view of the importance of professional training adequately grounded in critical reflection and academic discipline.
>
> (Tomlinson 1993: 20)

As the Articled Teacher scheme in Hillingdon progressed, the responsibilities of the school towards the articled teacher within the partnership became more and more clear. They were seen to include:

- the provision of an appropriate training environment;
- the appointment of mentors to undertake the coordination of a programme of relevant learning experiences;
- support for the training offered to mentors;

- support of the work of the mentor through whole-school commitment;
- provision of the necessary (funded) release time for the mentor;
- monitoring of the quality of school provision offered to the student throughout the course; and
- close liaison with the scheme consortium, respecting all guidelines in relation to timetabling, student responsibilities in the classroom, off-site courses, assignment deadlines, and the assessment of student progress.

The responsibilities of the higher education institution included:

- the devising and teaching of an appropriate programme of professional training;
- the drawing up of a set of professional competences to provide the basis for the training and assessment of students;
- provision of a framework for the assessment of the professional competence of students;
- support in relation to the assessment of classroom competence;
- preparation of suitable foci for school-based enquiry work;
- marking and assessing the students' coursework with written feedback; and
- liaison throughout the course with the other members of the partnership in the administration and organisation of the scheme.

Finally, the third partner, namely the LEA, provided what Hendy has called the 'adhesive the education service needs' (1993: 154), although in this case it was rather what the teacher training partnership needed. He mentions elsewhere in this article the key part played by LEAs as mediators and enablers, emphasising yet again their coordinating and networking role in relation to such work. Certainly the LEA played this very role as a partner in the Articled Teacher scheme and is ready to continue playing it in future SCITT schemes.

A description of the coordinating role played by the LEA in the Articled Teacher scheme explains perhaps why few primary schools wish to take on alone the responsibilities of the lead school within the SCITT version of school-based teacher training. For the Articled Teacher scheme, LEAs were required to:

- cost the feasibility of the scheme;
- contact all local schools (GM and LEA) with an invitation to take part;

- supervise the advertisement campaign, dealing with replies and arranging school visits;
- set up and take part in consortium interviews;
- oversee the placing of successful candidates into appropriate schools; and
- keep in touch with the articled teachers before the scheme started.

The LEA also kept a 'finger on the pulse' once the scheme was up and running, acting as a focus for views, publicising opinions, responding to requests for information and for help, and keeping open the channels of communication so that the partnership remained open and user-friendly. It also took care of all administrative matters relating to bursary and mentor payments, travel arrangements and accommodation for training sessions, as well as acting as counsellor and guide when articled teachers were failing or when schools were in doubt, liaising between partners when there was need.

The outcome of several very successful years of the scheme has been its closure. It has been intimated that it proved more costly than anticipated and did not always attract in sufficient quantity the number of students for whom a traditional course would have been impractical. A more mischievous observation would be that perhaps the LEA role was becoming too central for the liking of the Government, since evaluation of the scheme had recommended LEAs should be given an additional strategic role in monitoring and quality control. It is certainly not irrelevant to observe that in his speech at the North of England Education Conference on 4 January 1991, when the Secretary of State, Kenneth Clarke, announced the reform of secondary ITT through a much closer partnership between schools and higher education institutions, LEAs were not mentioned once. As the same Minister later in March that year promoted the notion that the natural progression for schools was to move from local management of schools to grant-maintained status, that is, all schools should sooner or later opt out of local authority control, the omission of any reference to LEAs in his plans for new secondary initial training course structures is hardly surprising (DFE 1992). His example has since been emulated by his successor, John Patten, who also omitted any role for the LEA in the accreditation criteria for primary initial teacher training (DFE 1993b).

It is surely not unreasonable to query why the LEA, with its unique experience and position within the community, should be deliberately excluded as a key partner in the tripartite management of school-based teacher training. The current criteria for initial training courses require that students should have the opportunity to work with experienced teachers in at least two schools. The LEA, as an impartial partner, could mediate between schools and also negotiate appropriate pairings. School-centred training is likely to recruit from local candidates, providing a welcome supply of home-based newly qualified teachers. Together the schools and LEA could supply a local pool of newly qualified teachers to satisfy need. The larger the ITT consortium, the more cost-effective its operation, and the more effective its end product. However, size also creates complexity and time-consuming administration. In the primary sector could a single lead school have the time and human resources needed to head such an organisation? Once again, in the light of the experience acquired through the Articled Teacher scheme, the LEA is uniquely placed to play the vital role of supporting and coordinating the training commitment of primary SCITT consortia, ensuring that communications are kept open with their higher education partner.

The LEA, as leader as well as partner, can also recognise other significant benefits which close association with higher education can bring to its schools. Hillingdon therefore responded to the DES draft circular of July 1990 which sought to encourage further school experience links between 'shire' higher education institutions and London LEAs. Such involvement offers mentors the invaluable opportunity to reflect upon their own practice in the classroom. The resultant initiative is now in its third year and evaluation meetings for schools after each school experience, for both PGCE and B.Ed. students, have emphasised the value of the experience for the professional development of those concerned.

The LEA is also aware that this exciting collaboration can lead to further higher education participation in the planning of induction programmes for newly qualified teachers. Earley made this very point in his book on induction which argued that 'it was usually the case that LEAs with developed partnerships in relation to initial teacher training were similarly placed in relation to induction' (1992a: 16). Certainly, examples of collaboration between LEAs and higher education across the country have often led to the development of competence-based profiles or professional development portfolios as a vital link in the NQT training continuum. In all of this, the higher education/LEA partnership has been pivotal, while the LEA has usually played a subsequent key planning role *vis-à-vis* its schools in their joint formulation of a quality induction programme, stressing the continuing development of the newly qualified teacher.

However, before turning to the question of induction and the role of the LEA, I offer one concluding comment concerning the management of teacher training. It is clear that the full potential of a teacher training partnership, linking higher education, LEAs and schools, is still to be realised. If the notion of school-based schemes is to succeed, then whatever the message conveyed by government pronouncement and circulars, the key part to be played in its management by the LEA must be recognised.

THE LEA AND INDUCTION

There is encouraging evidence of recent positive collaboration between the LEA and schools in relation to induction, even if this can hardly give us cause for self-congratulation since good induction practice was strongly urged as long ago as 1972 in the James Report (DES 1972). Despite some guidelines from the Department of Education and Science over the 1970s and 1980s, the support that probationers received varied considerably across the country. In 1988, an HMI report on new teachers in school confirmed that many did not receive the support to which they were entitled. LEAs and schools were urged to 'review their practice to ensure that induction is effectively arranged and delivered' (HMI 1988: 11).

The final paragraph of this report makes very clear the lead role LEAs were expected to play in future arrangements. It was suggested that 'there is a need for closer liaison between schools and local authorities in defining their respective responsibilities for the induction of new teachers' (1988: 11). Since then, the government has used GEST funding to highlight the role to be played by LEAs in the recruitment of new teachers and, more recently, the need for imaginative induction policies and programmes. Once again, the LEA has been called upon as visionary, partner and planner in the support of its schools.

Hillingdon is one of many LEAs which have responded through carefully devised induction policies.

The National Foundation for Educational Research (NFER) carried out a most thorough research project to investigate the role of LEAs in the professional development of new teachers (Earley 1992a). The main findings revealed that:

- virtually all LEAs provided schools with written guidelines on induction;
- all LEAs arranged a central induction programme and over three-quarters saw this as an important incentive for NQTs when applying for posts;
- LEA induction programmes were seen particularly as opportunities for NQTs to meet and share experiences in a neutral setting;
- LEAs support school-initiated induction primarily by providing support materials and advice, structured classroom observation, the monitoring of practice and the training of mentors;
- nearly eight out of ten LEAs had arrangements in place which avoided unnecessary duplication between LEA and school-initiated induction; and
- the majority of LEAs rated their induction programmes as 'good' or 'more than satisfactory'.

However, the final section of this NFER report causes some unease about the future. LEA respondents feared that delegated funding, with a consequent lack of central LEA resourcing, might reduce significantly the LEA role in induction. It might be necessary for the LEA of the future to focus its resources on one or more of the principal areas of support, such as mentor training, ITT links, supporting school-initiated induction or developing LEA induction programmes. A reservation is expressed about the degree to which schools would give priority to induction if the LEA was no longer able to provide the support to which schools have become accustomed. As Earley has noted, drawing from his most recent research on induction, despite the potentially fruitful partnership between LEAs, schools and higher education in relation to induction, the waning influence of LEAs may mean that future newly qualified teachers may not be properly inducted (Earley and Kinder 1994).

Such concern is understandable. However, where schools recognise from experience that a quality school/LEA integrated programme is a *sine qua non* for good recruitment and where they are persuaded that investing in people is vital to school improvement (Earley 1992b), then they will supplement from delegated funding whatever support the LEA has been able to offer from its reduced budget. They will in effect follow its example and lead. The influence of the LEA will not be perceived as waning if it continues to provide a positive strategy on behalf of the schools it serves. In this the LEA can be seen as an advocate on behalf of the ongoing process of professional development upon which the assurance of quality teaching and learning is founded.

THE LEA AND CONTINUING PROFESSIONAL DEVELOPMENT

It is perhaps unwise to speak of 'the' LEA in this context as though LEAs had responded uniformly to the 1988 Education Reform Act and the subsequent erosion of local influences and powers. There can be no doubt that all LEAs attach the very highest priority to the delivery of quality professional development services but as Ranson points out, individual LEA strategy has been influenced by the role it played through previous decades. For proof of this one would only have to compare the differing stories told by the four LEAs studied in his book (Ranson 1992).

Hillingdon adopted a similar approach to Kent, as discussed in Ranson (1992), with the customer placed from the outset at the centre of the management of education. Moves were swiftly implemented towards marketing the authority as a caring employer, with market research and working parties set up to identify the changing needs of clients and customers and the setting up of client steering groups. Quality was placed at the forefront of service management, emphasising a new approach to quality assurance and establishing procedures for logging client satisfaction. The Hillingdon Service Level Agreement booklet must have been one of the first to be published, with schools given a series of options on how to 'buy back in' from their delegated funding.

As I have stressed throughout the chapter, this particular market strategy approach had been made possible by the excellent LEA/school relationships forged throughout the 1980s, when headteachers, LEA officers and advisers had explored together a broad range of issues relating to professional training and management development. This is not to suggest that LEAs which have reacted differently did not enjoy the same partnership. However, the nature of the response has also inevitably depended upon the local political climate, current management vision and personality, and the inherent ethos distilled over the years.

The determination of LEAs to provide the continuing professional development to which schools were accustomed was challenged once again by severe budgetary difficulties. Hillingdon found itself in the unenviable position of contemplating possible redundancy for the very curriculum advisers upon whom its success in the 'market' would depend. Clearly the level of in-borough approval and buying back by schools determine how much in-house professional development activity can be retained. If delegated funding is not 'returned' through a service-level contract, then the LEA must inevitably be diminished in expertise and involvement. One could then envisage its reduction to a purely statutory role, concerned solely with admissions, special educational needs, educational psychologists, home to school transport, and youth and adult education. Even a distant, undemocratic, bureaucratic Funding Agency could attempt to discharge such truncated responsibilities.

Fortunately schools are aware of this danger. They do not want this fate to befall their LEA. They are warmly aware of the unique role the LEA has played in their professional affairs in the past. They have adequate proof of the grasp the LEA holds of local issues and they value the relationship which has grown over the years. If they wish to buy back professional development services now, it is a tribute to the past and to the LEA colleagues they have come to know and trust. Outside agencies are simply 'not one of the family'. In Hillingdon, this commitment to, and support of, the LEA was perfectly summarised in an article published by primary headteachers in the local newspaper. Entitled 'Why we must stick with the Borough' it stressed that the professionals upon whom schools relied centrally had a sense of commitment towards them which would be lost if the service was sold out. It was imperative that headteachers, governors and staff should have access to locally coordinated induction, professional development and ongoing support.

CONCLUSION

All this surely conveys a powerful message which makes a mockery of those who trumpet the demise of the LEA. This is the true spirit of partnership and an appropriate answer to quango proposals which threaten a return to the bureaucracy from which LEAs and their schools have long escaped. I look back on a teaching career which began in the 1950s and remember vividly the dispiriting feeling of working alone, aware of the isolation not only of one school from another, but of one department from another in the same secondary school. As a head of department I lacked any semblance of the INSET support which schools now expect and deserve from their provider LEA.

And yet, in recent years, there has been the fear that we could return to that lonely post-war wilderness. The road for LEAs has become much harder. Signposts have been deliberately altered along the way. Requests for direction have been ignored. It would seem that the present Government has little wish to see the journey completed. There is even as I write a move afoot to change the whole map relating to the territory, and therefore efficacy, of local government. Education would seem not to be considered a key operational factor in determining the new shapes and boundaries.

Nevertheless there are whispers of optimism and some evidence of a welcome revival of confidence amongst LEAs. Moreover, even where a large number of schools have opted out of LEA control, there is a consensus that there is still a wide range of statutory and non-statutory responsibilities which require substantial, expert and well-resourced LEA support and personnel.

It has been a long, hard road but, respected for its proud record over the years in helping to promote the professional formation and development of its teacher colleagues, and carrying with an ever-growing assurance its new role as visionary, planner, co-ordinator, enabler and advocate, the tried and trusted partner, the LEA, may at last be coming in sight of home.

Part III

Partnership and professionalism

Chapter 13

The politics of partnership

Tony Edwards

Even in 1990, it required no foresight to question whether teacher education had a future 'in anything like its present institutional forms' (Edwards 1990: 180). In the four years since, the Conservative Government has vigorously promoted school-centred initial training; moved from encouraging more equal partnership between schools and higher education to wishing 'the school and its teachers' to be 'in the lead in the whole training process'; launched pilot projects in which consortia of schools take full responsibility for training programmes and may choose not to use 'outside expertise' at all; and handed the oversight and funding of all initial teacher education to a Training Agency appointed by and answerable to the Secretary of State.

These reforms have come in quick succession, with only nominal consultation and no government evaluation of their effects. On the surface they are about improving training by making it more practical, and Ministers deny any deeper purpose of severing its links with higher education. Yet the suspicions which they seek to allay are reasonable, given the increasing prescriptiveness of government interventions and the loud echoes each time of the Right's systematic campaign against educational theory. In a speech to the 1992 North of England Education Conference that accelerated the pace of reform, the then Secretary of State Kenneth Clarke attributed the damagingly impractical nature of teacher training to its continued domination by the 'colleges' and by the 'orthodoxies of the past'. That refrain, regularly repeated by his successor John Patten, is echoed in the Prime Minister's commitment to 'a much-needed reform of teacher training that takes influence from fashionable theorists and gives it to schools' (interviewed in the *Daily Express*, 17 February 1994).

It is some time however since the theorists felt fashionable. As a *Times* editorial on Clarke's speech recognised, the main 'ideology on the march' in teacher education has been that of their opponents, whom the paper described as 'a politically-minded minority' marching from the Right and 'determinedly imposing its dogmas about teaching methods and classroom organisation' (6 January 1992). This chapter examines what has been a highly politicised restructuring of initial teacher education. It is about the politics of partnership at the institutional level, but is primarily about the ideological environment within which the various arrangements described elsewhere in the book have taken shape. Although a personal view, this perspective reflects the extent to which the work of the Universities Council for the Education of Teachers (UCET) during the writer's time as its chair and co-chair has been reactive, and usually resistant, to successive government initiatives (see Edwards 1994).

AN EQUAL PARTNERSHIP?

In its formal responses to the government's 1992 and 1993 reform proposals, UCET affirmed its belief in an equal partnership of schools and higher education in the training of new teachers. This was not a grudging acceptance of new facts of life. More equal and better defined arrangements were already being established before the government's intervention, as a matter of principle and good practice (Booth *et al.* 1990) and because heavy pressure on delegated school budgets required arrangements to be formalised which had previously been left to goodwill. But 'partnership' carries no clear implication of equality. It can involve a senior–junior relationship or a 'sleeping' role, and equality is much harder to manage than either.

Certainly the relationship of schools and higher education prior to Circular 3/84 was markedly unequal. The post-Robbins move towards a fully graduate teaching profession was achieved through the devolving of provision and validation to higher education. If there was little government control over form and content, there was no professional voice in it either. With some local exceptions, the relationship between schools and higher education was hierarchical. Schools were rarely consulted or even informed about the courses for which they provided the necessary practical placements. The professional culture might give priority to practical skills, as might students and many of their tutors, but it was the academic components of training which were formally dominant. The Department of Education and Science Circular 3/84 terminated the freedom of colleges, polytechnics and especially universities to do things their way. But subjecting all courses to the Secretary of State's criteria, with an Accreditation Council created to monitor compliance, did nothing for professional control. Initial training had to be more practical and higher education staff had to renew their classroom experience, but the membership of the Council was deliberately distanced from teacher 'representation' because the unions were regarded as too 'educationist' in outlook and therefore as part of the problem which the government was seeking to solve. Nor, despite its recent rhetoric about schools playing 'the leading role', has the government paid serious attention to the profession's views about the forms of training being prescribed. Indeed, much of this chapter is about government efforts to achieve a much more extensive transfer of training to schools than the profession generally wishes to accept.

A more substantial role for schools has certainly been advocated from within education as a powerful means of professional development, and of breaking down the traditional isolation which denies many good teachers the influence outside their own classrooms which their qualities deserve (Hargreaves 1989). But when, for example, the Association of Teachers and Lecturers argued in its formal response to Circular 9/92 that active involvement in training heightened the profession's awareness of the 'complexity and depth' of expertise demanded of teachers, its support for a larger role stopped well short of wanting to take the business over. Even where a wholesale transfer of responsibility has been thought desirable, it has been on conditions very unlikely to be met – namely, the special resourcing of 'training schools' by analogy with teaching hospitals, and the creation of a General Teaching Council to monitor the training process and safeguard professional standards (Beardon et al. 1992; Hargreaves 1990; Warnock 1988). As will be argued later in the chapter, recent Conservative Governments have ignored the greater cost of their preferred training models. They have also continued to refuse the creation of a General

Teaching Council. What they have actively promoted is the right of schools to decide for themselves whether or not to be free-standing and self-sufficient providers of training.

It is a crude error redolent of higher education's self-interest, Berrill (1994) argues from within a training consortium, to assume that school-provided training is inherently a descent into unreflective apprenticeship. For him the question is not whether theory and reflection are essential to teacher training, because they clearly are, but whether and how schools are to be empowered to provide them. My counter-argument is emphatically not that schools should leave the 'theory' to higher education, as though theory were a mystery which should reserved for those licensed by their academic qualifications and engagement in research, but that they should not do it all. Theory, understood as generalisation from the critical scrutiny of practice, is an activity in which good schools regularly engage. The contribution of higher education is to add a wider frame of reference and a particular commitment to independent inquiry.

The 'equal' partnership of schools and higher education therefore requires not that each does the same but that each 'accepts the other's distinctive authority and strength' (Cameron-Jones and O'Hara 1993: 37). But there is a third 'partner' in training, increasingly inclined to dictate the terms on which the others work and to do so on the crude assumption rightly deplored by Berrill – that 'theory' is what is done in higher education and that it is so largely in opposition to what is done in schools that it should be crowded out. In the next section of this chapter, I consider what would be lost if the contributions of higher education were too severely curbed. I then examine, in the context of current reforms, some necessary conditions for those contributions to be effective.

CONTRIBUTIONS OF HIGHER EDUCATION TO THE TRAINING PARTNERSHIP

When the sociology of education was almost as prominent in initial teacher training as its detractors believe it still is, the status of teaching was a common syllabus item. The conventional explanation for teaching's failure to be more than a 'semi-profession' was that it lacked the control over entry and over violations of the professional code which 'full' professions enjoyed, and that it also lacked 'a body of abstract knowledge, largely created and organised by the profession itself, which is sufficiently impressive and sufficiently mysterious to keep the public at a respectful distance and officials from being too intrusive' (Edwards 1992: 284). From that unfashionably socio-logical perspective, recent Conservative Government reforms threaten to undermine professional status still further.

Certainly the teacher associations have suspected the motives of recent Conservative governments in treating the training of teachers so differently from preparation for the other major professions, and in intervening so prescriptively in its form and content. They have defended a strong base in higher education as essential to the teaching profession's autonomy and public esteem, and seen the reforms as potentially undermining the concept of 'qualified teacher status'. The strength of these anxieties can only be understood in the context of the profession's long struggle to end the segregation of most teacher training from the rest of higher education, and its determination to avoid any revival of 'extinct and ineffective forms of apprenticeship' (Taylor 1991: 63; Grace 1991). There has therefore been a strong professional interest, as well as strong arguments of principle, behind the profession's defence of higher education's role in teacher training. However, recent Conservative governments have seen only the self-interest and not the principle. In their general hostility to professional institutions and cultures, they have tended to dismiss as a self-serving conspiracy against the public the 'expert' knowledge claimed by the providers of services. Educational knowledge or 'theory' has been treated as an especially objectionable case of unjustified restrictive practice, being rejected as both useless and subversive.

To take the charge of uselessness first, the argument has been that teaching is essentially a 'practical activity' for which 'theory' is largely or entirely irrelevant. That view, with its accompanying assertions that teaching can be learned 'simply by doing and emulating good role models' (Cox 1989), has been too well publicised to need illustrating here. It is a view which seriously oversimplifies teachers' work. For while a great deal of classroom practice undoubtedly comes with experience from knowing what works without necessarily knowing or being able to articulate why, it involves much more than the instant application of what has been learned on past occasions. Using the term which has come to dominate discussion of effective teaching (Barrett *et al.* 1993), the 'reflective practitioner' decides on appropriate action or chooses between alternatives by exercising professional judgement informed both by familiarity with those particular circumstances and by conscious reference to more general knowledge and understanding of how children learn. Any approach to professional competence that breaks it down mechanistically into discrete skills ignores teachers' endlessly creative responses to new situations and tasks.

What higher education should contribute to teacher training is a wider range of evidence about teaching strategies and curriculum developments than even the best schools can provide, and a habit of making the theories embedded in practice explicit so that they can be more easily examined and compared. What it cannot provide is a set of prescriptions for confident application. Yet its failure to do that has provided some of its critics with a conveniently easy target. Writing in the polemical tradition which also treats higher education as being inherently subversive, Lawlor (1990) caricatures conventional 'teaching practice' as the opportunity for educationists to inflict on schools through the agency of their students the politically correct doctrines with which those students have been imbued. That account, patronising in its attribution to trainee teachers of such vulnerability to indoctrination, also reflects a view of educational theory as sets of ideas (or in this case of errors) which are produced at a distance from practice and then contaminate professional commonsense. Similarly, Kenneth Clarke, in the speech cited earlier which accelerated the drive towards school-based training, identified the acid test of the 'models' offered by higher education as whether they 'can actively be made to work effectively by the average teacher in the real classroom' because only then could the hold of 'dogmatic orthodoxies' about teaching methods and classroom organisation be broken.

Educational theory is rarely framed for that kind of direct application, nor should dogmatic orthodoxies be any part of it. Schön (1987) is often cited, as he is by Berrill (1994), for his scepticism about the relevance of 'scientific knowledge' to professional practice. He is sceptical about knowledge devised and tested on some academic high ground and then 'brought down' to the messy low ground of practice, because he sees well-defined and directly applicable solutions as being dependent on well-structured problems. Certainly the professional dilemmas faced by teachers fall into his other category, being complex and unpredictable and prone to value conflict. It is therefore essential that new teachers are helped to be 'reflective-in-action' – that is, to experiment with and evaluate different methods in their own classrooms and to have the confidence to become quickly involved in discussion of whole school issues. It is among the many unfounded assertions used to justify recent reforms that new teachers need 'particular combinations of knowledge and skill to meet the increasingly diverse needs of schools' (DFE 1993a: 1). Even if schools were not changing as rapidly as they are, such direct matching of tasks with competences would be unrealistic. When new demands and new technology are challenging traditional methods so profoundly, then a high level of general professional knowledge from which practical solutions to new problems can be creatively derived is greatly preferable to more specific recipe knowledge with, at best, limited application and early obsolescence.

In this context, Schön's defence of practical competence acquired through 'practice' is sometimes misunderstood. For he also emphasises the value of 'reflection-on-practice', which for teachers would draw on knowledge of curriculum and pedagogy in different contexts and of their social and moral dimensions. 'These are the forms of professional knowledge based on research, theory and scholarship that have traditionally been made available through higher education' (Furlong 1994: 120), and which constitute that wider frame of reference which higher education should contribute to teacher training. Even Kenneth Clarke claimed to recognise the importance of time 'away from the hurly burly of the school to think and read and discuss', though he gave no indication of the kinds of topic on which that time might profitably be spent.

There are good reasons why they should not include his imagined 'dogmatic orthodoxies'. When Lord Skidelsky in the first House of Lords debate on the 1993 Education Bill attacked educational theory for being chronically 'under-developed' in comparison with medicine, law and accountancy, he did so on the grounds that 'there is no theoretically based good practice which defines professional teaching'. Yet he also unwittingly provided the explanation of why 'theories of how to teach' remain 'highly disputable'. It is because (in his words) educational theory contains such 'large elements of politics and ideology, and such strong connections with wider social aims', that there will always be disputes about what to teach, how to teach it, what constitutes an 'educated' person, what part of the population should be encouraged (or allowed) to aspire to that condition, and so on. It is therefore impossible for these debates to be resolved. It is also essential that they are allowed to continue.

Many of the debates will occur within schools, broadening out from immediate issues to more general considerations. Nor has higher education a monopoly of research relevant to innovation or to improving practice, though much of that research will be done by teachers in the course of study for higher degrees and the declining scope of LEA activities adds to the value of higher education institutions as independent centres for curriculum development and evaluation. For teaching to be an appropriately research-minded profession, it is essential that much of its knowledge base should be produced by teachers – as the school-based studies carried out within the National Oracy Project effectively illustrate (Norman 1992; see also Altrichter *et al.* 1993). But higher education has several characteristics which enhance its value as a base for educational research. It has the freedom not to be tied by the criterion of immediate usefulness, and a tradition of intellectual independence which creates an obligation as well as a right to question established beliefs and practices. That scope for asking and trying to answer awkward questions is very different from what some of their critics suppose university education departments have been up to – namely, to use their 'hold over teacher training' to allow 'a particular philosophy to spread through the system' (Lady Blatch, quoted in the *Daily Telegraph*, 5 October 1993). The charge, too familiar to need documenting here, is well illustrated in O'Keeffe's (1990) exposition of why teacher education has been at the heart of the 'intellectual crisis' in British education through its promotion of egalitarian notions of educational opportunity and a romantic child-centredness. Part of the reform strategy of recent Conservative governments has therefore been a deliberate narrowing of the scope of initial teacher training by largely excluding the wider contexts of schooling, and focusing instead on the immediate tasks of classroom management, instruction and assessment. Thus the first set of criteria with which ITT courses for school education had to comply included sufficient

work in both subject-teaching and 'educational studies' to enable
new teachers to respond 'flexibly' to the cultural diversity they
would find in an 'ordinary' school and to 'guard against preconceptions based on the race or sex of pupils' (DES 1984,
Annex, para.11). The much narrower list of competences in
Circular 9/92 (DES 1992) is presented without any explanation
for its selectiveness or why previous accreditation requirements
had been judged redundant. If some of the existing contributions
of higher education to teacher training undoubtedly display a
'value-laden choice of issue', to borrow Halsey's admission about
the 'political arithmetic' tradition in British social science, they
also reflect a refusal to detach the investigation of teaching and
learning from the social conditions in which they occur. However,
political objections to the choice of issues have extended to
denying Halsey's accompanying claim to 'objective methods of
data collection' (Halsey et al. 1980: 1).

Except in rare instances when the findings are politically
convenient, as in Turner's (1990) indictment of teachers' contribution to falling standards of literacy, the disdain of recent
Conservative governments for educational research has been
increasingly apparent. Thus the first head of the National
Curriculum Council noted the blanket attribution to researchers
of 'outmoded views on egalitarianism blended with idealism',
and the avoidance by 'right-wing think tanks' of systematic
analysis of proposals which relied on asserting and reiterating
their prejudices (Graham 1993: 137–8). Disregard for inconvenient
facts has been blatant, for example, in the politically expedient
claims that 'progressive' teaching is pervasive in primary schools
and that reading is rarely taught at all, despite all evidence to the
contrary (Osborn and Broadfoot 1992; Pollard et al. 1994; Raban
et al. 1993), and in the continuing adherence to 'unmanipulated'
comparisons of school performance when value-added and
contextualised assessment is advocated from the most non-
doctrinaire of sources (Audit Commission and OFSTED 1993).

It has to be recognised, of course, that ideology is a matter of
belief rather than knowledge, and that recent Conservative
Governments have been unusually ideological in their ambitions
to transform culture as well as institutions. Teaching and teacher
education have therefore been obvious areas for ideological intervention, and neither argument nor evidence from non-believers
are likely to be taken seriously (Wilkin 1994). Strong objections

from higher education and teacher associations alike to the wide remit initially proposed for the Teacher Training Agency were therefore expressions of deep concern that the funding of educational research and of higher degrees should not be subjected to such potentially close political control. When Berrill (1994) dismisses university appeals to academic freedom as institutional self-interest, he misrepresents my (and others') argument by shifting its target. Whereas he sees mainly resistance to theory being taken over by schools, my objection is to increasing state centralism and the authoritarian intolerance of dissent that has come with it.

It is not that higher education has a unique capacity to see through the policies of the day. Schools have been asking their own searching questions about the effects of government reforms on the quality of education (Bowe and Ball 1992). But as I argued earlier, higher education has a particular obligation to subject even 'authorised' knowledge to critical scrutiny. That is how John Patten described, in a speech at Trnava University in Slovakia (7 November 1993), the essential role of universities in a free society. They are, he claimed, 'the best place to nurture the thinkers and questioners' and those who challenge the 'received wisdom of the age'. If they are to fulfil that task, then their commitment to free inquiry has to be upheld by government even when its outcomes are politically inconvenient. At least in a Slovakian context, the past Secretary of State for Education both recognised universities' right and assigned them the duty to be constructively subversive. At home, in relation to teacher education, that role has been travestied as the preaching of a 'single philosophy' and therefore as needing to be curbed by transforming the conditions in which higher education's contributions to teacher training are to be made.

MANAGING THE PARTNERSHIP OF 'EQUALS'

It was partly because he could see no prospect of equality between the training partners that Hargreaves (1990) presented a stark choice between continued domination of initial training by higher education and a handing over of full responsibility to schools. Government reforms have not yet been so radical, though the declared preference has been for schools to take 'the leading role' and the pilot projects of school-based training may be indications of particular hopes. The notion of a single 'leading' role suggests a pervasively unbalanced relationship rather than one in which the partners take responsibility for different and complementary parts of integrated training programmes. Unbalancing the partnership the other way by restoring the hierarchical relationship of the past is also unacceptable, so that the Committee of Vice-Chancellors was overstating (or perhaps over-abbreviating) its case against the 1993 reforms by arguing that 'universities and other higher education institutions, with their tradition of independent enquiry and presentation of best practice, must continue to play *the leading role* in teacher education'. At a time of unprecedented changes to their organisation and work, it is understandable that schools generally have wished the lead in coordinating and administering ITT to remain with higher education rather than be added to their own multi-plying responsibilities. But that lead should not extend to the effective integration of ITT's various components, which is a joint task. If one partner remains uncertain of its role or uninformed about large areas of the whole programme, then the relationship remains unacceptably hierarchical.

There are practical reasons, however, why institutions of higher education should retain their coordinating role. However committed to a full part in teacher training, schools are likely to see it as a marginal activity. As such, it is vulnerable to being found incompatible with their primary tasks or crowded out by other priorities. The current government has sought to allay fears that its experiments in school-based training herald a wholesale take-over by insisting that schools are free to choose the scale of their involvement, and whether or not to become involved at all. But when it urges schools to enter into five-year training contracts with institutions of higher education so as to ensure continuity in the arrangements, it runs against the voluntarism which it affirms and against the advice of professional associations that schools retain the freedom to disengage from their training role if their circumstances or priorities change. At the very least then, the continuing substantial presence of institutions for which initial teacher training *is* a primary task is a stabilising factor in the system as a whole.

That schools have not been more eager to take a greatly enhanced role in teacher training has disappointed Conservative Government advisers inclined to oversimplify that change as a shift from 'theory' to 'practice'. While there has been reluctance to take on extra work even for ready money, the costing of the reformed partnerships has brought its own problems because the models of training that recent Conservative governments have supported are significantly more expensive than what these governments have wished to replace. This is partly because the dispersal of more training to schools has considerable diseconomies of scale, but mainly because schools, contributions were previously not costed at all. The official argument has been that payment for what schools were already doing had been subsumed within the education budget so that only their new responsibilities had to be paid for, a claim that headteachers, hectored to be businesslike, have understandably been keen to challenge. The consequent official assumptions have been that the new requirements can be met by an appropriate transfer of funding because higher education institutions need less to do less, and that government should not provide funding guidelines because the exact division of labour between the partners will vary according to circumstances and the outcome of local negotiations. The second assumption is reasonable. The accompanying expectation that more expensive forms of training can be funded within existing resources simply through a redistribution of funds is not shared by higher education or by schools. Instead, it has created a situation in which realistic costing carries the risk that each partner's contribution will appear financially unviable.

At the time of writing, and apart from the school-based projects funded directly by the Department for Education, funding for the school side of the partnership still comes through higher education. This has produced some hard argument about what is taken out of the funding allocation for ITT (itself not earmarked at institutional level) for higher education institutions' central expenditure. It has been at least difficult to persuade headteachers, who know how their budgets are decided and how much their LEA retains, to accept that heads of education departments in higher education control a much lower proportion of the total budget and are often unable to specify how the rest is spent. However, the latter have been inhibited from arguing too hard against the current top-slicing because they do not wish to make teacher training too obvious a special case when, like schools, their institutions cannot afford to subsidise internally any of their activities. They face the more fundamental difficulty too that departmental budgets are unlikely to separate initial training from the other primary tasks of in-service provision and research. The government itself has recognised the folly of treating *initial* teacher training as though it were, with practice, a sufficient foundation for a professional career, and has pressed for much more continuity with induction and with continuing professional development. That is how education departments commonly organise their teaching programmes, with most staff working across the 'boundaries'. The competing claims of teaching and research are common to all areas of higher education as the rewards and penalties of research ratings become greater between and within institutions. That 'education' stood up well to comparison with other subjects in the 1992 research assessment ratings reflects a high investment of staff effort, and a commitment to providing 'useful knowledge' in such critical areas as testing and school effectiveness even where that has meant demonstrating the complexity of the issues rather than providing too-easy solutions. Such research does not lie alongside teacher training, but provides much of that wider frame of reference which higher education brings to the examination of effective practice.

It is unlikely that the Teacher Training Agency's take-over of funding for ITT, with the funding being earmarked overall and monitored for its equitable distribution between the partners, will resolve the difficulties outlined earlier. Indeed, the case against its initially wide remit was that the Agency's creation produced an insoluble problem; either it took responsibility for research and higher degrees to an extent politically inappropriate for a body so directly answerable to government ministers, or a more limited role separated activities which are so interdependent as to be inseparable. The Agency survived, by weight of political numbers if not of reason, strong arguments that it was unnecessary and politically dangerous. It did so amid ministerial reassurances that it was simply a mechanism for raising standards of training and encouraging more diversity in training routes, and that the attribution of darker purposes was simply the fearful constructions of interests unwilling to change. There was, they argued, nothing to worry about. Accreditation was merely being transferred from one quango to another, with greater flexibility for providers because the focus would be on institutions rather than particular courses and with less political control than before because, though appointed by the Secretary of State and working to his or her criteria, they would be free to make their own decisions within what an Education Minister described as 'unequivocal statutory objectives of high quality and cost effectiveness' (Squire 1994). Addressing a UCET conference in March 1994, the Department's Deputy-Secretary hoped that conference members would 'welcome the detachment of accreditation from the Department for Education and its transfer to an independent specialist body'. It remains to be seen how open the Agency will be to the experience and concerns of the profession whose training it controls, how interventionist it will be in managing the training partnership, whether it can resist the translation of cost-effective into cheap, and whether it can avoid measuring quality by conformity to political priorities.

Chapter 14

Professional development and control: a General Teaching Council

John Tomlinson

There are three kinds of obstacle to the teaching profession assuming more responsibility for its own education and training:

- the determination of governments to retain and extend their control over teachers and teaching. This has been especially evident in the conservative New-Right projects of the 1980s and early 1990s; these sentiments are reinforced by a fear of resurgent trade unionism;
- the lack of organisation and a single focus for 'the teaching profession'; and
- the conceptual and political problems now thought to be connected with the notion of 'profession' and professionalism.

Despite this, it remains possible to mount strong arguments in favour of:

- the value of the idea and ideal of a profession in the modern ('post-modern') world;
- a General Teaching Council as a focus and publicly responsible body;
- the value to policymakers on matters of pre-service and in-service education and training of advice and initiative from within the body of teachers as well as extraneously.

The purpose of this chapter is to examine these propositions and thereby develop the argument in favour of a degree of professional control over the education and training of teachers, as an essential element in a self-regulating profession, open at the same time to public scrutiny of its standards and procedures.

TEACHING AND THE IDEA OF A PROFESSION – THE LONG ROAD TO A GENERAL TEACHING COUNCIL

England is usually seen as the kind of society in which a weak corporate state and the strength of parliamentary élites encouraged the development of professions.

> The English model – of a professional corporation legitimized in early modern times by a royal charter (a guild or college) and solely responsible for the education and entry into the profession of its members, which was not swept away by a revolution – became something of an exception in the history of professionalization.
>
> (Siegrist 1994: 9)

That may be true in the case of, say, medicine or law, but not for teaching. Until the expansion of public education in the late nineteenth century, teaching was closely associated with the Church, and the ordained leaders of the profession usually sought their promotion within the Church. Even in the Middle Ages, the classical period of vocational organisation, among the various corporations there was no craft, guild or mystery of teachers – the close connection between the teacher and the priest militated against the rise of a professional organisation of teachers. As late as the first half of the nineteenth century, head teachers and university tutors were generally in holy orders and looked for advancement to an archdeaconry or higher office in the Church.

The idea of a teaching *profession* is thus associated with the advent of secularisation and expansion as the state began first to subsidise and then directly fund and control the public education system. Yet in England the state did not make the new teachers civil servants, 'fonctionnaires', and thus the tension between state and profession, administrator and practitioner, was built in from the beginning. Moreover, if professional status was to be won, it must be on new terms, not simply accorded by tradition. Those in holy orders saw the significance of events. Thus when Edward Thring in 1869 called together colleagues who were to form the Headmasters' Conference, he said that the main object of the gathering would be to put forward, with one voice, 'pronounced opinion from the most important profession in England' (Webb 1915). Five years later the Headmistresses'

Association was formed. The leaders knew they were pioneering education for women; they came from a very different background and had no impedimenta from the past:

> The object Miss Buss had in drawing her friends thus together was to form, in the women teachers of England, a *true professional spirit*, a spirit informed by high ideas of work and character, holding that education involved much more than learning and that the future good should always be held more important than any immediate advantage.
>
> (Webb 1915)

It is not surprising then that the first proposals for self-regulation of the teaching profession appeared in the mid-nineteenth century. The College of Preceptors was founded in 1846 and received its Royal Charter in 1849. The Medical Registration Act was passed in 1859 and within two years a Scholastic Registration Act was proposed. Bills were put forward on three occasions between 1879 and 1896 but all failed. The 1899 Education Act made provision for setting up a register of teachers and the Board of Education Act of 1901 laid upon the Board a duty to establish a Teachers' Registration Council. However, the resulting Council was divisive, treating elementary and secondary sectors differently, failed to gain the support of teachers and ended in 1906. Efforts continued, and in 1912 an acceptable Teachers' Registration Council was established by order of the Privy Council. In 1929 it became the Royal Society of Teachers. This was a voluntary society, intended as a precursor to compulsory registration for all teachers. The 1944 Education Act did not include that requirement, the RST did not have influence on the supply and training of teachers and it and the Register were abolished by an Order in Council in 1949 (DES 1970; GTC 1992a; Taylor 1994). The government's anxiety to ensure a sufficient and appropriate supply of teachers had overcome any impulse to share power with the profession.

In the 1950s the teachers' organisations began to bring pressure on government to set up a General Teaching Council. Such a Council would have three chief purposes:

- to maintain a register of those qualified to teach;
- to control professional discipline; and
- to advise on standards of entry to the profession and for continuing professional development.

Events in Scotland moved much faster. Following a dispute over the level of entry requirements a committee was set up chaired by Lord Wheatley. It reported in 1963 and recommended 'that there should be established a General Teacher Council for Scotland broadly similar in scope, powers and functions to the Councils in other professions' (quoted in GTC 1992a: 8).

The Teaching Council (Scotland) Act was passed in 1965 and the Council set up the following year. Ross comments that:

The powers granted to the General Teaching Council for Scotland are not unduly great but, in contrast with the situation in England and Wales they do, while recognising ultimate authority of the Secretary of State for Scotland, give the teaching profession a recognised place in the organization and management of the profession. Instead of being left to provide observations on policy initiatives emanating from government, the Scottish teachers are able through the Council to initiate policy discussions.

(Ross 1990: 127, quoted in Taylor 1994: 54)

In England, two years later, the new Secretary of State, Edward Short, announced his intention to set up a General Teaching Council and appointed a working party chaired by (Sir) Toby Weaver, a deputy secretary at the Department of Education and Science and representative of teachers' associations, LEAs, universities and teacher-trainers. However, 'although the Weaver Report in 1970 considered the case for a professional council already to have been accepted, and did much detailed ground-work which is still valid, it recommended a division of functions under two separate Councils, and this failed to command professional support' (GTC 1992a: 8).

It should also be noted that, through the report, the government put down a caveat which reflected its historical concerns and must still remain valid:

Because the government must be responsible to Parliament for securing an efficient education service at reasonable cost, we accept the general principle that it must retain sufficient reserve powers to ensure that in the last resort its purposes were not frustrated by action of the Teaching Council.

(DES 1970: 9)

The rest of the 1970s was preoccupied with the economic crises following the oil price rises after 1973. James Callaghan made his

'Ruskin Speech' in 1976 and a Conservative government was elected in 1979. When the movement for a General Teaching Council next gathered shape and direction, from 1983, the political climate had totally changed. The New Right governments of the 1980s had a deep distrust of trade unions or any organisation that might work 'in restraint of trade' and against the interests of the consumer. Their project was to reduce the power of the producer and increase that of the consumer through the mechanism of the market. A prolonged dispute with the teachers' unions led in 1987 to the Teachers' Pay and Conditions Act, which removed their bargaining rights and for the first time, introduced national conditions of service. In the same period new regulations were being introduced concerning teacher training, the appraisal of teachers, the curriculum and the assessment of pupils. It was not a climate conducive to introducing a measure of self-government of the teaching profession. The stance adopted by the government was that there must be broad agreement among teachers, LEAs and parents before they could consider a GTC; and when that agreement was indeed made manifest, that the movement should start on a voluntary basis. It is unclear whether that proposal was made in ignorance of the history from 1929 to 1949 or because of it.

None the less, the situation (at the time of writing in 1994) is more consolidated and encouraging than at any time since 1846. The movement for a GTC (GTC: England and Wales, a company limited by guarantee) has accrued in ten years a wide and strong body of support representing all the teachers' associations in schools, further education and higher education institutions, together with the LEAs, churches, governing bodies and, most significantly, parents. Moreover, the importance of the case is beginning to reach the generality of teachers. An information leaflet circulated in 1991 to all schools brought an overwhelming positive response (Sayer 1993: 119).

The House of Commons Select Committee on Education and Science in 1990 gave its backing to a GTC:

> We believe that the positive effect on morale from a properly constituted and effective council warrants such an effort. To move forward on this we consider that a lead from central government is essential and we therefore recommend that the Government create a General Teaching Council to work

for the enhancement of the profession.

(House of Commons Select Committee on Education,
Science and the Arts 1990: para. 26)

Debates in the House of Lords every year since 1989 have indicated strong and cross-party support for a statutory General Teaching Council.

At the time of writing this chapter, the Bill to create a Teacher Training Agency is before Parliament. The government has resisted moves to retain a division of responsibility for funding and quality on the one hand and accreditation of courses on the other. In the process the position of both the Higher and Further Education Funding Councils and the idea of a General Teaching Council have been undermined.

Yet the same Government has also recognised the absolute necessity to regain the support and commitment of teachers and has allowed the Dearing reviews of the National Curriculum to bring them back into consultation and the exercise of professional judgement in a manner unheard of for a decade. There are further signs that although the Teacher Training Agency will be given authority over education and training, the establishment of a General Teaching Council to maintain a register of teachers, attend to professional conduct and create a focus for the profession might be contemplated – provided any possibility that it would become a mega-trade union could be set aside. Of course, it could not become such an organisation. Pay and conditions of service would remain the domain of the trade unions and would be explicitly ruled out of the remit of a General Teaching Council.

We shall return at the end to the contemporary educational scene and what possibilities it may hold. It is now time to look at the enduring case for recognising and enhancing the professionalism required of teachers.

THE PROFESSION OF TEACHING

There is a considerable literature on the notion of a profession. In 1978, and speaking as a reflective practitioner, I identified four essential characteristics, namely:

- its practitioners must be learned;
- its practitioners must have some special executant skill – there

are special ways of doing the job as well as a body of knowledge to be mastered;

- its practitioners must have integrity, that is conscience to act where necessary contrary to public or political whimsey – in the interests of their clients;
- its practitioners must have organisation as a group – with a code of action and ethics.

(Tomlinson 1978: 353)

A review of the academic literature suggests that these are indeed the defining characteristics. Surveying half a century from Flexner's (1915) analysis, Leggatt reported that the most frequently mentioned characteristics were:

(a) Practice is founded upon a base of theoretical, esoteric knowledge

(b) The acquisition of knowledge requires a long period of education and socialization

(c) Practitioners are motivated by an ideal of altruistic service rather than the pursuit of material and economic gain

(d) Careful control is exercised over recruitment, training, certification and standards of practice

(e) The colleague group is well organized and has disciplinary powers to enforce a code of ethical practice.

(Leggatt 1970: 56, quoted in Taylor 1994: 44)

In a more recent essay, Downie (1990) argues for five characteristics which legitimise a profession:

Its knowledge base; the provision of a service within a relationship of beneficence and integrity and a set of legal and ethical rights and duties underwritten by a professional institution; a critical function ('the duty to speak out with authority on matters of social justice and social utility'); independence, which is not inconsistent with employee status or state funding; preparation that constitutes an education rather than 'mere training' (i.e. that nurtures a wide cognitive perspective and requires a commitment to the continued development of knowledge and skills within a framework of values).

(Downie 1990: 159, quoted in Taylor 1994: 45)

I want to suggest that, if you actually do it conscientiously, teaching *feels* like a profession, according to these canons. There is a self-forgetting concentration on the needs of the pupil – and a continuing agony better to understand those needs. There is an imperative to be sure you know and understand enough of the content of what you are teaching and the process by which you have chosen to mediate it. There is a continual search for better ways of discovering whether learning has taken place – in the different domains of knowledge, understanding, skills and values. And there is a sense of serving a wider public purpose, within a collegiality of others engaged in the same work, on whose support and criticism you partly rely for your growth. That is how it feels. And those sensations are as true and similar in whatever setting you may work or whatever age the learners may be or whatever their personal and social advantages or disadvantages. It is that categorical nature of teaching that both makes the notion of a shared professionalism possible and makes it a necessity for the practitioner and the quality of the work.

But the public ought also to want teaching to be a profession. It is their best hope for the highest standards and their best protection. It is impracticable to monitor the work of 750,000 teachers daily. Processes of appraisal and inspection, and the assessment of pupils or students, though necessary, are unavoidably partial, retrospective and of ambivalent interpretative value. The surest safeguard is the inner conscientiousness of the teacher, for only the individual can know whether the work has been done according to the highest standards as understood by the best the profession knows.

I tried to express this in a Foreword to the GTC (England and Wales) *Proposals* (1992). Having acknowledged the strenuous recent attempts by government to raise educational standards by the two processes of greater centralisation and market forces – national standards and parental choice – I continued:

The market and controls, alone or together, cannot of themselves however, ensure improvement in the quality of learning. Teachers play a key part in creating quality. What is therefore needed now is the setting in place of the proper third element of the new world, namely a process which acknowledges the part teachers themselves play in creating quality and places collective responsibility for it upon them and in a way that is publicly accountable.

The consumer cannot always know the nature or extent of his or her own needs or potential. Often it is the very purpose of the educational process to provide that insight and confidence. Thus for an essential part of the transaction of education the learner must be dependent upon the teacher. However effectively the pupil is eventually brought to mastery of his or her own learning, during the process of acquiring that mastery, which is mainly what teaching and teachers are about, the learner cannot be autonomous or independent.

The real concern is with quality not standards, because 'standards' can be set at any level those inside or outside education may choose. By quality we mean the diagnoses, processes and outcomes which as nearly as we can judge meet the needs and realise the best potential both of those learning and of society. These lie in the hands of teachers in the final and most important respect.

Many other aspects can help or hinder – resources, structures and expectations all set the context. But the action itself lies with the teachers alone. If they do not feel quickened by their daily work and driven by an inner conscientiousness, the work will remain uninspired, no matter how much technically it may match a national curriculum programme of study or be set in a school of the parents' choice or a university with a high research rating.

That kind of quality must be rooted in the knowledge, skills and dedication of the teachers. It can spring from no other source, any more than a fine diagnosis and treatment in medicine can come from anywhere but the physician.

In consequence, there arises an absolute need for a professional ethic and a code of conduct. The responsibility must be placed with teachers continually to have a care for the improvement of their work. Unless that collective and individual responsibility is made explicit and given effective form, the educational reforms from which so much is hoped will remain inert, and will achieve less than their potential. It would be as though a demand had been created, the factories and distribution systems put in place, and that had been thought sufficient to complete the task. Producers are essential also if there is to be a product. And in education, as in other professions, the producers pre-eminently bring their own unique and essential contribution: the touching of one mind by another, one spirit by another's.

(GTC 1992a: 1–2)

I feel that our greatest danger is the discarding of the personal responsibility of the individual teacher through an excess of external direction, control and measurement. Somehow a balance between public accountability and private responsibility needs to be found. You cannot, as Jane Austen remarked, 'screw people to virtue'. The idea of vocation is so precious, yet so vulnerable. Its power was beautifully expressed by that astonishing Benedictine nun, Dame Laurentia McLachlan, the Abbess of Stanbrook:

> A vocation – any kind of vocation – is a very personal matter, a very real thing too, though so impalpable, and its effects are very enduring. It is in fact the whole secret of our life.
>
> (Corrigan 1990: 6)

The force of the moral sense of the teacher is also expressed in *A Man for All Seasons*, where Robert Bolt creates the following exchange between Thomas More and Richard Rich, an ambitious young man (whose false witness eventually contributes to More's downfall):

> *More*: Be a teacher – you could be a fine teacher, perhaps a great one.
> *Rich*: And if I were, who would know it?
> *More*: Your pupils, you, your friends, God. Not a bad public, that!
>
> (Bolt 1960: 4)

Those two quotations, about vocation and the springs of satisfaction for the teacher, illustrate the crossroads this country has reached. Is the teacher to be remodelled as an operative, carrying out the requirements of the nation measured by only external yardsticks?; or can public accountability be achieved without the destruction of inner satisfaction and personal responsibility?

The notion of a profession preserves that balance. The idea of a General Teaching Council, requiring both professional conduct and public scrutiny could be an essential operational element.

But let us make no mistake. More than the affection of recent Conservative governments for controls and market forces, and their fear of 'organised labour', stand in the way. If we are to succeed in preserving an ultimate and personal responsibility in teachers then a robust intellectual stance against some of the notions of the 'post modern' mind-set will also need to be mounted.

The intellectual movements of the last 150 years, prompted among others by Darwin, Freud, Wittgenstein, Einstein and Derrida, have given humankind a much diminished view of itself. The feeling has been underscored by the violent history of the twentieth century and the reflective darkness of some of its arts. Such humility as has been learned has been of immense value; but such belief in the possibility of nobility as has been lost has reduced us. In particular, the view that altruism is merely another form of self-interest attacks the very notion of personal integrity. It is that intellectual climate, reinforced by moral relativism, and the post-modern belief that only fragmentation is possible, as much as New Right politics and free market economics, that makes mock of those who would insist that humans truly can behave in the interests of others as well as of themselves. Yet it seems luminously clear that the survival of the species on the planet, the possibility of social cohesion in pluralist societies and the health of economies that have now to rely on the knowledge of individuals (which lies beyond the reach of supervision) all require a salience of personal responsibility exercised in the interests of others as well as of the individual. We have rediscovered and enthroned libertarianism at the very period when it is most dangerous. It is a Faustian defiance that will finish us, if not reformed.

If that analysis is true, then one social group whose work must assume special significance is that of teachers, who discharge public responsibility for the socialisation and value-world of the next generation. They must be expected to encourage personal and social responsibility in their learners, and accept it for themselves.

Seen in this wider intellectual and political context, the case for *requiring* teachers to take some responsibility for their own regulation and the development of their craft is irresistible. Of course, in the modern state, it must lie alongside whatever requirements for the curriculum, the organisation of education and accountability for public funds the government of the day may require. But a condominium of government and profession is the best assurance the public could have for the growth of quality in education.

CONCLUSION

I have argued that teaching is not afforded currently the status of a profession and have considered many of the historical and contemporary reasons, especially those deriving from government's view that it needs to retain control. Nevertheless, I have also tried to show that teaching does indeed meet the defining characteristics of a profession and that the sense of this has been demonstrated in both professional and political action over the last 150 years, and is especially strong and coherent now. A major force to be reckoned with is the post-modern view that a fragmented, pluralistic and incoherent intellectual and social landscape is the unavoidable future condition of western societies. Already arguments against such a view are gathering force (for example, Green 1994). It has been assumed by some that the post-modern view, of which free-market competitive policies and deregulation may be seen as a constitutive element, also removes any case for the recognition of professions and professional organisation in teaching. I have argued against this view on the grounds that although teaching is indeed involved in questions of social cohesion and control, and therefore can be feared by or manipulated by governments, the dominant defining characteristic is the personal responsibility of the teacher to the client.

How far may we reasonably look to increased professional control of the training of teachers? Some see the predilection of recent Conservative governments for more school-based initial training as a transfer of control to the profession. It is not. It is an abdication to individual schools, indeed to a selection of teachers within certain schools. It lacks any cohesive framework of method, values or review. In any case, entirely school-based initial teacher training will remain a small part of the total and will probably prove impracticable in primary schools. A simultaneous and contrary reform, the introduction of the Teacher Training Agency, would appear to run directly counter to strengthening professional involvement. A small group of politically selected persons, even though some may have a teaching background, who have the task of determining the distribution of courses between institutions, the length and content of courses and the funding of the whole system, is unlikely to wish to engineer the complexities of collecting and focusing advice and feedback from the profession. A continuation of a fairly mechanical application of criteria set down by the Secretary of State seems most probable.

By contrast, where effective partnerships between many schools and an institution of higher education have been built up, a thoroughgoing professionalism of approach can be created from the several perspectives of subject and education tutors in the higher education institution joined with teachers, heads of department and those with general management responsibilities in schools. There is already mature experience among school teachers of being a mentor, whether 'subject-based' or 'general', to both students in training and beginning teachers, and a similar experience in further education. And there is a burgeoning literature analysing and developing that experience (for example, the journal *Mentoring*). To become involved in this dialogue is to realise how rich are the veins of experience and thinking about teaching in schools, colleges and higher education institutions in this country. For example, I listened recently to a group of colleagues from my own university, local schools and three LEAs discussing the kind of evidence that could be gathered from the work and behaviour of student teachers to give meaning to the descriptions of 'competence' contained in the CATE advice attached to Department for Education Circular 14/93. They moved from that easily into how evidence could be defined and then collected and analysed for the control of quality in the school-based elements of the course. Hearing their discussion and admiring its depth and direction, I was forced to the conclusion that it was grounded in learning in the principles of education and a capacity to reflect critically on experience rather than on any view that 'knowledge' might be simply 'transmitted'. It suggests very strongly that those capacities and elements of learning are needed more rather than less in the current reforms towards a better partnership between higher education and schools. There is thus a moral as well as a practical imperative to retain such capacities and elements, whatever the current utilitarian pressures.

Seen in the light of these powerful developments in the field, it is possible that such a centralised and over-powerful body as the Teacher Training Agency, though it would have its attractions to politicians of any party, would not survive a change of government, should one occur. Moreover, the profession collectively has shown itself capable of working on this essential aspect of self-regulation, namely professional education and training, through the initiative for a General Teaching Council. It has done so regardless of the trade union affiliation of those concerned and in cooperation with parents and employers. That is unprecedented but now rests on an organisation built carefully over ten years which has published significant documents on initial teacher education and training, the induction of teachers and continuing professional development, (GTC 1992b, 1993a, 1993b). GTC (England and Wales) is currently at work on the nature of teaching and standards of professional conduct. It would therefore appear to be a time when teachers and those who work with them should keep their nerve. An opportunity to offer advice about the education and training of teachers by a means that will ensure real influence may be made within five years. The profession needs to keep working at its ways of thinking and speaking collectively so that it can act responsibly should that day arrive. The experience will of itself make the event more likely.

Chapter 15

Entering the unknown universe: reconstructing the teaching profession

Michael Barber

The need to raise standards of education for all young people is almost universally recognised. This is partly a matter of economics. The British economy, and indeed the wider European economy, would appear to depend on having a well-educated, adaptable, continuously learning work-force which is able to generate and implement innovation.

The case for raising standards, however, goes far beyond this. As we watch with growing anxiety the fragmentation of crucial aspects of society – the community and the family for example – it seems increasingly clear that education, both in a narrow academic sense and in the broadest sense, has a critical role to play in attempts to maintain and develop a successful democratic society. The challenges of the next century will pose for future generations problems which at present we can hardly imagine. The success or failure of education in the 1990s will determine their ability to respond effectively.

Finally, and at least of equal importance, there is the question of individual personal fulfilment. The idea of encouraging all children to reach their full potential has wide currency these days. However, it is inadequate. Education is more successful when founded on a belief in the unlimited potential of every human being. Individual development depends not only on educational success but on a realisation that education never ends.

This range of demands on the education service places extraordinary responsibility on teachers. HMI reports tell us repeatedly that the quality of teaching is the most important determinant of successful learning. Everyone, from government ministers to teachers and parents, accepts that this is true. Yet, in spite of that consensus, virtually none of the whirlwind of reforms in the last decade has given priority to teachers, their professional skills or their professional development.

In this chapter I argue that if the education service is to succeed in the next decade or so, this will have to change. I advocate a reconstruction of the teaching profession and suggest, tentatively, the form such a reconstruction might take. In the conclusion I propose a means by which it might be accomplished.

THE CASE FOR RECONSTRUCTING THE PROFESSION

I have chosen to use the word reconstruction because I believe 'reform' does not express sufficiently the kinds of development that I wish to see. In any case, the word 'reform' has been used so much in the last few years that it has almost ceased to have significant meaning.

Much of my argument is based on an extended metaphor drawn from an important book. It is called *Wrinkles in Time* (Smoot 1993). The book describes the remarkable series of scientific experiments that have enabled Smoot and his colleagues to work out, apparently, what happened in the first two trillionths of a second after the Big Bang that set the universe in motion.

According to Smoot, everything that we have ever seen, from even the most powerful telescope or the most distant satellite, amounts to less than 10 per cent of the universe. The rest, which no one has ever seen or come to understand, is known as 'dark matter'. It is the unknown universe. And perhaps most amazingly of all, Smoot reveals in an aside that this dark matter, the unknown universe, may not obey the laws of physics.

What has this got to do with the teaching profession? From 1988 onwards, politicians have attempted to reorganise the entire known educational universe. They have dealt with structure, funding, curriculum, assessment and testing, inspection, the provision of professional development and initial teacher education. Everything has changed, yet oddly everything, it seems, has stayed the same. Classroom practice would be clearly recognisable to a teacher who had retired in 1975 or 1985 and pupils tend to be organised in similar ways. In spite of the tremendous progress over a generation, it is still true that large numbers of pupils leave school with a sense of failure and a lack of self-esteem and without sufficient knowledge, understanding and competence either to pursue successful careers or to lead lives which are socially, culturally or personally fulfilling.

How can this be? It seems that the reforms of recent years completely missed something. I would argue that, although they turned the known universe on its head, they missed the unknown universe altogether. They missed that crucial part of education that is to do with the classroom interaction of learner and teacher and with the extraordinary ability of teachers to generate sparks of learning, even in the most inauspicious circumstances. Yet each of these sparks of learning is a seminal event of incalculable importance to society.

When I refer to the unknown universe, I am referring to the critical and major element of all education that is to do with educative relationships, where all learning originates, between learner and teacher, learner and learner, and parent, learner and teacher. It is that part of all education that does not obey the laws of physics, that defies logic, but, at the same time, is the key to educational success. It is also the major part of the agenda of school and college improvement.

Though this unknown universe defies logic, it is not impossible to study. The problem is that it does not receive the attention it deserves. Even the word that describes a large part of it, 'pedagogy', is out of fashion. But we can and must learn more about it. We must then attempt to ensure that our deeper insights into the learning process become the collective possession of the teaching profession. The time has come to shift the focus of educational thinking from the known universe, which we have become tired of reorganising, to the unknown. This is the key, on the brink of the new century, to bringing about the quantum leap in standards which is universally sought.

There are many aspects of teaching and learning where teachers' skills, although already extensive, could become more refined and better developed. For example, we need to consider the use of teachers' assessments to inform their own teaching, the nature of questions used by teachers, both when they are addressing whole classes and individual pupils, and the relationship between teachers' expectations (which have been given attention) and learners' self-esteem (which has not).

Although these are essentially classroom and school or college matters, ensuring they are given due priority is a matter of policy.

Indeed it is because policy has led to endless reorganisations of the known universe, that the unknown universe has been neglected. If this order of priorities is to be reversed, then a whole series of new policy questions will need to be pushed to the top of the agenda. These questions include:

- How can initial training, induction and continuing professional development be more effectively related to each other?
- How do we persuade teachers and lecturers to give higher priority to their own learning?
- How do we disseminate the silent successes of many teachers, schools and colleges across the country, so that everyone benefits?
- Are we spending enough on professional development? Is it well distributed? Does it take account of the age and skill profile of the profession? Does it match the demands that will be made of the profession ten or fifteen years from now?
- Why is the profession so deeply unattractive to so many of our most able graduates? How do we change that?
- If teachers are overworked, as they are, does all their work need to be done by fully qualified teachers? Could we make better use of administrators and paraprofessionals?

The process of answering these questions would lead inexorably to a reconstruction. In short, there is a critical educational agenda that is being neglected at the precise moment in history when we can least afford to do so. This leads to my second theme, and an attempt to identify the obstacles in the way of changing the agenda.

THE BARRIERS TO RECONSTRUCTING THE PROFESSION

There have been four huge barriers to changing the agenda. Each will be difficult, but not impossible, to overcome.

The first barrier has been the political approach to education policy. The unknown universe of education is difficult territory for politicians. They find it difficult to understand fully, and generally avoid trying to travel too far into it. It usually seems preferable to them to remain where they have been in the last decade, reorganising the known universe. The habitual announcement of initiatives has after all become the accepted route to political success. Sound bites are perceived to be more important than sound policies. Engendering progress in the unknown universe is not so easily susceptible to sound bite treatment. It takes time, patience, investment, thought and courage. If government ministers are to support development in the unknown universe, they will have to change their approach and attempt instead to create a framework in which improvement can take place. They should take responsibility for setting the tone for educational debate and for highlighting the need for progress. They should also seek to recognise and elaborate achievement wherever it takes place. In addition, they should lead by injecting ambition and urgency into a national crusade for higher standards and they should set targets, recognise the lessons of the school effectiveness research and give the whole enterprise a sense of direction. Finally, they should collaborate with the profession to help to bring about its reconstruction.

This is a very different role from the one Conservative government ministers have played in recent years. It would require them to take the long view but it would be more productive educationally, and probably more productive politically too.

The second barrier has been the approach of some of the leaders of the teaching profession itself. The unknown universe of education is by definition an area which demands professional leadership. Yet all too often the current leaders of the teaching profession have been as blinded as the politicians by the agenda of initiatives. Furthermore, they have too often been bitterly divided among themselves and absorbed by short-term issues, appearing to be more interested in recruiting the next union member than in promoting educational improvement. If the education reform debate is to move forward into more productive territory, then a new approach to leadership will be required. The teacher organisations will need increasingly to focus on the longer-term interests of their members, even where this means occasionally sacrificing their short-term concerns. In the long run, the pay and conditions of the teaching profession depend on the respect in which it is held in public and therefore ultimately on the success of the education service as a whole. For this reason alone, the teacher organisations should align themselves with the whole process of school and college improvement.

The third barrier is the constraint on teachers' time, which prevents them giving sufficient attention to their own learning.

If the unknown universe of education is to be given top priority in all schools and colleges, then finding the time and providing the incentive for teachers to learn will have to become a central goal of policy. Much of the next section of this chapter is concerned with proposals which could make this possible.

The fourth barrier is that there is no forum at present in which the future of the profession can be properly thought about, discussed and advanced. At national and local levels, governance of the teaching profession is uneasily divided between the Department for Education, OFSTED, the Teacher Training Agency and the School Teachers' Review Body. The Funding Agency for Schools and the Further Education Funding Council also have a role. Not one of these organisations has the responsibility for looking at the overall long-term development of the teaching profession. Furthermore, because of the way they are constructed, they encourage and condone the endemic short-termism among teacher organisations because they do not offer the profession as a whole any significant degree of responsibility for its own development and progress.

The kind of reconstruction of the profession that I envisage can only be undertaken by a body which has the confidence of both government and the teaching profession and which is committed to the priority of the long-term development of the teaching profession. At present, such a body does not exist. It may be that a General Teaching Council would fill this vacuum. Certainly such a council would be a tremendous step forward in promoting this agenda, and would give a strong public message about the need to improve the status of teachers in society. Anyone who opposes the creation of a GTC must surely suggest an alternative since the *status quo* is patently indefensible.

Supposing a GTC or an alternative were created, and suppose it began to examine the questions I have set out, what answers might it suggest? The third section of the chapter attempts to begin such debate by making a number of tentative proposals.

AN AGENDA FOR RECONSTRUCTION

Any reconstruction will require that solutions emerge, both refined and coherent, after a period of professional and political debate. In order to begin the debate and to give it a cutting edge, the proposals that follow err on the side of radicalism.

A respect for research

There is evidence that we are on the brink of a revival of research, not in the form of unreadable, depressing tracts about how schools cannot compensate for society but in the huge and fertile regions concerned with the effectiveness of teaching, classrooms, schools and colleges. Much of the work in this area will be developed by practitioners themselves working in association with higher education. The quality of British research in education is recognised worldwide. By contrast, the British education system has been relatively slow to take its findings into account. There are signs that this is changing: certainly the development of more research on school effectiveness and other aspects of education would be a welcome step in the reconstruction of the teaching profession.

Higher entry qualifications

One of the most welcome developments of 1993 was the government's acknowledgement in its final circular on primary initial teacher training (DFE 1993b) that it would be disastrous to reduce significantly the entry qualifications for those who want to teach at the nursery and infant stages of education. If the profession is to become more successful in the future, then, if anything, entry qualifications should be raised rather than reduced, with an emphasis not only on academic qualifications, but also on personal qualities and experience. It is interesting that the National Commission on Education Report (1993) suggested that raising entry requirements might make teaching more attractive to good honours graduates, since the public message would be that teaching was a highly skilled and demanding occupation which required multi-talented people. This line of thought should be explored further.

Initial teacher education and induction

The debate over recent years reveals very clearly that continuous reorganisation of the initial phase of teacher education will never solve entirely the problems associated with it. Initial teacher education is a beginning. It cannot possibly make fully rounded entirely competent teachers, however hard higher education institutions and their partners, schools and colleges, work. Evidence suggests that initial teacher education is at present broadly successful and certainly much better than in many parts of the United States. It is also clear from the evidence, including OFSTED's recent report on the new teacher in school (OFSTED 1993c), that the induction phase has been shamefully neglected by policymakers in this country. It is surely time we began to see initial teacher education and induction as one continuous process, which becomes based increasingly in schools and colleges, though never entirely so. In the best practice around the country, following their initial teacher education, students find themselves on a structured induction programme which offers them not only support in school or college but also opportunities to pursue studies at higher education level which lead to accredited diplomas. If we are to give all beginning teachers the best possible start in their careers, then we ought to ensure that this best practice becomes an entitlement for all of them. It would enhance the process if some teachers approaching early retirement were given a contract under which in the year they retired they provided support to teachers in their first year. This would provide them with a responsibility that many would welcome and would give beginning teachers the kind of support they often lack. It would also cost very little.

Better use of administrators

It has been a constant complaint of teachers over recent years that the burden of bureaucracy and administration is distracting them from their chief task of educating children and young people. Evidence of such problems has been seen in surveys by, among others, the Association of Teachers and Lecturers (Campbell 1991) and the National Union of Teachers (Coopers and Lybrand 1991). Government reforms have been a major cause of this complaint. However, the teaching profession itself also bears some responsibility. For too long, promotion in schools, or indeed in colleges, has been equated with moving away from the classroom towards administration. Given the message this conveys about priorities, it is hardly surprising if the administrative burden expands dramatically, particularly during a period of rapid change.

Under local management of schools there has been a welcome shift in some schools towards the employment of more administrators to carry out administrative tasks, so that teachers are able to focus on learning. It is absolutely essential that this process continues. High-quality administrators, with appropriate pay, conditions and opportunities for professional development, should not be seen as draining money away from the curriculum, but as enabling teachers and managers to concentrate upon it. As long as headteachers and college principals remain educators and leaders of the teaching profession, and there is no shift towards the American model where such managers are broadly administrators, then there is little danger of bureaucracy expanding to excessive levels.

A paraprofessional contribution

The employment of a greater number of administrators will not solve all the problems facing teachers. The quality of the teaching profession depends on finding much more time for teachers' own professional development. They should be encouraged to exercise 'a proper selfishness' (Handy 1991). When teachers are presented with the choice, they tend to support pupils' or students' learning rather than their own. Often in the long run this is at cost to the very learners whose interests they have at heart. It is interesting to contrast the position of school and further education college teachers with that of university teachers in this respect. Universities are proud to acknowledge that their staff are involved in research and developing their own learning, whereas in schools and colleges the same activities tend to be seen as a luxury. For these reasons, in addition to employing more administrators we need to see the development of a paraprofessional work-force in the education service.

This would enable a much improved pupil–adult ratio in schools, ensuring that pupils received more attention and that teachers found more time to work on the fundamentally important elements of teaching. It could also give more individual support to students in further education colleges.

Of course schools and colleges have in any case a long tradition of employing laboratory technicians, librarians and special needs support staff. Nursery schools are at the leading edge in this respect, having for many years demonstrated how teachers and other adults can collaborate effectively in the teaching process.

These are models on which to base the extension of the para-professional work-force across other areas of the curriculum.

Paraprofessionals could support teachers with some aspects of the education process, such as working with small groups or individuals, answering routine questions, assisting with the preparation of materials, or advising pupils or students on sources of information. They would provide in many cases an important bridge to the local community, and the increased variety of role models for young people would also be beneficial. Unfortunately, paraprofessional staff have generally been denied the kinds of professional development and career progression that would be taken for granted in many other lines of work. It is an issue for all education policymakers, whether at school, local or national level, to develop a proper career structure for paraprofessionals. The structure should also provide the means for those who wish, and have the potential, to gain the qualifications to become fully fledged members of the profession.

A professional review for all teachers every five years

It would greatly enhance the standing and quality of the teaching profession if all of its members were required periodically to discuss with peers their career and professional development and the development of their pedagogical and other professional skills. Each full-time teacher would, every five years, present a professional development profile to a group of his or her peers including teachers from other institutions. The result would be a serious discussion of these critical matters. The profession itself should also lay down minimum expectations for involvement in professional development over the five-year period. These might include, for example, obligations to participate in some courses or spend time watching skilled fellow professionals at work, or a requirement to spend a period of time working outside the school or college, either in a university, or abroad, or in industry. Although at first sight this would seem to be an imposition on teachers, I believe that such reviews would very rapidly become entitlements, just as curricular entitlement became a reality only when it became a requirement.

The interview with peers might lead to certain requirements being laid down by the group, in collaboration with the teacher being interviewed, in relation to the professional development of the teacher concerned. It may be that certain aspects of the teacher's work would need refinement, support or development over a specified limited period. Of course I am also implying that in a very few cases there might be teachers who would not come through their review. This is always an extremely difficult subject to discuss in professional circles but it cannot be avoided. If there were a routine system of reviews every five years, those teachers who at present drift through years in the profession, often suffering acutely in a personal way and certainly not achieving anything remotely approaching career satisfaction, would have the prompt they need to seek career guidance and counselling. Hopefully, in so doing they would have the full support of the institution at which they work. It seems to me the least punitive, and most supportive, means of dealing with a problem which ought not be neglected.

The statement that a system along these lines would make to the wider public about the teaching profession's determination to improve the quality of teaching and learning would have immeasurable benefit for the profession and the education service as a whole. For any such system to reap its full benefit however, it ought to be introduced at the initiative of the profession itself.

Promotion within the classroom

In the United States, in cities such as Cincinnati, the teacher unions have agreed with their school boards arrangements to enable teachers to be promoted to 'lead teacher' status without at the same time being moved away from children and away from the curriculum. Similarly, the state of New South Wales in Australia has introduced the concept of an Advanced Skills Teacher (AST). These are not merit pay schemes. Perhaps schools and colleges here should have lead teacher posts, which do not have management responsibilities attached to them but which would carry higher salaries. These lead teachers would be professional pace-setters, high priests of pedagogy, called on by others purely because of their teaching expertise. They might also take on some of the mentoring duties associated with initial teacher training or induction and perhaps become associate fellows of partner higher education institutions.

Appointment to these posts should of course be through the best equal opportunities practice, certainly not through patronage nor even simply an interview but through rigorous selection procedures in which the appropriate skills – in this case class-room skills – are tested or observed. There would be value in involving classroom teachers in the appointment process.

In any case the salary structure for all teachers ought to be altered, to offer much better pay on completion of five successful years in the teaching profession. Furthermore, given the proposals made earlier for administrators and the greater use of paraprofessionals, it could be anticipated that in the long run we would have fewer but much better qualified and more highly skilled teachers in our schools and colleges. There would there-fore be no reason why significantly higher salaries could not be paid to teachers in mid-career who wished to stay working in the classroom.

Professional development vouchers

Many teachers are investing their own money in professional development. This is a credit to the profession but far too haphazard for the system to rely on. At present, virtually all funding for professional development supports either national initiatives or the implementation of institutional change. Both of these are important, but the net result has been a neglect of the professional development of individual teachers. It has become more difficult for teachers to follow their own interests or to remedy what they perceive to be their own deficiencies, in spite of the fact that these are absolutely crucial to their success. Furthermore, current expenditure on professional development supports the short-term or occasionally the medium-term, but rarely, if ever, the long-term professional needs of teachers.

Certainly teachers' personal expenditure on professional development should be tax-deductible. In addition, teachers perhaps should receive a professional development voucher worth in the region of £300 to £500 *per annum*. They would thus be empowered to make decisions about their professional devel-opment. They might use the money on, for example, MA course fees. Alternatively they might decide to accumulate the money and use it to buy a one-term management course. Above all, such a voucher would empower teachers and enable them to make choices appropriate to their needs.

Professional representation in inspection teams

Teachers undoubtedly benefit from visits to other institutions and opportunities to see the work of other pupils or students. This was one of the chief development benefits of the moderation procedures introduced for school examinations and it is also one of the benefits of being a GCSE or 'A' level examiner. At present, particularly in city schools where there is the ever-present danger of teachers becoming ground down by the pressures upon them, teachers have far too few opportunities to see other pupils' work or the approaches used by teachers in other schools. Now that the new school inspection procedure has been implemented, surely we should take the opportunity it offers to enable teachers to visit other schools. Similar approaches could also be developed in relation to the inspection of further education.

Arrangements should therefore be put in place to enable every inspection team to include at least one practising teacher. It is interesting to note that inspections of teacher education courses can involve higher education teachers from other institutions. Such an arrangement would be of immense benefit to the teachers participating in the inspection process, just as very often in the case of classroom observation it is the observer who reaps the most benefit. It would also give greater credibility to the inspection process itself.

CONCLUSION

Whether or not the nine proposals made in the previous section are the right answer, there would be few, surely, who would argue that the questions raised are the wrong ones. Means have to be found to put such questions higher up the agenda of education policy and find answers to them. Partnerships can also begin to address such questions.

First, a debate about the long-term future of the teaching profession ought to be an element of every ITT course. If they remain in the profession, the beginning teachers of today will participate in the most radical reconstruction of teaching and learning in history. Their preparation cannot explain to them what this reconstruction will involve, since at present we are all at best guessing; but surely it can raise the questions and set a debate running about the possibilities.

Second, there are rich opportunities for schools, colleges and higher education institutions to make research an integral part of partnership. Such research can inform school and college improvement, teachers, schools and colleges can be involved in research projects and teachers can themselves be researchers making use of the expertise, data and resources of partner higher education institutions.

Third, schools, colleges and higher education can together contribute to the national debate, not least by advocating investment in teachers' own learning. If they are to do so successfully, they will need to go beyond asserting the importance of such learning and produce hard evidence for their case. This in itself is an area which requires research.

Nationally, as I have argued, there is no obvious forum in which the long-term future of the teaching profession can be debated. There are three possible ways this could be rectified. The first would be the establishment of a General Teaching Council (GTC) as discussed by Tomlinson in Chapter 14, with responsibility for maintaining a register of those eligible to teach, establishing qualifications for entry to the profession and advising government of the nature, scope and content of teachers' initial education, induction and continuing professional development.

However, three attempts in the last two years to legislate for a GTC have been defeated in the House of Lords, in spite of a degree of support across the political spectrum. Government to date has remained implacably opposed to the idea and the Department for Education's historic opposition also appears to be unchanged. For the foreseeable future therefore, it seems unlikely that the GTC will be established. The reconstruction of the teaching profession cannot wait for a GTC that may never come. The second option would be for the government to establish a committee of inquiry to examine the issues and make recommendations. This would ensure the matter had status, but would have possible flaws. The reconstruction of the profession cannot be imposed against the wishes of the bulk of teachers. Any body appointed by government would therefore have to build an effective working relationship with the profession and its leaders.

The third option, and in my view the most desirable, would be for the profession itself to establish a committee with a substantial degree of independence. The committee would have to earn the respect of the Department for Education and politicians of all parties if its proposals were to have any impact. This would be difficult but not impossible.

While progress of this kind at national level is awaited, there are opportunities for progress at local level, not least through partnerships between schools, colleges and higher education institutions. Many of the proposals in the previous section are within the power of school or college governors to begin to implement. However, although this would represent a step forward, it could not bring about the national reconstruction that is required. Until a powerful element of national policy is directed at providing teachers with the time and incentive to prioritise their own learning, standards of education in this country will not reach the levels the next century will demand.

Part IV

Conclusion

Chapter 16

Managing partnership: future directions

John Welton, John Howson and Hazel Bines

As the writers in this book have demonstrated, change is never an easy process. Everyone involved has to adjust to new perspectives and frequently there are also shifts in the balance of power. Where governments seek to make changes to social policy through legislation and regulation, they provide a significant reference point for planning about structure and practice. However, implementation is rarely simple, since it involves a complicated process of social and institutional change during which the groups and individuals involved seek to influence the beliefs and actions of others and the ways in which new systems and procedures are set in place. It is therefore widely recognised that government social policy is rarely implemented in exactly the way its architects intended (Barrett and Hill 1984; Welton and Evans 1986). Where there is a consensus, legislation enables and encourages policy along accepted lines. Where there is dissent, governments have greater difficulty in ensuring compliance. Weatherly and Lipsky (1977) described ways in which educational administrators and professionals developed coping mechanisms to manage the demands of reform and of their jobs, distorting the intentions of legislators where such intentions did not appear to be in the interests of clients. The gap between policy and action can be such that it may be more realistic to define policy in terms of the outcomes of legislation, rather than the original policy intentions of the government. Such a gap is likely to be greatest where a government attempts to impose requirements which run counter to recognised or emerging good practice.

Unlike the previous upheavals in teacher education such as followed the McNair Report (Board of Education 1944), the introduction of the B.Ed. degree and the massive closure and amalgamation programme of the 1970s, the current partnership movement and the resulting transfer of teacher education activities from higher education to schools and colleges are only being partly driven by the strategic initiatives and ideological position of central government. The move towards partnership started from within the profession rather than at Westminster. However, apparent consensus over the value and importance of such change masks a number of different ideological and practical concerns. The outcomes of present policy intentions may, therefore, be somewhat unpredictable.

As the writers in this book have shown, thinking about partnership has challenged established orthodoxies, and in so doing, has raised important management issues, many of which have yet to be fully resolved. The majority of such issues can be characterised as either strategic or operational. For example, at a national strategic level, any government faces decisions concerning the maintenance of the supply of teachers prepared in accordance with its criteria. Such decisions then need to be turned into operational plans for targets, courses and providers. At the institutional level, schools, colleges and higher education institutions have to make decisions about whether to include support for initial training or other aspects of teacher education within their overall strategic plans, and then decide on the most effective means for delivery. Whether at national or institutional level, changes in strategic thinking alter the reference points for operational planning, with possible consequences for roles, relationships, provision and practice.

As discussed in Chapter 1, moving the debate about partnership from the issue of the location and control of initial teacher training to the wider canvas of staff and institutional development issues considered in preceding chapters, requires a change in the concept of partnership. Government measures to apply market processes to social welfare organisations have introduced both a mechanism for encouraging competition between providers and a responsiveness to client need. However, what is left is a semi-regulated market, which still requires a strong element of strategic and operational planning at national, regional and local levels if it is to ensure the supply of teachers, and universal educational provision, to a required standard. The range of issues and practices discussed in previous chapters reinforces our belief that it is not possible to plan and manage initial teacher training in isolation from other elements of staff and school or college development. Initial teacher training cannot be divorced from continuing professional development, either conceptually or operationally. In addition to the arguments for a single professional voice, summarised so succinctly in Chapter 14, there is a need for vision and a set of operating principles for teacher education, which set the process of preparing a new teacher in the context of career-long professional development. This vision, which is widely understood in the context of staff development planning at institutional level, needs to be matched by a national vision and strategy for linking together initial teacher training, the induction and support of newly qualified teachers, further professional development and research.

The partners who are directly involved in managing teacher development have different responsibilities, but they need an overview of the process of teacher development, set in the context of institutional planning. The teacher training curriculum has to be planned towards the needs of the new teacher in school; the induction process has to build on the presenting characteristics of the new teacher; and induction should feed into a scheme for continuing professional development suitable for individual teachers, the teams in which they work and the institution as a whole. The failure of plans for senior management development during the past decade provides some evidence about how difficult this is to achieve.

At a national level, the different powers accorded to the Secretary of State relating to initial and in-service education, together with the division of responsibility within the civil service and Inspectorate, have so far militated against a coherent policy for the various stages of teacher recruitment and development. As discussed in Chapter 12, policies to reduce the planning power of LEAs have limited further the coherence of staff development provision at local and regional levels. As noted in Chapter 2, while the influence of the LEA has decreased, so the role of higher education as partner has increased. Nevertheless, higher education institutions do not manage teacher education as an activity isolated from their other roles. As discussed in Chapters 3 and 13, they should also provide: sources for ideas and experiences; libraries to support professional research and development; a focus for networking between teachers, schools, colleges and LEAs and, it should be noted, between national governments and international research and practice; and above all, critical and independent thinking.

Despite political rhetoric about the distance between theory and practice, and higher education and the classroom, the partnership between schools, colleges and higher education has been deepening and strengthening for some time. However, it is also changing continually in terms of contributions, functions and power. The effective management of partnership will therefore become increasingly important.

In this chapter we seek to draw together the range of management issues identified by contributors to this book, by focusing on such key aspects as teacher supply and teacher education provision, funding, managing the change in roles and responsibilities, quality assurance and staff development. We will then conclude with some consideration of ways in which partnership can contribute to educational improvement at institutional, local and national level.

PLANNING FOR TEACHER SUPPLY AND DEVELOPMENT

Although responsibility for the delivery of teacher education is moving towards schools and colleges, answers to the key national strategic questions still need to be decided by central government, either directly, or through a quasi-autonomous body such as the Teacher Training Agency. These questions include forecasting the demand for teachers and lecturers relative to demographic changes in the numbers of school-aged students, and the predicted demand for further and higher education. Any changes in the method of implementing strategic policy, such as a move towards work-based teacher education, need to be considered in relation to their potential effect on teacher supply.

In demographic terms, based on predictions by the Department for Education, assumptions about initial teacher training for school education are clear for the near future; between the academic years 1992/3 and 1996/7, recruitment targets for primary teacher education should decline by some 40 per cent, while recruitment targets for secondary training should rise by a similar amount. These targets will need to be achieved against the background of an economy emerging from recession and a school system threatened by a squeeze on government funding.

Historically, teacher training for further and adult education has been subject to a much looser planning framework since the bulk of teaching staff receive their initial teacher training as part-time students when already employed as lecturers. Nevertheless, as noted in Chapter 1, the neglect of further education is a strategic aspect of teacher education and development which must be addressed at a national level, particularly since the sixth-form colleges have been moved into the further education sector.

There are a number of unknown or unpredictable factors which may distort the teacher supply model. These include the effects of delegated institution-based budgeting on employment policies and the possible shift in government policy towards developing more nursery and other pre-school education. The latter may result in the need for more primary teacher training places, while the former seems to be reducing the predicted need for more secondary school teachers. For example, between January 1992 and January 1993 the number of primary school teachers in service (in England and Wales) rose by 1558, whereas the number of secondary school teachers rose by only 481. During the same period, there was an increase of 71,151 in the number of secondary school pupils compared with only 58,899 more primary school pupils (DFE 1993d, 1994). Thus it took an additional 122 secondary pupils to generate an extra teaching post compared with only 46 additional primary pupils.

Nevertheless, the seriousness of the potential operational problems in achieving the supply of intending secondary school teachers can be measured by the fact that in 1987, prior to the economic recession, there were only 1299 applications for places on PGCE courses for mathematics teachers. In that year, 70 per cent of applicants were accepted. By 1996, the strategic need has been predicted as requiring about 2400 training places. In operational terms, there could therefore be a shortfall of over one thousand if a more buoyant graduate job market forces applications back to their 1987 level (House of Commons Select Committee on Education, Science and the Arts 1990; DFE 1993e). The Teacher Training Agency is likely to find that encouraging applicants into teaching may be a significant part of its operational concern, as graduate unemployment falls and the economy continues its recovery from recession.

Another aspect of implementing current strategic plans for teacher supply involves ensuring the provision of teachers with the right mix of subject expertise, age phase and geographical distribution. However, the present geographical and institutional pattern of teacher education is largely the product of incremental change rather than a coherent strategy. The Higher Education Funding Council, like its predecessors, has never made public the basis for its distribution of cuts or new places. The process of cutting the numbers of primary teacher training places during the period 1992 to 1994 does not appear to have taken a great deal of account of the national patterns of demand and supply. Government policy of encouraging partnership between higher education institutions and schools may therefore not be possible in some areas due to the uneven geographical distribution of provision. The decrease in ITT places for primary education in particular means that some potential primary school partners are going to be disappointed, since uneven geographical distribution will lead to fewer primary trainee teachers being available to schools through their traditional higher education partner. While recruitment to teacher education is still channelled through higher education institutions, shortages in supply may place some schools in a weak bargaining position relative to higher education. As a result, some schools which seek the benefit of partnership may be forced to switch allegiance from their local traditional partners to higher education institutions in parts of the country which have been more favoured. Alternatively they may seek to use SCITT schemes to devise a course which allows them to continue to associate with an institution of their own choice.

In the secondary sector, however, it is the higher education institutions which may be in the weaker position. As the number of places is expanding, higher education institutions may find it difficult to identify schools willing to take more trainee teachers. In this case, scarcity has moved the balance of power to the schools as providers of places, a position which is reinforced by moves to charge for involvement and the option of non-cooperation if terms are not met. At present there is no mechanism which can compel schools to provide initial training places. Indeed they can always establish a SCITT or resort to the use of licensed teachers paid out of the other sources of public funding for teacher education, rather than establish or continue training partnerships with higher education.

At the present stage of the economic cycle where most teaching posts suitable for newly qualified teachers still attract reasonable numbers of applicants, secondary schools may therefore hold the ring in relation to partnership. However, those with a feel for the longer time-scale will be aware of possible future problems of recruitment and supply, particularly for certain 'shortage' subjects, and will see possible advantages in developing a close partnership with a higher education institution ahead of any period of teacher shortage. Unless schools want to take on all the burden of recruitment, linking with a higher education institution, or indeed a range of institutions, may provide a cheaper alternative to the process of struggling to find sufficient teachers to fill vacancies. Some far-sighted schools may therefore be prepared to forgo part of the real costs of participating in a partnership for the savings available on the recruitment process together with the marketing opportunities of presenting potential pupils' parents with a school fully and appropriately staffed. These schools may not necessarily demand full recompense for the training costs of working with students.

A neglected problem in managing teacher supply is the need to establish integrated provision for the further professional development of teachers, through their induction period towards more specialist curriculum and management roles and responsibilities. In this respect, government planning falls behind good strategic planning in schools and colleges by failing to recognise the importance of a coherent approach to planning, supporting and monitoring all stages of staff development. Without the intermediate management role of LEAs, national policy for in-service education is becoming an aggregate of separate decision making by different institutions. The absence of coherent planning for national and regional provision through higher education means that some schools and colleges lack convenient local access to institutions which can provide appropriate support for staff development programmes or for research and evaluation. Specialist and costly in-service provision, such as training for management or special education needs, may not be available and other provision such as training for administrators and paraprofessionals, as discussed in Chapter 15, remains patchy and fragmented. Supply has largely been viewed as a question of ITT targets and recruitment. It also includes, however, the supply of appropriate provision to meet demands in relation to the range of training and continuing professional development. Such strategic questions therefore need to be considered by all participants, if partnership, as discussed in this book, is to be fully realised.

FUNDING

The funding of initial teacher training involves key strategic decisions at institutional as well as national level. The historical link of initial teacher training with higher education has meant a serious decline in funding over the past decade, as a result of reductions in funding per student for higher education as a whole. Moreover, higher education is threatened with a further 'efficiency gain' of some 14 per cent over the next three years. It is doubtful whether teacher training courses can withstand such a cut from an already reduced base. The introduction of an Agency bidding for hypothecated funding will at least allow some debate about comparable funding levels for training teachers compared to the work-based training of other professions, particularly given the trend towards payment for the school-based aspects of teacher training.

The solution cannot just be found through the various attempts by institutions to recover their expenditure irrespective of the effect on the other partner. It is to be hoped that in any genuine partnership there will be a recognition that all partners have costs associated with delivering the course and that available funds need to be distributed on a *pro rata* basis. Another strategy would be to consider the current patterns of resource distribution, including a reduction in the level of central overheads charged by higher education institutions. Since internal funding mechanisms in higher education are more of an art form than a science, this seems a superficially attractive way to move the existing resources around. However, given many of the fixed costs associated with quality assurance, recruitment, record-keeping, student services, libraries, computer provision and all the other corporate functions of a higher education institution, certain forms of support might well be denied to teacher education if this model was pushed to its logical conclusion on the present levels of funding (Howson and Mitchell 1994).

Alternatively, partners could decide to re-allocate the responsibilities, and thus the funding, associated with teacher education. For example, in addition to taking responsibility, and receiving payment, for providing school experience, a school could be remunerated for taking the entire responsibility for recruiting students, monitoring and assessing progress or providing library and other study facilities. Similarly, a college could teach part of an initial training programme for further and adult education, or provide all the support for personal tutoring and mentoring. However, although partnership will undoubtedly involve such changes, their impact on long-term provision by the higher education institution in particular, and the administration and negotiation involved in identifying costs and price, will have to be considered.

The partnership model outlined in Circulars 9/92 and 14/93 for secondary and primary education respectively (DFE 1992; 1993b) has been introduced on the basis of existing funding, with apparently no obvious consideration as to whether it is more or less expensive than the models it supersedes. If the Teacher Training Agency does not conduct an early investigation into the basis on which the funding has been calculated, then it is probable that one or other of the partners will regard the funding as so inadequate that they will no longer be prepared to participate in initial teacher training. Some of the issues that are likely to cause strains are the widening gap between salary levels in schools and higher education, the problem of funding empty places on courses and the changing number of places required from year to year. A similar investigation is needed in relation to initial teacher training for further and adult education, to establish the costs involved in partnership and in the new approaches to training and other forms of staff development.

Any further weakening of the resource base for initial teacher education within higher education will have the consequence of reducing the scale of facilities available to support continuing professional development and research. Reduction of the finance available to support teachers undertaking long courses has already reduced the resources and facilities for individual professional development and qualifications or substantial research to support school and college improvement. Faced with reduced budgets, and choices between spending money on books or staff development, school governors may be understandably reluctant to pay for courses for staff to learn to undertake basic research.

MANAGING CHANGES IN ROLES AND RESPONSIBILITIES

As Fullan (1992) has noted, successful innovations and reforms are usually clear after they work, not in advance. The implementation of the new partnership model involves a complex process of managing change, with unpredictable results. Much of the writing on school-based teacher education and on partnership has focused on issues at the operational level. In writing about equivalent changes in policy and practice in the United States, Cornbleth and Ellsworth (1994) quote research that demonstrated four major sources of tension arising from strategic policies which changed the relationship between schools and higher education. These tensions stem from role overlap between school and higher education personnel, from different perceptions of responsibilities, from the difficulty which staff have in giving up traditional roles and from unresolved issues of power and authority. All of these problems are recognisable in the earlier chapters of this book. They may only be temporary problems which will be resolved as the implications of strategic changes become clear and as programmes and relationships develop. However, the process of clarifying concepts, relationships and practice needs to be built into both the strategic and operational stages of implementing change.

In the initial stages of partnership, schools, colleges and higher education institutions are faced with reconciling different organisational cultures, structures, processes and roles. For example, at a very practical level, the planning and recruitment cycles of schools and higher education institutions are not in phase with each other. Recruitment to ITT courses (through higher education) begins a full year before schools start to decide whether they are able and willing to provide facilities for classroom experience. Schools like to arrange their commitments for the following year when they are writing their timetables during the previous summer term, by which time their higher education partner will have had to make firm offers to candidates. Conversely, if recruitment becomes more difficult in certain subjects, higher education institutions may not be able to deliver an agreed number of students to schools and may also not be able to pay for students who fail to register or drop out in the first few weeks of the course.

There is, therefore, rightly much anxiety about managing the change in the relationships between higher education, schools and colleges. Where partners learn to trust each other, solutions will emerge which make the best use of the resources available to fulfil needs. However, careful attention to roles and responsibilities will be required.

In contrast to the strategic issues, some of the problems relating to operational planning are much more straightforward. They can be settled more easily than the strategic issues providing that the central question of the leadership of the partnership is resolved and a planned approach adopted towards the systematic management of change. As outlined in Chapter 1, the shift away from the historical model of teacher training delivered and controlled by higher education towards a partnership model has led to a new distribution of roles and an increased sense of ownership of the training process by all those involved. Schools, colleges and higher education institutions which move towards a closer partnership need to negotiate their mutual understanding of:

- the unique contribution which each partner brings to the partnership;
- the nature of their core purpose as school, college or higher education institution;
- the extent to which their core purpose might be altered by a change in their responsibilities;
- the added value of the partnership;
- what each partner needs from the partnership;
- what advantage each partner gains from the partnership;
- what each partner might lose from the partnership;
- the explicit expectations of the roles and responsibility of each partner to provide information, agreed services and resources to the other partner; and
- the means for quality assurance in relation to the contribution of each partner and the operation of the partnership.

For some schools and colleges, the result of such reflection will lead them to withdraw from teacher education, making the point that they are primarily concerned with children and young people and that teachers have not been trained to facilitate adult professional training. For others, maintaining the enthusiasm with which a partnership was established will require vision and leadership. Much will depend upon the willingness of those in the partnership to be open and frank with each other, to be ready to identify and overcome barriers to change.

The nature of the partnership between higher education, schools and colleges is likely to be represented in both formal contracts or agreements signed when partnerships are established and the continual negotiation and redefinition of operational understandings and arrangements. Contracts or agreements will reflect the formal definition of partnership at the local level and will identify relationships and responsibilities, the structure of courses, the transfer of resources and arrangements for quality assurance and control. Where partnership includes joint initiatives for training mentors and other support staff for initial teacher education, the contract may also extend from informal training into arrangements for incorporating in-service pro-grammes and access for research. In practice, once drawn up and signed, such formal agreements and contracts will rarely see the light of day in successful partnerships. They cannot easily deal with the day-to-day minutiae associated with the operation of such a complex activity as a teacher education programme and will need to be supplemented by examples of custom and practice which should be consistent across the partnership.

A school or college does not have to provide facilities for learner teachers and higher education institutions do not have to supplement their initial teacher education programmes with higher degree programmes and a full range of support services for schools and colleges in their region, although many do, both to provide service and to enrich the professional base for initial teacher training and research. There should therefore be no exclusivity in the contractual relationship between partners in teacher education, and no requirement in particular for INSET to be undertaken in conjunction with a single local higher education institution, even where they are in partnership for the delivery of initial training. In practice, few if any higher education institutions are either large or diverse enough to have the capacity to be able to meet effectively all the professional development needs of partner schools and colleges. As noted in Chapter 2, schools and colleges may therefore wish to pick and choose their INSET partnerships using different criteria from those which have influenced a choice of partnership in relation to initial teacher training. However, as noted in this and other chapters, there are clear advantages in planning the two together, since a planned development of partnership activities for INSET as well as ITT may bring a stability to educational programmes and resource planning which is beneficial to all parties.

QUALITY ASSURANCE

Schools, colleges and higher education institutions are subject to different forms of quality control, and while they share some aspects of a common culture of quality assurance, this cannot be taken for granted in any form of partnership. Successful partnerships therefore need to make strategic decisions about developing joint processes of quality assurance and control to take account of both the regulatory frameworks and management cultures of each of the participating organisations.

Quality assurance should be addressed in a number of ways. It will need to be considered in relation to: the design, delivery and outcomes of courses, including compliance with accreditation criteria where appropriate; the structure, coherence and content of programmes; approaches to teaching, learning and assessment; and the standard of achievement demonstrated by those completing a particular course. The quality of staff and learning resources will also need to be evaluated, as will the ways in which particular aims and objectives for different programmes are met. For example, whereas ITT courses focus on developing professional competences appropriate to the beginning teacher, INSET programmes could be evaluated with reference to the ways in which they meet both individual and institutional needs. The quality of research activity, however, may be assessed on different criteria, for example the contribution made to new knowledge or to the solution of problems. The quality of partnership is also extremely important, and could be defined in terms of the level of mutual understanding and commitment, the effectiveness of communication and coordination, the efficient use of available resources and the degree to which partnership encompasses the continuum of professional development.

As schools and colleges take on a greater part of the delivery of teacher education, there will therefore need to be very clear understandings about the aims and the procedural elements of quality assurance. For example, procedures will need to be established to ensure consistency of judgement between teacher, teacher tutors or mentors, higher education tutors and external examiners, and to overcome variations between the standards expected of initial training students either in the same or different school or college contexts. This will require standardisation of forms of profiling, agreement about the weighting to be given to different components of the profile and common approaches to the assessment of competences or other learning outcomes to be achieved. Some of these issues could be overcome if teachers in partner schools are able to visit each other and watch different students at work, much as higher education tutors used to do under the former models.

Participation by higher education staff in development activities based in schools and colleges, and similar participation by teachers from schools and colleges in higher education programmes, would help to deepen mutual understanding of quality issues. Such contacts would not only enhance the working knowledge of how others in the partnership operate but would also provide the opportunity for joint research into the criteria for effective practice. There also needs to be a national debate on quality assurance including the value of current criteria, evaluation procedures and the way in which judgements of quality are used to inform funding and other allocation of resources. For example, judgements of the quality of research are based largely on academic criteria. If, however, research is to be developed as an aspect of partnership concerned particularly with support for institutional development, the practical value of research ought to be given more consideration.

The role of external and government bodies also needs to be debated. For example, it is clear that OFSTED is likely to focus more in future on the quality of partnership as well as the quality of courses (OFSTED 1993d) and will want to monitor schools' views about training. The impact of the range of quality assurance bodies and procedures will also need to be monitored. Further, schools that have undergone a recent full inspection in relation to the education they provide for pupils may be less willing to participate in an inspection shortly afterwards concerned with initial teacher training. If a school has a lot of students, the question may arise as to whether such students should take lessons during the period of an inspection concerned with the quality of education for pupils within the school. This is less of a problem for those partnerships operating a model where students change schools on a regular basis, since arrangements can more easily be made to accommodate a school wishing to miss a term for an inspection or any other reason. Partnerships where students spend the bulk of the year in one school will, however, have to consider such issues. Finally, more attention needs to be given to the use of the range of data collated by external bodies, to ensure that local and national trends, issues and problems are monitored carefully.

STAFF DEVELOPMENT

We have already touched upon the way in which the work involved in achieving mutual understanding of quality issues and performance requires extended contact between partner institutions to develop mutual understanding, procedures and experience. Partnerships that are formed for a single student, for a single academic year or less, such as those found in some distance learning and franchise programmes, may face more difficulties in building up a shared culture of quality assurance. The time and resources involved in developing this shared culture also need to be written into partnership agreements. The greater the amount of interchange and joint work between staff in schools, colleges and higher education, the stronger the likelihood of developing shared understandings of the formative and summative processes involved in the assessment of student teachers and the evaluation of work carried out for INSET courses. Joint observation of student teaching, joint in-service programmes for school or college mentors and higher education staff, good documentation about the aims and principles of course design, delivery and evaluation, and a regular review of practice through partnership meetings supplemented with external consultants and research, all have the potential to increase the amount of shared understanding that underpins the professional formation of teachers.

It would be logical to expect that once a partnership has been established, curriculum planning and the development of courses should be relatively straightforward. However, pressure on resources and changes in personnel throughout the partnership will mean that unless time is set aside for staff development and a continual review of curricula and courses there will be the danger of fragmentation and misunderstanding.

Currently, resources for staff development have to be found from the existing resource base. It is unlikely that sufficient funding will exist to allow for the quality of staff development and training which is necessary to ensure continued improvements in the quality of professional development. Nevertheless, funding for mentor training will have to be found as part of the cost of a partnership model. At the same time it is an aspect of staff development which can also meet institutional needs, since mentoring can support a range of professional development needs, including initial training, induction, continuing professional development and preparation for a management role. The benefits, as well as the costs, of staff development therefore need to be considered in this light.

For the concept of partnership to be more than empty rhetoric those responsible for the strategic planning of teacher development must ensure sufficient funds to enable successful training to take place. The development of new partnership models has coincided with requirements for greater accountability for delegated budgets, the accumulative effect of the 'efficiency gains' demanded of higher education and government cutbacks on public expenditure. This means that the whole partnership model could be under threat if it is not adequately funded. In addition, there is little or no earmarked provision for developing the capabilities of staff to undertake research into the practice of teacher education. Such research now needs to be part of the process of planning, managing and maintaining change and development.

MANAGING EDUCATIONAL IMPROVEMENT THROUGH PARTNERSHIP

A theme running throughout this book has been the need to see the development of strategic and operational planning for teacher education as a process of managing change, requiring critical reflection and research. Further, we have argued that initial teacher training should not be isolated from the succeeding stages of professional development, or from research. These are among the most important aspects of the partnership between schools, colleges and higher education, and most at risk in the absence of a coherent national strategy for teacher education and development.

The climate for social welfare management introduced by recent Conservative governments has encouraged competition for control of the values, content and resources for teacher education. There is therefore a danger that the prime motivation for an institution to seek involvement in partnership may be benefits to the particular institution, as expressed in:

- the way in which partnership helps the institution to meet its immediate needs;
- the impact of partnership on the material/financial resource income available to the institution;
- the contribution of partnership to institutional creativity;
- access to a network of experience, information and support; and
- an enhanced public reputation.

Although such institutional benefits are important to consider, the common and collaborative value of partnerships, and the ways in which they can contribute to educational improvement, also need to be calibrated. In particular, there needs to be a commitment to the quality of the partnership itself, and the means by which it may enhance professional and educational development in the interest of the education service as a whole. If partnership is to foster such improvement, however, careful consideration must be given to the ways in which change will be achieved.

The voluntary nature of the partnership, together with the increasing need to put a monetary as well as a professional value on every activity, dramatically alter the relationship between participants, requiring:

- joint planning;
- excellent communications;
- sharing and renewing knowledge and understandings;
- well-designed and regularly reviewed systems for working together;
- developing and maintaining appropriate forms and styles of leadership;
- staff development; and
- monitoring and evaluation.

Taken together, these aspects demonstrate the interdependent nature of schools, colleges and higher education, as partners in both the process of institutional development and the professional development of individual teachers. They highlight the value of

joint planning of resources for educational development, including provision of teacher education courses at all levels and
cooperation in research. Partnership is not just about institutional
gain, but rather about cooperating to provide complementary
resources for professional and institutional development, and in
so doing, enhancing the range of opportunities for educational
improvement, and ultimately, the experiences and achievements
of learners in the education service as a whole.

Bibliography

Ainscow, M. and Hopkins, D. (1992) 'Aboard the moving school', *Educational Leadership*, November 1992, 79–81.

Alexander, R. (1990) 'Partnership in initial teacher education: confronting the issues', in M. Booth, J. Furlong and M. Wilkin (eds) *Partnership in Initial Teacher Training*, London: Cassell.

Altrichter, H., Posch, P. and Somekh, B. (1993) *Teachers Investigate their Work*, London: Routledge.

Audit Commission (1993) *Adding Up The Sums: Schools' Management of their Finances*, London: HMSO.

Audit Commission and Office for Standards in Education (1993) *Unfinished Business: Full-time Educational Courses for 16 19 Year Olds*, London: HMSO.

Avis, J. (1994) 'Teacher professionalism: one more time', *Educational Review*, 46, 1, 63–72.

Ball, S. (1990) *Politics and Policy Making in Education*, London: Routledge.

Barrett, E. and Galvin, C. with Barton, L., Furlong, J., Miles, S. and Whitty, G. (1993) *The Licensed Teacher Scheme: A Modes of Teacher Education Project Survey*, London: Department of Policy Studies, London University, Institute of Education.

Barrett, S. and Hill, M. (1984) 'Policy, bargaining and structure in implementation theory: towards an integrated perspective', *Policy and Politics*, 12, 3, 219–40.

Barth, R. S. (1991) *Improving Schools From Within*, San Francisco and Oxford: Jossey Bass Publishers.

Beardon, T., Booth, M., Hargreaves, D. and Reiss, M. (1992) *School-led Initial Teacher Training: The Way Forward*, Cambridge: University of Cambridge Department of Education.

Becher, T. (ed.) (1994) *Governments and Professional Education*, Buckingham: Society for Research into Higher Education/Open University Press.

Berrill, M. (1994) 'Initial teacher education: cross-roads or by-pass?', *Cambridge Journal of Education*, 24, 1, 113–15.

Bines, H. (1992) 'Quality or survival?: the consultation document on the reform of initial teacher training for secondary education', *Journal of Education Policy*, 7, 5, 511–19.

———— (1994) 'Squaring the circle? Government reform of initial teacher training for primary education', *Journal of Education Policy*, 9, 4, 369–80.

Bines, H. and Thomas, G. (1994) 'From bureaucrat to advocate? The changing role of local education authorities', *Support for Learning*, 9, 2, 61–7.

Bines, H. and Watson, D. (1992) *Developing Professional Education*, Buckingham: Society for Research into Higher Education/Open University Press.

Board of Education (1944) *Teachers and Youth Leaders: Report of the Committee appointed by the President of the Board of Education to consider the Supply, Recruitment and Training of Teachers and Youth Leaders (McNair Report)*, London: HMSO.

Bolam, R. (1993) 'Recent developments and emerging issues', in GTC (1993a) *The Continuing Professional Development of Teachers*, London: GTC.

Bolt, R. (1960) *A Man for All Seasons*, London: Heinemann.

Booth, M., Furlong, J. and Wilkin, M. (eds) (1990) *Partnership in Initial Teacher Training*, London: Cassell.

Bowe, R. and Ball, S. with Gold, A. (1992) *Reforming Education and Changing Schools*, London: Routledge.

Boydell, D. and Bines, H. (1994) 'Beginning teaching: the role of the mentor', *Education 3–13*, 22, 3, 29–33.

Bridges, D. (1993) 'School-based teacher education', in D. Bridges and T. Kerry (eds) *Developing Teachers Professionally*, London: Routledge.

Cameron-Jones, M. and O'Hara, P. (1993) *The Scottish Pilot PGCE (Secondary) Course 1992–3*, Edinburgh: Moray House Institute, Heriot-Watt University.

Campbell, J. (1991) *Primary Teachers' Workload*, London: Association of Teachers and Lecturers.

Clarke, K. (1992) 'Speech for the North of England Education Conference', 4 January 1992, London: DES Press Office.

Coopers and Lybrand (1991) *The Costs of Implementing the National Curriculum in Primary Schools*, London: National Union of Teachers.

Cornbleth, C. and Ellsworth, J. (1994) 'Teachers in teacher education: clinical faculty roles and relationships', *American Educational Research Journal*, 31, 1, 49–70.

Corrigan, F. (1990) *Friends of a Lifetime, the Nun, the Infidel and the Superman*, London: Fount Paperbacks.

Council for National Academic Awards (1986) *The Credit Accumulation and Transfer Scheme*, London: CNAA.

———— (1990) *Complex Modular Inservice Education Schemes: A Review of CNAA Provision*, London: CNAA.

———— (1992) *Competence-based Approaches to Teacher Education: Viewpoints and Issues*, London: CNAA.

Cox, C. (1989) 'Unqualified approval', *Times Educational Supplement*, 6 January 1989.

DENI (1993) *Review of Initial Teacher Training (ITT) in Northern Ireland*

(Reports of the three working groups); *Competences* (Working Group 1). Belfast: DENI.

DES (1970) *A Teaching Council for England and Wales: Report of a Working Party appointed by the Secretary of State for Education and Science*, London: HMSO.

————— (1972) *Committee of Inquiry into Teacher Training (James Report)*, London: HMSO.

————— (1975) *Training of Teachers for Further Education: Report of the Further Education Sub-committee of the Advisory Committee on the Supply and Training of Teachers*, London: HMSO.

————— (1977) *Training of Adult Education and Part-Time Further Education Teachers: Report of the Further Education Sub-committee of the Advisory Committee on the Supply and Training of Teachers*, London: HMSO.

————— (1978) *Training Teachers for Education Management in Further and Adult Education*, Discussion paper by the Further Education Sub-committee of the Advisory Committee on the Supply and Training of Teachers, London: HMSO.

————— (1985) *Better Schools*, London: HMSO.

————— (1984) *Initial Teacher Training: Approval of Courses*, Circular 3/84, London: DES.

————— (1989) *Initial Teacher Training: Approval of Courses*, Circular 24/89, London: DES.

————— (1992) *Reform of Initial Teacher Training: A Consultative Document*, London: DES.

DFE (1992) *Initial Teacher Training: Secondary Phase*, Circular 9/92, London: DFE.

————— (1993a) *The Government's Proposals for the Reform of Initial Teacher Training*, London: DFE.

————— (1993b) *The Initial Training of Primary School Teachers: New Criteria for Courses*, Circular 14/93, London: DFE.

————— (1993c) *School-Centred Initial Teacher Training*, Letter to headteachers of selected schools (March 1993), London: DFE.

————— (1993d) *Statistical Bulletins*, 1/93, London: DFE.

————— (1993e) Written Evidence to the School Teachers' Review Body, Statistical Tables and Annex, unpublished, September 1993.

————— (1994) *Statistical Bulletins*, 3/94, London: DFE.

Downie R. (1990) 'Professions and professionalism', *Journal of Philosophy of Education*, 24, 2, 147–59.

Earley, P. (1992a) *Beyond Initial Teacher Training: Induction and the Role of the LEA*, Slough: National Foundation for Educational Research.

————— (1992b) 'Getting off to a good start', *Times Educational Supplement*, 4 December 1992.

Earley, P. and Kinder, K. (1994) *Initiation Rights*, Slough: National Foundation for Educational Research.

Edwards, T. (1990) 'Schools of education – their work and their future', in J.B. Thomas (ed.) *British Universities and Teacher Education*, Lewes: Falmer Press.

———— (1992) 'Issues and challenges in teacher education', *Cambridge Journal of Education*, 22, 3, 283–91.

———— (1994) 'The Universities' Council for the Education of Teachers: defending an interest or fighting a cause?', *Journal of Education for Teaching*, 20, 2, 143–52.

Elliott, J. (1993a) 'The assault on rationalism and the emergence of the social market perspectives', in J. Elliott (ed.) *Reconstructing Teacher Education*, London: The Falmer Press.

———— (1993b) 'Professional education and the idea of a practical educational science', in J. Elliott (ed.) *Reconstructing Teacher Education*, London: The Falmer Press.

English, F. (1975) 'The three-cornered contract', *Transactional Analysis Journal*, 5, 4, 383–4.

Flude, M. and Hammer, H. (1990) (eds) *The Education Reform Act: Its Origins and Implications*, London: The Falmer Press.

Fullan, M.G. (1991) *The New Meaning of Educational Change*, London: Cassell.

———— (1992) *Successful School Improvement*, Buckingham: Open University Press.

Furlong, J. (1992) 'Reconstructing professionalism: ideological struggle in initial teacher education', in M. Arnot and L. Barton (eds) *Voicing Concerns: Sociological Perspectives on Contemporary Education Reforms*, Wallingford: Triangle Books.

———— (1994) 'Another view from the crossroads', *Cambridge Journal of Education*, 24, 1, 117–21.

Furlong, J., Hirst, P., Pocklington, K. and Miles, S. (1988) *Initial Teacher Training and the Role of the School*, Milton Keynes: Open University Press.

Galton, M. (1989) 'Primary teacher-training: a practice in search of pedagogy', in V. McClelland and V. Varma (eds) *Advances in Teacher Education*, London: Routledge.

Gaunt, D. (1992) 'Coordinating inservice education for teachers', in H. Bines and D. Watson (eds) *Developing Professional Education*, Buckingham: Society for Research into Higher Education/Open University Press.

Gilroy, J. and Day, C. (1993) 'The erosion of INSET in England and Wales: analysis and proposals for a redefinition', *Journal of Education for Teaching*, 19, 2, 141–57.

Grace, G. (1991) 'The state and the teachers: problems in teacher supply, retention and morale', in G. Grace and M. Lawn (eds) *Teacher Supply and Teacher Quality*, Clevedon: Multilingual Matters.

Graham, D. (1993) *A Lesson For Us All*, London: Routledge.

Graham, J. (1989) 'Professional development portfolios and their implications for portability in modular schemes', *British Journal of Inservice Education*, 15, 46–50.

Graves, N. J. (ed.) (1990) *Initial Teacher Education: Policies and Progress*, London: Kogan Page.

Green, A. (1994) 'Post modernism and state education', *Journal of Education Policy*, 9, 1, 67–83.

GTC (England and Wales) (1992a) *Proposals for a Statutory General Teaching Council for England and Wales*, London: GTC.

———— (1992b) *The Induction of Newly Appointed Teachers*, Papers by J. Calderhead and J. Lambert, London: GTC.

———— (1993a) *The Continuing Professional Development of Teachers*, Papers by M. Williams and R. Bolam, London: GTC.

———— (1993b) *The Initial Education and Training of Teachers for Primary Schools*, by R. Goodyear and V. Little, London: GTC.

Hagger, H., Burn, K. and McIntyre, D. (1993) *The School Mentor Handbook*, London: The Falmer Press.

Hall, V. and Wallace, M. (1993) 'Collaboration as a subversive activity: a professional response to externally imposed competition between schools?', *School Organisation*, 13, 2, 101–17.

Halsey, A., Heath, A. and Ridge, J. (1980) *Origins and Destinations: Family, Class and Education in Modern Britain*, Oxford: Clarendon Press.

Handy, C. (1991) *The Age of Unreason*, London: Heinemann.

Hargreaves, A. (1992) 'Cultures of teaching; a focus for change', in A. Hargreaves and M. G. Fullan (eds) *Understanding Teacher Development*, London: Cassell.

Hargreaves, D. (1989) 'Judging radicals by results', *Times Educational Supplement*, 6 October 1989.

———— (1990) *The Future of Teacher Education*, London: Hockerill Educational Foundation.

Hendy, J. (1993) 'LEAs provide the adhesive the education service needs', *Education*, 18, 9, 27 August 1993.

Hirst, P. (1979) 'Professional studies in initial teacher education', in R. Alexander and E. Wormald (eds) *Professional Studies for Teaching*, London: Society for Research into Higher Education.

HMI (1984) *Teaching in Schools: The Content of Initial Teacher Training*, London: HMSO.

———— (1988) *The New Teacher in School*, London: HMSO.

———— (1989) *The Implementation of the Local Education Authorities Training Grants Scheme (LEATGS): Report on the First Year of the Scheme 1987–88*, London: DES.

———— (1991a) *The Professional Training of Primary School Teachers: A Commentary based on the Inspection of Twenty Initial Teacher Training Courses*, London: DES.

———— (1991b) *School-based Initial Teacher Training in England and Wales*, London: HMSO.

House of Commons Select Committee on Education, Science and the Arts (1990) *The Supply of Teachers for the 1990s*, Vols 1 and 2, London: HMSO.

Howson, J. and Mitchell, M. (1994) 'Course costing in devolved institutions: perspectives from an academic department', *Higher Education Review*, (in press).

Jackson, J. A. (ed.) (1970) *Professions and Professionalization*, London: Cambridge University Press

Kerry, T. and Shelton Mayes, A. (1994) (eds) *Issues in Mentoring*, London: Routledge.

Lauglo, J. and Lillis, K. (eds) (1988) *Vocationalising Education: An International Perspective*, Oxford: Pergamon.

Lawlor, S. (1990) *Teachers Mistaught*, London: Centre for Policy Studies.

Lee, M. (1990) 'Conceptualising staff development in further education', *British Journal of In-Service Education*, 16, 2, 107–15.

Leggatt, T. (1970) 'Teaching as a profession', in J.A. Jackson (ed.) *Professions and Professionalization*, London: Cambridge University Press.

Leighton, P. and Aldrich, R. (1988) 'Student experiences of teaching practice 1985–86: a study in professional education', *Education Today*, 38, 1, 53–65.

LeGrand, J. and Bartlett, W. (1993) *Quasi-Markets and Social Policy*, London: Macmillan.

McIntyre, D. and Hagger, H. (1992) 'Professional development through the Oxford Internship Model', *British Journal of Educational Studies*, 40, 3, 264–83.

McIntyre, D., Hagger, H. and Wilkin, M. (1993) *Mentoring: Perspectives on School-Based Teacher Education*, London: Kogan Page.

Maclure, S. (1993) 'A General Teaching Council for England and Wales?', in *Briefings for the Paul Hamlyn Foundation, National Commission on Education*, London: Heinemann.

Marsden, S. and Tuck, R. (1988) *Ab-Initio Training of Staff Development Tutors Employed in Further/Higher Eduction*, Leeds: YHAFHE.

Müller, D. and Funnell, P. (eds) (1991) *Delivering Quality in Vocational Education*, London: Kogan Page.

NATFHE (1994) *Annual Report for 1993 of the National Executive Council*, London: NATFHE.

National Commission on Education (1993) *Learning to Succeed*, London: Heinemann.

Norman, K. (ed.) (1992) *Thinking Voices: The Work of the National Oracy Project*, London: Kogan Page.

OFSTED (1993a) *The Articled Teacher Scheme: September 1990–July 1992*, London: OFSTED.

———— (1993b) *The Licensed Teacher Scheme: September 1990–July 1992*, London: OFSTED.

———— (1993c) *The New Teacher in School*, London: OFSTED.

———— (1993d) *Working Papers for the Inspection of Secondary Initial Teacher Training*, London: OFSTED.

O'Keeffe, D. (1990) 'Equality and childhood: education and the myths of teacher training', in N. Graves (ed.) *Initial Teacher Education: Policies and Progress*, London: Kogan Page.

Ormston, M. and Shaw, M. (1993) *Inspection: A Preparation Guide for Schools*, London: Longman.

Osborn, M. and Broadfoot, P. with Abbott, D., Croll, P. and Pollard, A. (1992) 'The impact of current changes in English primary schools on teacher professionalism', *Teachers College Record*, 94, 1, 138–51.

Pollard, A., Broadfoot, P., Croll, P., Osborn, M. and Abbott, D. (1994) *Changing English Primary Schools? The Impact of the National Curriculum and Assessment at Key Stage One*, London: Cassell.

Raban, B., Clark, U. and McIntyre, J. (1993) *Evaluation of the Implementation of English in the National Curriculum at Key Stages 1, 2 and 3: Final Report to the National Curriculum Council*, Warwick: University of Warwick.

Ranson, S. (1992) *The Role of Local Government in Education: Assuring Quality and Accountability*, London: Longman.

Ranson, S. and Tomlinson, J. (eds) *School Cooperation: New Forms of Local Governance*, Harlow: Longman.

Ross A. (1990) 'A General Teaching Council for England and Wales', in N.J. Graves (ed.) *Initial Teacher Training: Policies and Progress*, London: Kogan Page.

Rothwell, S., Nardi, E. and McIntyre, D. (1994) 'The perceived value of different role activities in the Oxford Internship Scheme', in I. Reid, H. Constable and R. Griffiths (eds) *Teacher Education Reform: The Research Evidence*, London: Paul Chapman.

Sayer, J. (1993) *The Future Governance of Education*, London: Cassell.

Schön, D.A. (1983) *The Reflective Practitioner*, London: Temple Smith.

———— (1987) *Educating the Reflective Practitioner*, London: Jossey Bass.

Shaw, R. (1992) *Teacher Training in Secondary Schools*, London: Kogan Page.

Siegrist, H. (1994) 'The professions, state and government in theory and history', in T. Becher (ed.) *Governments and Professional Education*, Buckingham: Society for Research into Higher Education/Open University Press.

Smithers, A. (1993) *All Our Futures: Britain's Education Revolution*, London: Channel Four Television.

Smoot, G. (1993) *Wrinkles In Time*, London: Little Brown.

Squire, R. (1994) 'Why we need a training agency', *Times Educational Supplement*, 13 May 1994.

Taylor, A. (1993) 'Partnerships with everyone are paramount', *Education*, 182, 19, 5 November 1993.

Taylor, W. (1991) 'Ideology, accountability and improvement in teacher education', *Evaluation and Research in Education*, 5, 1/2, 57–66.

———— (1994) 'Teacher education: backstage to centre stage', in T. Becher (ed.) *Governments and Professional Education*, Buckingham: Society for Research into Higher Education/Open University Press.

Theodossin, E. (1992) *Invisible Assets: FE in the Educational Market*, Bristol: Further Education Staff College.

Tomlinson, J. (1986) 'Public education, public good', *Oxford Review of Education*, 12, 3, 211–22.

———— (1993) *The Control of Education*, London: Cassell.

Tomlinson, J.R.G. (1978) 'A profession in its relationship to society', *British Dental Journal*, 144, 11, June 1978.

Triggs, E. and Francis, H. (1990) *The Value to Education of Long (Award-Bearing) Courses for Serving Teachers*, London University: Institute of Education.

Turner, M. (1990) *Sponsored Reading Failure*, Warlingham: IPSET Education Unit.

Usher, R. (1989) 'Qualification, paradigms and experiential learning in higher education', in O. Fulton (ed.) *Access and Institutional Change,* Milton Keynes: Society for Research into Higher Education/Open University Press.

Warnock, M. (1979) *Education: A Way Ahead,* Oxford: Basil Blackwell.

———— (1988) *A Common Policy for Education,* Oxford: Oxford University Press.

Waterman, C. and De Lyon, H. (1993) 'Not yet dead', *Education,* 182, 12, 17 September 1993.

Watson, D. (1989) *Managing the Modular Course,* Milton Keynes: Society for Research into Higher Education/Open University Press.

Weatherley, R. and Lipsky, M. (1977) 'Street level bureaucrats and institutional innovation: implementing special education reform', *Harvard Educational Review,* 47, 2, 171–97.

Webb, B. (1915) *New Statesman,* 1915, Vol. V, Nos 129 and 130, 25 September and 2 October 1915. Special supplement on English Teachers and their organisation. A report prepared for the Fabian Research Department.

Welton, J. and Evans, J. (1986) 'The development and implementation of special education policy: where did the 1981 Act fit in?', *Public Administration,* 64, 2, 200–7.

Whitty, G., Barrett, E., Barton, L., Furlong, J., Galvin, C. and Miles, S. (1992) 'Initial teacher education in England: a survey of current practices and concerns', *Cambridge Journal of Education,* 22, 3, 293–309.

Wilkin, M. (1990) 'The development of partnership in the United Kingdom', in M. Booth, J. Furlong and M. Wilkin (eds) *Partnership in Initial Teacher Training,* London: Cassell.

———— (1992a) (ed.) *Mentoring in School,* London: Kogan Page.

———— (1992b) 'The challenge of diversity', *Cambridge Journal of Education,* 22, 3, 307–22.

———— (1994) Ideology and the Initial Teacher Training Curriculum 1960–1990, Doctoral thesis, University of Cambridge (unpublished).

Williamson, G. (1989) 'Meeting teachers' needs', *Education,* 174, 18 August 1989.

Winter, R. (1991) *The ASSET Programme,* Vol 1 'Professionalism and competence', Essex County Council Social Services Department and Anglia Polytechnic University.

Index